The Community College

EXPERIENCE

PLUS

FULL EDITION

Amy Baldwin

PULASKI TECHNICAL COLLEGE

PEARSON

Prentice
Hall

Upper Saddle River, New Jersey
Columbus, Ohio

Library of Congress Cataloging-in-Publication Data

Baldwin, Amy.

   The community college experience: PLUS/Amy Baldwin.—
   Full ed.
   p. cm.
   ISBN 0-13-221560-8
   1. College student orientation—United States.
   2. Community colleges—United States.
   3. College students—Conduct of life.   I. Title.
LB2343.32.B24 2007
378.1′543—dc22

2005029413

Vice President and Executive Publisher: Jeffery W. Johnston
Executive Editor: Sande Johnson
Development Editor: Jenny Gessner
Editorial Assistant: Susan Kauffman
Production Editor: Alexandrina Benedicto Wolf
Production Coordinator: Holcomb Hathaway
Design Coordinator: Diane C. Lorenzo
Photo Coordinator: Valerie Schultz
Cover Designer: Jeff Vanik
Cover Image: Corbis
Production Manager: Pamela D. Bennett
Director of Marketing: Ann Castel Davis
Marketing Manager: Amy Judd

This book was set in Goudy by Integra. It was printed and bound by Courier Kendallville, Inc. The cover was printed by Phoenix Color Corp.

Pearson Education Ltd.
Pearson Education Singapore Pte. Ltd.
Pearson Education Canada, Ltd.
Pearson Education—Japan

Pearson Education Australia Pty. Limited
Pearson Education North Asia Ltd.
Pearson Educación de Mexico, S.A. de C.V.
Pearson Education Malaysia Pte. Ltd.

10 9 8 7 6 5

ISBN 0-13-221560-8

BRIEF CONTENTS

CONTENTS

PART I   *Getting Started*

1 Understanding Your College   2

Who Are You? 32

Managing Your Time and Stress 62

PART II   *In the Classroom*

 Navigating Technology   92

Diversity and Relationships   120

Listening and Taking Notes Effectively   148

7 Reading Skills   172

Study Skills and Test-Taking Strategies   196

Writing and Speaking Effectively   226

10 Thinking Creatively, Analytically, and Critically   258

11 Information Literacy and Research Writing   276

PART III   *Beyond the Classroom*

12 Staying Healthy   298

13 Taking the Next Steps   318

T he *Community College Experience: PLUS* meets the unique needs of community college students. Some students face unbelievable obstacles and life experiences before stepping through our doors. These students are often the first in their families to enroll in college; they juggle multiple responsibilities while they work on a degree.

With their backgrounds and "full plates" in mind, this full edition of *The Community College Experience: PLUS* provides not only the basic information community college students need to be successful in college, in the workplace, and in life (information often overlooked in other college success textbooks), but also real-life critical thinking and problem-solving scenarios. This book focuses on how students can think about information critically and apply it to their own lives. Only then does such information move from being simply words on a page to being a map leading to a higher degree.

Chapters in this edition of *The Community College Experience: PLUS* are designed to help students become more aware of themselves and to realize the impact of higher education on their lives, their family, and their community. A common denominator shared by instructors at most community colleges is their desire to equip their students with the knowledge that *they have options.* Knowing who they are and what they want allows these students to make better choices.

One of the most notable additions to the book is the incorporation of VARK learning styles in the Community College Student Profile, in the PLUS (Personality + Learning style = Understanding Situations) Exercises, and through the Learning Styles Application feature at the end of each chapter. Chapters 6 and 8 provide note-taking and test-taking strategies that apply to VARK learning style preferences. The VARK learning style information sets this book apart from other college success textbooks because it moves beyond merely determining what a student's learning style preference is. Instead, *The Community College Experience: PLUS* integrates that information throughout the text so students are consistently reminded as to how this information affects their learning and interactions with others.

This edition contains new material on health issues, research writing, using technology, and thinking creatively and analytically, as well as expanded chapters on diversity and study strategies. These additions will help students better manage their journey through higher education towards a certificate, degree, better job, different career, and a more fulfilling life.

When I first set out to write the shorter edition of *The Community College Experience* (2005) for my students, I noticed a void in the market. Most college success or study skills books do not speak to the typical community college student—someone with many other challenges and priorities to manage than the traditional student who is 18 to 22 years old, doesn't work full time, and doesn't have a family and household to manage. Not surprisingly, I found many other instructors and administrators at community colleges who felt the same way. They wanted a text that better reflects the information their students need, a text that meets their students where they are—first-generation, first-time students.

The earlier, shorter edition of *The Community College Experience* owes its success to the growing importance of community colleges and their students. Whether it is because of a presidential agenda that includes more funding for community college programs, an awareness that almost half of first-year college students attend a community college, or just recognizing the flexibility and convenience that they offer, community colleges are raising their profiles nationwide. With their distinct needs, they are finding that their voices are being heard in their communities and at the nation's capitol. Despite setbacks in funding and uncertain financial times for some community colleges, the future looks bright for these institutions of higher learning and for their students.

Special Features

The Community College Experience: PLUS offers several features that enhance its relevance and usefulness:

Community College Student Profile. Each chapter begins with a profile of a community college student, including a photo and questions and answers that pertain to the chapter topic. Readers have a chance to see others who, just like themselves, are learning to cope with the pressures of college and succeeding.

Clear, honest, and practical information. Each chapter covers a specific college survival topic with honesty and clarity and provides practical advice. Students of all levels and knowledge bases can benefit from the information presented. The topics covered in each chapter are what community college students need to know to succeed.

Embedded exercises within the text. Each chapter has at least one reflection, practice, critical thinking, collaboration, and PLUS (Personality + Learning style = Understanding Situations) exercise. These exercises appear throughout the text so that instructors can incorporate them more easily into their lecture or discussion.

Integrity Matters. Each chapter includes information about integrity, both academic and personal. Students who read this book will understand how integrity is essential to education and a good life.

Each chapter ends with the following activities:

Learning Styles Application. Students are given a learning styles application chart that provides tips for each VARK learning style.

Path of Discovery: Journal Entry. Readers are asked to reflect on and write about a topic presented in the chapter.

From College to University and From College to Career. These sections apply the chapter's topic to the world beyond the community college.

Students can see how these essential keys to college success are building blocks for fulfillment.

Chapter in Review: Questions. These are questions based on Bloom's Taxonomy. Each question reflects one or more of the six levels: knowledge, comprehension, application, analysis, synthesis, and evaluation.

Case Scenarios: Consider. A few case studies are presented to allow students to apply what they learned from the chapter to real-life scenarios.

Research It Further: Ideas. Research ideas are presented for students to explore and report their results. The ideas are engaging and provide students with practical information once they complete the projects.

The ability of readers to use and respond to many of the above features is improved by this book's **Companion Website (www.prenhall.com/baldwin)**, noted throughout the text by the CW icon. Based on and enhancing the book's content, the Companion Website offers many valuable tools for broadening and deepening the reader's understanding of the material. The site allows hands-on interaction with the text, thus stimulating greater learning and retention.

Acknowledgments

First, I would like to offer my sincere appreciation to the following individuals, who reviewed the manuscript for this full edition and offered suggestions for improving it: Christina Chapman, Lewis & Clark Community College; Sara Connolly; Margaret Puckett, North Central State College; Kim Smokowski, Bergen Community College; and Sharon M. Snyders, Ivy Tech Community College.

Prentice Hall executive editor Sande Johnson and publisher Jeff Johnston receive my highest acknowledgment for their encouragement and support during this project. Development editor Jennifer Gessner was instrumental in shaping the book throughout its journey. Thank you to marketing manager Amy Judd, for her tireless efforts—as a result of her work, I have met and worked with some very dedicated community college faculty. I also wish to thank editorial assistant Susan Kauffman.

At Pulaski Technical College, I would like to thank Purnell Henderson, Dan Bakke, Wendy Davis, Debbie Kirby, Kim Halpern, Ann Fellinger, Rashunda Johnson, Joey Cole, Allen Loibner, Danny Martin, Dorothy Martin, and Angie Macri–Hanson. Thank you also to my friends who supported my endeavors: Meghan Harper, Camille Napier, and Gail Fry.

I appreciate the work of those who helped to produce this book, including Prentice Hall production editor Alexandrina Wolf; Holcomb Hathaway production coordinator Gay Pauley; Prentice Hall cover coordinator Diane Lorenzo and cover designer Jeff Vanik; interior designer John Wincek of Aerocrafter Charter Art Service; and copy editor Sally Townshend. Thanks, too, to the team at Integra, who paged the book.

My thanks to Neil Fleming (www.vark_learn.com), for allowing us to use the helpful VARK Learning Styles Inventory and apply the VARK concept to our charts. His material will help readers better understand and use their learning preferences.

Finally, I offer my greatest appreciation and acknowledgment to my students at Pulaski Technical College, who serve as the inspiration for this book.

What Does the Community College Student Look Like?

Larry, 33, is in his second semester at a community college. Despite his strong family support when he was in his mid-teens, he got involved with the wrong crowd. His teachers did not consider him "college material" and predicted that he would be in prison before he was 25. In fact, some of his friends did end up there, but Larry escaped the same fate by getting focused before he graduated from high school. Nonetheless, it took him almost 15 more years before he got serious and started taking classes at the local community college. He now wants to serve as a motivational speaker for other students who may be tempted to make the wrong decisions.

Laura, 38, was once a single mother who struggled to provide for her only child. Last year after her son graduated from high school and was on his own, she enrolled in a community college, because she envisioned something better for herself and her future. Not knowing what she wanted to do, she took classes that interested her and fulfilled the requirements for an Associate's of Arts degree. As she began her second semester, she was inspired by her teachers to pursue social work, and she now has a "thirst for knowledge." With the help of counselors and instructors, she overcame a learning difficulty. Now, Laura encourages other students to advocate for themselves to get the help they need.

Cassie, 18, is taking day classes because she works at night to help pay for her college tuition. Her low ACT and SAT test scores kept her from enrolling in the four-year university 50 miles away. Her ultimate goal is to be a veterinarian. She started her Associate of Science degree at the community college in her area by taking remedial classes to improve her math and reading skills.

These stories are representative of students who attend community colleges everywhere. Enrollments are skyrocketing, changing the face of the college graduate. Today's college students come from a wide variety of backgrounds, represent numerous ethnicities, and possess various abilities.

What do all these people have in common with you? They discovered that an education is key to realizing dreams and achieving goals. They know, as you do too, that the first step to a satisfying career and a life filled with possibilities is enrolling in college. In addition, like you they chose to start their academic careers at a community college.

The reasons that students, like you, are choosing to enroll in a community college are just as diverse as the community-college population. A resounding reason, though, is that community colleges offer services, classes, and personal attention not typically found at a university. You will see these "extras" in the types of classes and degrees offered, as well as in the personalized attention and assistance you will receive.

No doubt, you have your own story as to why you are attending a community college, but the common denominator you share with your classmates and the students profiled in this text is that you all took an important step to improving your lives through education. With guidance, determination, and hard work, you will succeed in your quest.

Why Choose a Community College?

Whatever your reason for starting your education at a community college, The College Board lists its own reasons to attend a community college:*

You don't want to pay a lot for college. Historically, community colleges' costs average less than four-year universities' tuition and fees, in part because their missions include providing education to people who cannot afford to go to a traditional university.

You are not sure if you want to get a degree. Community colleges are a great place to start taking classes if you are unsure of your future goals. If you decide that college is not for you, you won't have a large tuition bill looming over you.

You don't know what degree program you want to enroll in. Because community colleges offer technical, business, and industrial classes as well as university-transfer curriculum, you have more options to choose from. You can take classes in computers, music appreciation, welding, and business communication—all in the same semester.

Your GPA from high school or another college is low, and you want to work on improving your skills and your grades. Community schools are well known for their open admission policies, smaller classes (one-on-one attention), and student services. Thus, a community school is the best place to improve your reading, writing, and math abilities because you have more contact with your instructors and the opportunity to take classes that help you refine basic skills.

You want to pursue a degree in a technical, business, or industrial field. If you are more technical-, business-, or industrial-minded, a community college is an ideal place to pursue a certificate or degree in such fields as networking, landscape management, carpentry, computer-aided drafting, paralegal technology, and autobody repair. Most four-year colleges do not offer such programs.

You need a flexible schedule because of work and family responsibilities. Just as community colleges cater to students who need help developing their skills and students who cannot afford high-priced universities, community colleges are also more likely to offer classes that fit the busy schedule of a working student. Many community colleges offer Web-based courses; telecourses; early-morning, evening, and weekend classes; and accelerated classes.

---

*Six Benefits of Community Colleges. Copyright © 2005, collegeboard.com. Reproduced with permission. All rights reserved. www.collegeboard.com.

Other reasons you decided to enroll in a community college may include:

- The college is near your workplace, which makes it easier to get to class and back to work.
- The school has on-site day care that is affordable and accredited.
- You know someone who went to a community college, and now she has a great job.
- You took one class for fun, such as creative writing, and now you want to take more.
- Your high school counselor encouraged you to ease into college.
- The community college is smaller than the four-year university, and you want personal attention in class.
- You received a scholarship to attend the school.
- The community college has a larger variety of programs to choose from and great internship opportunities.
- You want a "practical" degree.
- The college is closer to home so you can spend more time with your family.
- You are not ready to make a four-year commitment to a degree, but you want to complete a program.
- The community college has fewer distractions, such as fraternities and sororities, so you can concentrate on academics.

The Benefits of Higher Education

Perhaps the most important reason people enroll in college is to get a better job. No doubt, higher education can help you find career success, but there are other reasons completing a degree (or just taking a few classes) can improve your life. The more formal education you have, the more likely you are to earn more money. Earning more money allows you to provide better for yourself and your family. Education can improve your life by increasing your understanding of yourself and the world around you. The more you know and understand other people, cultures, and yourself, the better able you are to influence your community in a positive way. Knowing more about yourself also improves your self-esteem and personal happiness. Moreover, higher education gives you the lifelong learning skills necessary for your health and well-being. Life, liberty, and the pursuit of happiness may be a cliché these days, but they are the primary results of an education.

- Going to college improves your life through a better career, more money, and better lifestyle choices because you are more informed.
- Going to college improves your freedom to make those choices—the more you know, the better choices you make and the more liberty you have to make those choices.
- Going to college makes you more satisfied with your life because you feel proud of your achievements.

Why Read This Book?

After reading the reasons why over 5 million students are attending a community college, you may be able to add a few more. But whatever your reason, you can be sure that you made the right choice. Your community college experience will enrich your life regardless of how long you stay, what degree or certificate you complete, or where you go afterward.

The purpose of this book, then, is to help you make the most of your community college experience. In the chapters, you will find information about college life and culture, the expectations of professors, study and test-taking skills, and managing your financial and educational future. You will also discover practical information to help you prepare to transfer to a four-year university or enter the workforce directly.

Remember, though, that this book is only one source of assistance for you as you make your way through decisions and deadlines. You can also look to your instructors, peers, counselors, advisors, friends, and family to help you with all of the challenges of being in college while juggling work, family, and extracurricular activities.

Remember, you are not alone: Over 5 million other students are experiencing what you are going through—the anxiety, the uncertainty, the exhilaration, and the pride that comes from starting on such an important and life-changing journey. No matter how many classes you take or what degree you finally complete, you have now taken the first step to bettering yourself by improving your education.

REFERENCE

The College Board (2005). "Six Benefits of Community Colleges: It Might Be the Right Path for You." Retrieved August 14, 2005 from www.collegeboard.com/article/0,3868,4-21-0-8169,00.html.

The Community College
EXPERIENCE
PLUS

1 Understanding Your College

R achel has learned that there is a different set of expectations in college than there was in high school. As she related, some "rules" do not apply anymore—there are new responsibilities and methods of communication. College students like Rachel realize that understanding college culture and becoming familiar with the campus are two important parts of starting college. In addition to the other information, Rachel told you that her VARK learning style is both aural and kinesthetic. You will learn more about personality types and learning styles in the next chapter, but for now, it may be helpful to know that she learns best by hearing and participating in physical activities. Whether you learn best by hearing, seeing, participating, or reading, this chapter discusses the following topics, which will move you closer to being comfortable in college:

- What will college be like? What can I expect?

- What do professors expect from me? How can I meet their expectations?

- Should I worry about my grades? Are they important?

- How will I find my way around campus?

- How can I find the help I need when I need it?

COMMUNITY · COLLEGE ·

Student Profile

NAME: **Rachel McCorkle**   AGE: **18**

MAJOR: **Art**

1. What was the biggest adjustment you had to make when moving from high school to college?

   The biggest adjustment was realizing that because I can set my own schedule, I need to be responsible.

2. Describe your college's culture. What is expected of you and others who are enrolled in college?

   It is really relaxed and friendly. There is time to get to know each other. In college, we are expected to come to class because we are paying to be here. We also have to be responsible for our own work. You have to rely on yourself—there's no one to tell you that you are not doing well.

3. What types of communication materials were you familiar with in high school? Which ones are new?

   The communication materials are the same as they were in high school. We had a student newspaper, literary magazine, and website. However, few of my high-school teachers handed out a syllabus, so that is a new way to communicate.

4. What is your VARK?

   Aural and kinesthetic.

What Is College Culture?

QUICK AND EASY?

LOSE WEIGHT OVERNIGHT WITHOUT DIET AND EXERCISE!

LUNCH IN TEN MINUTES OR IT'S FREE!

BUY GIFTS ON THE INTERNET—NO WAITING IN LINES, NO LOOKING FOR PARKING

A COMPLETE GOURMET MEAL FOR YOUR FAMILY—IN 5 MINUTES

As these common slogans show, we are bombarded by offers to get something without effort and without sacrificing our precious time. We have come to value anything that is quick and easy. Unfortunately, the desire for "quick and easy" has spread from fast food and convenience items to higher education as well. Students who are strapped for time, but who also believe a degree will give them the financial stability and career success they want, often enroll in a community college because the programs are typically shorter than those at a four-year university—the "quick" students are looking for. Other students enroll in a community college because they believe that the courses are not as challenging as they are at other schools—the "easy" students are looking for.

Although the community colleges' degree programs are sometimes shorter, usually one or two years long, the reality is that more time may be necessary to complete a degree program if you enroll as a part-time student. You also may need developmental or remedial classes before you can start the required curriculum, which will delay the program's completion. Perhaps the biggest misconception about community colleges, however, is that the classes are less demanding.

Because of technical and industrial standards and licensing, many courses and programs are, in fact, very challenging. Instructors who teach in the technical, industrial, and business fields are expected to graduate students who can pass the licensing exams, which means the standards in the class must be high. If the courses are "easy," the graduates are unemployable. Likewise, students intending to transfer to four-year universities after completing their general education requirements will not be successful if the community college courses are not challenging. Community colleges want well-prepared and successful graduates; thus, the colleges must provide courses that require the best work from the students.

This chapter's objectives, then, are to introduce you to the culture of college, to reveal the truths about going to college and debunk the myths—the "quick and easy" myth, for one—and to prepare you to meet the challenges you will inevitably face. The first step, though, is to change your thinking from "quick and easy" to the belief that your college education is worth taking time to complete, and should be challenging and rewarding.

Reflection

EXERCISE 1.1

What are your early impressions of your community college? How do you feel about taking on such an exciting and important journey?

Companion
Website

Higher Education and the Role of the Community College

Part of understanding college culture is to understand what higher education is and what it does. According to the American Association of Community Colleges' website, more than 1,000 community colleges exist today. The first community colleges provided a liberal arts education; that emphasis changed to job training during the 1930s to deal with unemployment during the Great Depression. Today, the AACC claims, over half of all undergraduates attend a community college. What sets community colleges apart from traditional four-year universities is their versatility and accessibility. Many community college mission statements demonstrate a commitment to offering higher education and continuing education to those who may not be ready or feel they are ready to pursue a four-year degree. At a community college, you can complete the first two years of general education credits toward a four-year degree, or you can work toward a degree or certificate in a highly specialized field. If you need help transitioning into higher education because of such issues as remediation and cost, a community college can be the perfect match for you.

Regardless of why you enrolled at a community college, be assured you made a wise choice. Community colleges are constantly adapting to the changing needs of their community, business and industry, and students. They pride themselves on being student-focused teaching and learning institutions that are uniquely capable of responding to changes in the workforce so the students receive the highest quality education. Community colleges also lead the way in innovative scheduling and accommodations because the students demand it. It speaks volumes when a community college reacts to students' special work and family needs by offering night, weekend, online, and special session classes. Because of their commitment to you, community colleges will continue to be a great way for people to start or continue their education or upgrade their skills.

What Does Your Community College Value?

As you will learn in Chapter 2, determining your values is an integral part of understanding yourself better. The same is true for what your college values; understanding its values enables you to better appreciate the college's mission and services. To determine your community college's values, as well as its goals, look at its mission statement, its extracurricular activities, the types of degrees it awards, and its faculty and staff. All colleges and universities value students' success. Because schools value producing educated, dynamic members of the community, they focus their goals on helping their students achieve success. They may do this by offering tutoring and counseling services or by providing developmental courses for students who lack the preparation needed to be successful in college-level courses.

Colleges and universities also value diversity, although they may define the term differently, because without diversity, there is little need for college. Diversity—in people's backgrounds, in their opinions, and in their interests and activities—creates an environment in which ideas and values can be developed and shaped. Your school may celebrate ethnic diversity by sponsoring multicultural groups, promoting cultural celebrations, or working to include all types of people in decision making. Your school may value a diverse faculty, attracting and hiring professors from all parts of the world, with different world views.

Although you will find similarities between what you and people in the academic world value, you may occasionally find that your college's values do not mesh with yours. At the very least, you will meet one person (most likely dozens) who openly or implicitly challenges what you believe.

Making the Transition: What Is Expected

For some students, the move from high school to college seems fairly simple—both require reading, writing, testing, and attending class. Students taking the step from work to school may also see some similarities between their jobs and their classroom work—both require working hard, staying motivated, and following the rules. Despite the similarities between the cultures, some students have trouble adjusting to the "climate" of college because they are not sure what is expected of them. In order to be successful, students must know what is expected of them beyond the questions on the next test; they need to know how college works and how to navigate through not only their courses, but also the common challenges they will face as they work toward a degree or certificate.

Exhibit 1.1 illustrates some of the differences and similarities between high school, a full-time job, and college. Notice that the greatest differences occur between high school and college; although there are some similarities between a full-time job and college, there are also distinct differences.

With your transition into college in mind, consider the following information about what you can expect in college. Even though the expectations are different, you are in control of your success.

Attendance

Movie director, actor, and writer Woody Allen said, "Eighty percent of success is showing up." Definitely, in college classes, you can't be successful unless you attend regularly. That means you must go to class every time it meets whether or not you feel like it and whether or not there is something "important" going on. Unlike high school, college professors may not take attendance or make an issue of students who do not attend; however, do not be fooled by an instructor's laid-back attitude about your attendance. If you do not attend regularly, you will miss valuable information about assignments, tests, and grading—information the instructor is not obligated to review with you. Especially in courses that build on concepts (such as math and English), your lack of attendance can keep you from being successful later in the semester. Also, think of regular attendance as your leverage for negotiating. If you have an emergency that prevents you from taking a test on time, your regular attendance and your status as a good student can help get an extension.

Students who have held jobs better understand the importance of attendance. They know that they do not get paid if they do not show up, or they

EXHIBIT 1.1   *Comparisons and contrasts.*

HIGH SCHOOL	FULL-TIME WORK	COLLEGE
Attendance is mandatory to meet requirements	Attendance is mandatory to stay employed	Attendance may not be mandatory
At least six continuous hours spent in class each day	At least eight continuous hours spent at work each day	Different amounts of time spent in class and between classes each day
Very little choice in what classes you take and when you take them	May have little choice in work assignments and when the work is to be completed	More flexibility in which classes you take, in when you work on assignments, and in how soon you complete them before the due date
Moderate to no outside work necessary to be successful	Moderate to no overtime work necessary to complete job duties	Substantial amount of outside work to complete assignments and to be successful
Teachers check homework and keep you up to date on progress; they will inform you if you are not completing assignments and progressing well	Supervisors check completion and quality of work at regular intervals; they will inform you if you are not meeting the standards for the position	Professors may not check all homework or provide feedback on progress at regular intervals; they may not inform you if you are not meeting the standards of the course
Teachers go over material and expect you to remember facts and information	Employers provide basic information and expect you to use it to complete the job effectively	Professors provide concepts and theories and expect you to evaluate the ideas, synthesize the ideas with other concepts you have learned, and develop new theories
Frequent tests over small amounts of material allow grades to be raised if needed	Supervisors create employee improvement plans to allow you to improve your ratings if needed	Professors provide the standards and grading criteria but often allow only a few chances (through infrequent testing/assignments) to meet them

may be fired if they miss too many days. However, just showing up is only part of succeeding in college and understanding the culture. To be a successful college student, regular attendance has to be combined with maintaining a positive attitude, preparing for class, asking for help when needed, acting with integrity, and staying motivated.

If you miss a class or intend to miss a class, you should mention the absence to your instructor. Although you may not need a doctor's excuse, you should be prepared to justify your absence, especially if you have missed an exam. Most instructors, though, do not care why you missed. In fact, they don't distinguish between excused or unexcused absences. Instead, they are more interested in whether you keep up with the work.

Attitude

A good attitude will take you far in the journey to achieve your goals. Sometimes it will be hard to maintain a positive outlook because you feel overwhelmed with the challenges of college, work, and family, but if you can maintain a good attitude, your chances of success are greater. Good attitudes are infectious, and you will soon find that your professors and classmates will reflect the good attitude you have.

Critical Thinking EXERCISE 1.2

Why is attendance important to success in college? Besides information and assignments, what can students miss when they do not attend regularly?

Companion Website

The other side of a positive attitude is a negative one, and at some point in your college career, you will feel as though the world is out to undermine your success. You may feel overwhelmed with the responsibilities of going to school and working, or you may feel frustrated that you have not progressed in your classes the way you hoped. There are numerous reasons that you may, temporarily at least, have a pessimistic outlook on your college education or your life. Bringing a bad mood into the classroom, however, can make your attitude worse and your outlook gloomier. Even though you may feel anonymous most of the time, instructors do notice when students are disgruntled and unwilling to learn. Although instructors may not know why a student is upset, they are still affected by the student's bad attitude. At the very least, they may see negativity as a sign of immaturity.

Common "bad attitude" mistakes that students make include

- acting as if they know more than the professor.
- rolling their eyes or shaking their heads when an instructor is presenting material or making an assignment.
- making negative comments out loud about the class, the instructor, or other students.
- resisting or refusing to do an assignment.
- slouching down in the seat, looking bored.
- getting angry about a low grade.
- walking out of class because of anger or boredom.

Presenting a good attitude in class is easier than you think. In fact, it just takes a little attention to the messages you send with your face, body, and language. Tips for presenting a good attitude include

- coming to class prepared with the appropriate books and materials.
- paying attention.
- demonstrating an effort to master the material and to complete assignments.
- providing positive or constructive feedback in class or privately.
- smiling and being friendly!

The belief that instructors only like students who make As or students who gush with compliments about the course is false. The truth is that professors like students who show a genuine interest and demonstrate effort in the course, regardless of the grades they earn. It is the student with the good attitude, then, who gets the most from the instructor because he or she realizes that a student with a good attitude is someone who is willing to learn.

Effort

Gone are the days of an A for effort. In high school, students who merely complete work are usually rewarded with a passing grade. However, in college, effort must be coupled with quality. Putting forth the effort to write a paper and turn it in is only part of the requirement. You also have to adhere to the standards of the course. If the instructor asks for a 10-page paper that argues a contemporary topic and uses 5 sources, you must follow those guidelines. Although a high-school teacher may have given you credit for submitting a 7-page paper on a contemporary topic that used only 3 sources and contained numerous grammatical errors, a college instructor will not. Usually, you will not receive any credit for an assignment if you did not follow the guidelines or requirements.

Also gone are the days when spending more time studying or writing a paper equals a higher grade. Students who complain about low grades by saying, "But I spent two weeks writing the paper" will not get any sympathy from the professor. Does this mean that you should not spend time working on assignments or studying? Definitely not. This means that you should pay attention to the quality of the work you produced given the time you spent. The quality of work is what you are graded on, not the number of hours you spent.

Students who are well-prepared for class improve their chances of success.

You will also find that you must increase your effort to get the grades you used to get in high school. You will have more reading, writing, and critical thinking to do each week, and most of the work will be done outside of class. Professors view class time as a small fraction of the course. A common rule for calculating how many hours you have to devote to a course is to study three hours for every hour you are in class. Therefore, if you are taking a 3-hour class, you should study 9 hours a week for that one course. If you are taking 12 hours a semester, you should devote 36 hours a week to studying. That means 48 (36 hours to study and 12 hours to attend class) hours of your week will be occupied with schoolwork—in class and outside class.

Honesty

Later chapters discuss the issue of integrity—the foundation for honesty—in depth, but it is worth mentioning here as well because honesty is such an important component to learning. It can be said that student learning is not possible without honesty and integrity. For example, if a student cheats on all the exams in a class, what has she learned about the subject? Student learning, therefore, relies on integrity.

In addition to being honest about doing the course work, you must be honest with yourself about your progress. If you do not understand the material and are making poor grades, take the time to honestly assess your preparation for the course or your abilities. Maybe you are not spending enough time studying and reviewing for the class, or maybe you need to take a lower-level course so that you can brush up on any skills you lack. It is better to admit that you need help or need better preparation than to spend valuable time performing poorly.

Instructors' Expectations

In addition to attendance, attitude, and effort, there are a few other expectations when you take college classes. For instance, when an instructor hands out a written assignment to be turned in at a later date, the assignment must be typed. In fact, unless otherwise stated, assume that all out-of-class writing assignments should be typed—they are easier to read and look more professional. If you do not know how to type or use a word processor, either find someone to type your assignments for you, or better yet, learn how to use a computer with word-processing software. The sooner you learn, the easier future assignments will be.

When you handwrite an assignment, the instructor also expects your handwriting to be legible. Handwriting that is messy or incomprehensible or is written with anything other than blue or black pen on white paper makes the instructor's job more difficult. Some instructors will ask you to rewrite the assignment or will lower your grade if your work is unreadable. If you have a disability that prevents you from writing legibly, be sure the instructor is aware at the beginning of the semester.

Another expectation instructors have is preparation—yours. Be prepared *before* you get to class by reading the assigned pages or completing the homework. Too often, students think the instructor will provide a complete overview of the material and that preparing for class is a waste of time. Nothing could be further from the truth. Instructors who assign reading or homework expect students to prepare—they may even administer quizzes to ensure that students are prepared—and to ask questions about anything they do not understand. It may be assumed that if you do not ask questions or participate in a discussion, then you understand the assignment. Professors often hold students accountable for the assigned reading on exams even though it was not discussed in class.

It is a common belief among seasoned students that instructors think that their classes are the only ones being taken, and studying for them is the only activity students do all week. More realistically, college professors expect that your first priority is your college classes. At a community college, you may find instructors who are more understanding about your multiple responsibilities, but remember their first concern is that you learn the material and meet course objectives.

Location

Where you sit in the classroom is just as important as being prepared to meet instructors' expectations. If you arrive early enough before class, you should be able to sit up close, which is where you want to be. Sitting in the back of the class where you can barely see or be seen or heard is the least advantageous place because you can be distracted easily or tempted to do other things. Sitting in the front row or as close to the front as possible maximizes your chances of success.

Students who sit up front are usually more engaged, more willing to answer questions and discuss topics, and more likely to get positive feedback from the instructor. Professors like students who sit up front and seem interested, even if they don't speak up during class. Moreover, students who sit close to the front (within the first few rows if the room is large or in the front row if the room is small) are more likely to pay attention, take good notes, and get good grades.

Maturity

Maturity is the foundation for many of the other components of college culture. Without a mature attitude and outlook, the other parts are unattainable. There are, however, less obvious actions that can help you present yourself as a dedicated, mature student. The first one is paying attention during lectures, presentations, guest speakers, and films. Although this sounds like an obvious suggestion, it is often forgotten after the first few weeks of the semester. Chapter 6 discusses the skills for improving your attention, but for now, work on looking at the front of the room and avoiding distractions.

A common barrier to paying attention, besides staring out the window, is doing homework in class. Instructors frown on students who use class time to study for other classes or complete assignments that were due at the beginning of class. Just remember that the instructor sees you, acknowledges that you are not paying attention because you are working on other classes, and remembers everything, especially when you need a favor.

Some colleges have policies about cell phone and pager use. If your college does not, turn your cell phone and pager off in class. Unless you work in a field that requires your immediate attention in the event of an emergency or you have a gravely ill family member, turn off all electronic devices while in class. In some cases (e.g., chemistry lab), the distraction can be potentially dangerous. In most cases, however, it is annoying at best, rude at worst. Students who answer social calls in class appear immature and unconcerned about their education—or anyone else's.

An important way to demonstrate maturity in college is to understand and appreciate constructive criticism from your professor. When you receive advice or comments about your work or progress in the course, look at it as an opportunity to learn more about yourself and the expectations of college. A professor's job is to educate you and help you learn more about the world; it is not her job to undermine those efforts by putting you down.

Some students feel any feedback that is not positive destroys their self-confidence. The opposite should be true—positive feedback does not help you learn, nor does it necessarily challenge you to do better. Of course, we all want to hear something nice about ourselves, but we also should be open to the challenge of receiving criticism about the quality of our work. It takes a mature person to value constructive criticism and learn from it.

Chapter 5 discusses diversity and relationships in depth, but it is worth mentioning here that dealing with diversity, conflict, and controversy takes a certain level of maturity. Effectively meeting any challenge to your belief system or values demands that you act with integrity and openness. Because the purpose of getting an education is to stretch your mind and expand your ideas, maturity helps you put all that new information into perspective.

Responsibility

No doubt you already juggle numerous responsibilities, and going to class and studying are just more tasks you must complete each week. Handling your responsibilities skillfully takes a positive attitude, respect for yourself, and maturity. Obviously, as a student you are responsible for taking notes, studying for tests, and attending classes regularly. But you also are responsible for asking questions when you do not understand or when you think you are being treated unfairly.

The University of South Carolina developed and adopted a creed it expects all of its students to follow while enrolled in the university. Here are two of the tenets of the Carolinian Creed that emphasize the student's responsibility:

> I will practice personal and academic integrity.
>
> I will respect the rights and property of others.

In addition, you are also responsible for taking control of your education if it is not going the way you want. As Laura Thomas, a community college freshman, admits, "I realized after my first semester of college that my instructors work for me. It is my responsibility to tell them what I need. They can't help me if they don't know what I am struggling with."

Collaboration

EXERCISE 1.3

Working in a group, write a five-minute scene in which a student demonstrates maturity and responsibility in the classroom. Perform the scene for the class, and ask your classmates to determine which actions demonstrate maturity.

Companion Website

The Right Stuff

Ever since kindergarten, you've been expected to bring your supplies with you on the first day of school. Crayons, glue, and No. 2 pencils have now been replaced by computer disks, laptops, and ink cartridges. The computer has changed the landscape of education by providing students with word processing and access to research databases and the World Wide Web. Most colleges provide computer labs, e-mail accounts, and printing capabilities for student use. Because college campuses offer access to computers, your professors expect you to have a working knowledge of how to use one. Instructors may require you to word-process assignments or correspond in a chat room.

If you do not have the necessary computer skills, seek help from computer lab technicians, special computer classes, and classmates.

Other "right stuff" items include paper (for taking notes and printing papers), pens, a dictionary, writing handbook, and thesaurus. As you take more classes, specialized reference books and supplies may be needed to help you study and complete assignments.

College Culture Shock

The preceding discussion listed only a sampling of college expectations and experiences. You will encounter many other aspects of college culture, some of which may be uncomfortable or even shocking to you. As stated previously, all colleges value diversity, whether in the student body population or the backgrounds of its faculty. You will find diversity in ideas and theories among the offered subjects. Some ideas and theories may challenge your beliefs and values. Still others may contain material you find disrespectful, distasteful, or disturbing (See Exhibit 1.2 for some examples).

EXHIBIT 1.2   *Samples of possibly controversial subjects and topics.*

SUBJECTS

Art	Music	Philosophy	Theatre	Literature	Composition
Cultural Studies	Gender Studies	Political Science	Religion	Sociology	Economics
Anthropology	Law	Biology	Chemistry	Astronomy	History

TOPICS

The existence of God, higher being

Conservatism and liberalism

Nudity in art, photography

Profanity and adult situations in music, theater, literature

Sexuality, including homosexuality and adultery

The creation of the universe

The theory of extraterrestrial life

Evolution

The beginning of life

Scientific investigation and experimentation (stem cells, cloning)

Socioeconomic theory

Besides reading and discussing controversial or uncomfortable issues, your college may produce student and faculty work that contains language, images, or situations you find offensive.

What should you do if you encounter college "culture shock"? First, remember that the purpose of higher education is to provide you with a wider worldview and understanding of diversity—even if that diversity involves different ideas, theories, and methods of representing those ideas and theories. Second, remember that you have the right to an opinion and a feeling about what you encounter in college. There is no reason you should hide your feelings or attitudes about what you are learning and encountering. With this said, the third point to remember is that with your right to an opinion, you also have an *obligation* as a college student to examine your previously held beliefs and evaluate how they are being challenged in your courses or as you participate in college activities. You also have an obligation to appreciate that there is more than one way to view an "offensive" idea or presentation.

Types of Learning Experiences

Some learning experiences involve one-to-one support, such as peer mentoring and tutoring.

n addition to *what* you learn at a community college, you should consider *how* you learn. Colleges and universities frequently use learning communities, sometimes called "cohorts," to group students together so

they can cultivate a supportive learning community. For example, 20 students have the same weekly class schedule and possibly a scheduled study session with smaller groups. Students who participate in learning communities build an instant support and study group because they are all going through similar experiences adjusting to college life and course workload.

Two other learning experiences you may encounter involve one-to-one support: peer mentoring and peer tutoring. New students are paired with students close to finishing their degrees in a mentor relationship. The peer mentors provide orientation, advice, and support during the new students' first semester or year. They may also help with time management skills, goal setting, and degree planning. Peer tutors, on the other hand, are not usually paired with an individual student. Instead, you will encounter peer tutors at a tutoring lab or at certain times during the week. Peer tutors provide students with help in specific academic areas. The benefit of both peer mentors and tutors is that you have others to help you who are not too far removed from the college experience. They are more likely to understand your needs and goals, and they can provide insight that faculty and administrators may not be able to share.

Service learning opportunities are community service projects that are integrated into your academic experience. You may take an Introduction to Education course where part of your class work takes place at a local elementary school. As part of your work in the community, you may be required to find a solution to a common issue in the community and keep a reflective journal about your experiences.

Grades

Grades are an important part of your education, and at the same time they are unimportant. How can that be? How can something be both important and unimportant? Grades are important because they often reflect your level of achievement on an assignment or in a course; they are also important for obtaining and maintaining scholarships and financial aid. In addition, grades are important to family, friends, and employers who may be supporting you financially and emotionally. Many people view grades as a reflection of a particular level of success. For instance, most people view a student who has straight As as someone who is smart and successful.

Although most people, especially students, place great significance on grades, they are what educators call "non-measures" of student learning. For example, an A in an algebra class does not necessarily indicate a student knows how to solve quadratic equations. Likewise, an A in a literature course does not automatically mean that a student knows how to explicate a poem. Grades, in these instances, may not reflect what a student has learned in a course. Instead, they may reflect that a student merely turned in all his homework on time or that he is a good test taker.

If grades sometimes indicate a level of success in a course and sometimes don't, what are you to do? How will you ever know when to worry about your grades and when to concentrate on learning the material? The purpose of this section is to help you answer these questions by explaining how professors grade and how you can make good grades in college. This section also discusses what you can do to de-emphasize making a good grade and emphasize mastering the course material. This is not to say, however, that grades are never important. They are important because they describe the work you have done in a class. However, grades alone are not the magic carpet to college success; they are only part of the story of your achievements. Your goal should be to strike a balance between caring about your grades and caring about improving your skills and increasing your knowledge.

Grades can be indications of

- a certain level of success on an assignment or in a course.
- the time and work you put into an assignment or a course.
- the knowledge and skills you obtained.

Grades are not indications of

- your worth as a person.
- your educational and career potential.
- an inability to learn.

Banner and Cannon (1999), in their book *The Elements of Learning*, define grades as "evaluations of your work, not of your character or intelligence. You may be a wonderful person but a failure as a biologist. You may find it impossible to do satisfactory work in history but may excel in all other subjects" (p. 160). They assert, therefore, that grades have limitations. Certainly, they are a necessary part of evaluation, much as you are evaluated on your job. However, as Banner and Cannon point out, grades do not show the whole picture of who you are. Grades, then, are only part of the story of your education.

How College Professors Grade

As stated earlier, college professors grade a student on his or her ability to meet the standards of the course or of a particular assignment. The following box shows a potential set of grading criteria, or standards, for a college-level paper. In this case, the criteria are for an A paper.

Grading Criteria for an A Paper

- An excellent introduction with engaging hooks, setup, plan, and main idea
- An original, significant thesis that offers insightful interpretation or thought
- An inventive and logical organizational plan
- Smooth and varied transitional expressions, phrases, and sentences that provide unity and coherence
- Strong conclusion that ends the essay effectively
- Expressive, clear style with sophisticated sentence structure and word choice
- No more than three major grammatical errors

INTEGRITY MATTERS

The Family Educational Rights and Privacy Act (FERPA) is a federal law that protects students' educational records. Under this Act, professors and other college officials cannot discuss your academic record with anyone who is not authorized by you to receive that information.

Grading Scales

Knowing how your college assesses student performance is a start to improving your overall outlook on grading. The following is a typical grading scale in college:

90–100 = A   80–89 = B   70–79 = C   60–69 = D   0–59 = F

Some colleges may use a + or − next to a letter grade such as A− or C+. Usually, colleges that allow for pluses and minuses also alter the grading scale to designate the different grades; for example:

94–100 = A   90–93 = A−   87–89 = B+   84–86 = B   80–83 = B−

Calculating Your Grade Point Average

Each semester, the registrar calculates your grade point average, or GPA, and posts it to your transcript. Because the calculation requires a little mathematical skill, it is important to know how your registrar determines it. Hours are the number of hours you are in class each week. Classes are usually three credit hours. Science classes that have labs usually carry four credit hours. Depending on the course and the program, credit hours can be as many as six or as few as one. To know how many hours a course carries, check the description in the college catalog because some classes meet for more hours a week than they are worth in terms of credit.

Letter grades carry a point value called quality points. The following example shows how many quality points each letter grade is worth.

LETTER GRADE	QUALITY POINTS
A	4
B	3
C	2
D	1
F	0

Courses that are designated developmental or remedial usually do not figure into your GPA, so they do not carry any quality points. If you audit a course or receive AP or CLEP credit for a course, you will not receive quality points. In other words, although you receive credit on your transcript for taking the course or taking a course equivalent, the grade will not factor into your grade point average. Before you figure your GPA, determine your grade points for each class by multiplying the quality points for the grade you received by the number of hours the class is worth. For instance, if you took a four-hour class and you made a B, multiply 4 (hours) by 3 (quality points for a B).

If you took 15 hours (5 three-hour courses) during the semester, and you received an A, B, and three Cs, then calculate your grade this way:

HOURS	GRADE	(QUALITY POINTS)	GRADE POINTS
3	A	(4)	3 × 4 = 12
3	B	(3)	3 × 3 = 9
3	C	(2)	3 × 2 = 6
3	C	(2)	3 × 2 = 6
3	C	(2)	3 × 2 = 6
15 Hours			39 Grade Points

Finally, divide the grade points total by the hours total (39/15). Your GPA is 2.6.

Practice

EXERCISE 1.4

Angela has an A in English Composition I, Bs in both College Seminar and Algebra, and a C in her Biological Science class. What is her GPA for the semester? (Assume the biology class is four credit hours and the other classes are three credit hours.)

Companion Website

What Does Your College Look Like?

Now that you have a better understanding of how your college works and what is expected of you, it is time to examine how your college looks. Getting to know the campus layout and the people who work there is important to understanding the culture.

The Campus

Find a map of your campus and study it for a few minutes. How many buildings does it have? How much parking space? How much "green" space or landscaping? Are there any unique features to your campus that make it an inviting and exciting place? Familiarizing yourself with the campus is probably the first activity you did when you enrolled. If you have not taken a tour or simply walked around campus, you should do so within the first few weeks of the semester. You should be able to locate the library, the student center, student parking, the bookstore, the business office, and the registrar's office—just to name a few destinations.

BUILDING OR AREA	AT MY COLLEGE
Student center or union	
Library	
Bookstore	
Administration building	
Theater or auditorium	
Snack bar or food court	
Athletic training facilities (indoor or outdoor)	
Science labs	
Technical and industrial training facilities	
Computer labs	
Separate divisions (e.g., technical and industrial, computer information systems, allied health, business, general education)	
Individual departments (e.g., accounting, drafting, welding, natural sciences)	
Student parking	
Benches and tables for meeting outside	
Quiet study space inside	

The more you know about your campus layout, the easier it will be to find what you are looking for when you need it most. Using your campus map or your memory, complete the campus checklist activity by checking off the types of buildings or departments within buildings that you know are present at your college.

If your college has more than one campus, familiarize yourself with the layout of the other college property. You may have to travel to a satellite campus to take a test or pick up materials for a class. If you have the time, and the other campus is not too far away, ask for a tour.

The People on Your Campus

Equally important to understanding where buildings and services are located is knowing who does what on your campus. Exhibit 1.3 shows basic titles and job descriptions for college officials (your college may use different titles or may have more positions than those listed).

Critical Thinking

EXERCISE 1.5

What would the ideal college campus look like? What buildings would it have? How would it be organized? Draw or describe a model college campus.

Companion Website

19

EXHIBIT 1.3   *The titles and responsibilities of campus officials.*

POSITION	WHAT THEY DO	WHY YOU SHOULD KNOW THEM
Board of Trustees	A group of people charged with overseeing the college operations and planning	The board of trustees is the last stop along the way to making a major change on campus. Controversial issues such as censorship, demonstrations, and firing faculty may be addressed to the board directly, depending on the circumstances.
President	The head of the school	Like the board, the president is one of the last stops for concerns about campus issues if attempts to resolve them are not successful.
Dean of Students	Sometimes called Vice President for Instruction; takes care of matters concerning curriculum, classes, degree programs, and instructors	If you have concerns about a grade, and all attempts to address the matter with the instructor and the department dean are fruitless, the dean of students can intervene. Potentially volatile issues, such as sexual harassment, should be brought to her immediate attention.
Dean of Student Services	Sometimes called Vice President of Student Services; oversees all student-related services such as contacting prospective students, enrollment, and counseling	You may actually meet the dean of student services when you enroll, and he will be an important contact person if you need assistance with any aspect of your classes.
Registrar	Handles registration and transcripts	You may visit the registrar if you recently applied for admission or if you transferred. Also, you may contact her if you receive a grade that is not correct or have to apply for an incomplete grade.
Director of Disability Services	May have other titles; handles the services provided to students with documented disabilities	If you need assistance with learning difficulties or disabilities, schedule an appointment with him. The more contact you have, the more information and help you will receive.
Career Counselor	Helps you discover what career you may be interested in and are best suited for; may also help you plan your academic career so you are prepared to enter the workforce	Stop by her office as soon as you get enrolled. You can take a skills and interest inventory that will help you think about the classes you want to take and the degree you want to complete. A career counselor can also help you with building a resume and provide tips for interviewing.
Director of Financial Aid	Handles financial aid for students and has access to scholarship information	If you need financial aid, the earlier you can see someone in this office, the better. Time is the key to getting what you need—apply early and follow up on the application. The financial aid office is usually very busy the week classes start, so plan ahead.

EXHIBIT 1.3 *Continued*

POSITION	WHAT THEY DO	WHY YOU SHOULD KNOW THEM
Library Director	Manages the library services for students and faculty	Talk with the director or any library staff when you need help finding a source. They can help you with the research process.
Director of Distance Education	Provides oversight for courses delivered to students at a distance; a new position at some schools	If you are interested in taking a course online or through compressed video, see her for information about how the courses work and what to expect.
Director of Campus Safety	Maintains a safe environment on campus, issues tickets, takes reports of incidents on campus, and reports annual crime statistics	If you ever become involved in or witness a crime on campus, you will need to talk to a campus officer. Because the officer's job is to maintain a safe environment, be willing to alert him to potential problems on campus.
Dean	Manages a group of departments or, if the division is small, a group of individual instructors	A dean is the next stop when you have an issue concerning a class or instructor. After you have talked with the instructor, you may see a dean to get more advice or help. Deans should be notified immediately of potentially volatile situations such as verbal threats from or physical assault by another student.
Department Chair	Oversees a department's instructors and curriculum	You may visit a department chair when considering a major in the department or if you need to talk about a certain class or instructor (after you have already talked to the instructor).
Professor, Instructor, or Lecturer	Is responsible for teaching you	There are many different names and ranks for the people who deliver content, motivate you to think critically, and assess your progress. They are the people you will have the most contact with on campus and the first people you should talk to when you have a problem.
Advisor	Helps students plan their schedules and their degrees before registration and during the semester	An advisor is another key person to your success in college. Consider the advisor the personal trainer who sets goals with you and helps you achieve them.

You should make a list of those administrators and faculty you may have to contact during your college career. For example, write down the names, titles, phone numbers, and e-mail addresses of your professors, department chairs, advisors, financial aid officers, and deans you have encountered. Keep the list in a safe place so that when you need to ask a question or get advice, you won't spend a lot of time searching for it.

When a Problem Arises

A time may come when you have a problem in one of your classes. If it does, be assured that the college's employees will work with you to resolve it. There are, however, rules and procedures regarding how to resolve a problem at a college. Knowing and following these procedures will ensure that a problem is handled appropriately and quickly.

The first step to resolving a conflict in class is to define what the problem is. Is it a communication problem? Is it a problem with the course material? Is it a problem with the course standards? Once you have defined the problem, your next step is to discuss the problem directly. If the problem is with your instructor, make an appointment during her office hours to discuss the issue. If you are emotional—angry, upset, nervous—wait until you have calmed down to discuss the problem. Your goal in meeting with the instructor is to resolve the conflict.

In order for the conflict resolution process to work, you must complete the first two steps. If you are not satisfied with the result or if you feel the problem has gotten worse, not better, move to the next step: talking to the department chair or dean. You will no doubt be asked if you have met with the instructor. Again, your goal at this step is to resolve the issue. Occasionally, the instructor may be called in to help resolve the issue. Staying calm and focused on resolving the conflict will be to your advantage. In the event the problem is not solved at this level, your last stop is with the dean of students or vice president for instruction. Starting at the top will only delay resolution.

Collaboration

EXERCISE 1.6

Working with two other classmates, determine the most helpful people on campus whom you have met so far. Describe how they helped you and what your overall impression of them is. Share your descriptions with the class.

Companion
Website

College Communications

Communicating in and out of class with instructors and students is a major part of the college experience, but don't forget that the college communicates with you in a variety of formats. College communications, in fact, are a great place to find information about courses, programs, scholarships, activities, and policy changes. It is important that you regularly read those publications the college produces in order to stay up to date with what is going on.

College Catalog

The college catalog is one of the most essential documents you will receive during your academic career. All of the information you need to apply for financial aid, to choose courses, and to graduate is contained

---

Reflection

EXERCISE 1.7

What are the advantages of knowing the people on your campus?

Companion
Website

in the catalog. It also sets forth what you are required to do to complete a degree. The academic calendar is usually placed at the beginning of the catalog. There you will find the dates for registration, dropping courses, and final exams.

Another important reason to read and keep your college catalog is that if the college changes any requirements of your degree program, you will be able follow the guidelines that were published the year you began the program. For instance, if you are working on an office management degree and you have taken three semesters so far, you will not necessarily have to adhere to new requirements made at a later date.

Student Handbook

The student handbook is another valuable publication because it provides you with specific information about student conduct, academic standards, and student services. Usually, the handbook describes the career services, bookstore, computer labs, and financial aid offices. Academic information, including probation and suspension for misconduct and qualifications for making the dean's list, is found in the student handbook. Most schools view the student handbook as a legal document that outlines what students can do in certain situations, so be sure to read the handbook closely and keep a copy at home or in your book bag.

Reflection

EXERCISE 1.8

What useful information have you found in your college catalog?

Companion Website

Campus Safety Brochure

A smaller, but equally important, document that your college publishes is the campus safety and security brochure. Information found in the brochure includes policies on handling sexual assault, substance and drug abuse, and harassment. Also, you can find contact numbers for campus police as well as campus crime statistics, which is a federal requirement.

College Newspaper

College newspapers differ from the college catalog and student handbook in that students are usually the ones responsible for the content. Within a college newspaper, you will find articles announcing upcoming events, reports on changes on the campus, editorials on important student issues, profiles of programs, and advertisements for used books, musical groups, and anything else that students want to announce. The college newspaper is also a forum to explore controversial topics and to discuss sensitive issues.

Newspapers always need students to interview, write, edit, and publish. If you have any interest in working for the newspaper, contact the editor or visit a journalism or composition professor.

Literary Magazine

One of the more entertaining and creative publications is the literary magazine. Some colleges produce a booklet or journal of students' creative endeavors; short stories, poetry, essays, art work, and photography are just a sample of the items literary magazines publish. Unlike the newspapers that are printed every day or every week, literary magazines are usually published once or twice a year.

Bulletin Boards

Even with the increased use of the Internet, the bulletin board is still an important way to get a message to students. Found all over campus, bulletin boards usually advertise used books, needs for roommates and part-time jobs, and upcoming campus events. Within academic buildings, bulletin boards often announce four-year college programs, summer workshops, and other types of academic activities.

Classroom Materials

Anything that professors hand out in class is a communication tool. The syllabus is one of the most important documents you will receive in class, so be sure to read it carefully. Exhibit 1.4 shows the information typically found in the syllabus.

EXHIBIT 1.4   *Components of a syllabus.*

- Instructor's name, office location, office phone number, office hours, and e-mail address
- Prerequisites for the course
- Course description from the catalog
- Textbook information
- Course objectives (what you will accomplish by the time you finish the class)
- Course content (what topics will be covered throughout the semester)
- Assignments and due dates
- Grading criteria
- Attendance and late work policies
- Academic integrity statement
- Disability policy
- General policies for classroom conduct

Even though the syllabus is considered a contract between the instructor and the student as to what to expect during the semester, some students do not read the document thoroughly. By reading the syllabus closely, you can ask questions about how the course will be conducted. Remember to reread the syllabus around midterm to refresh your memory of important dates and assignments.

Other important information handed out in class includes directions for assignments, photocopied readings, study questions, and notes. Regard anything given to you by the instructor as important, even if you are told the information "won't be on the test."

Although grades and feedback are discussed further in a later chapter, consider the grades and written comments you receive as communication from your instructors; in fact, it may be the most important information you receive from them. Be sure to read any comments or suggestions written on papers and exams, ask questions if you don't understand them or cannot read the handwriting, and save all feedback until the semester is over.

College Website

The college's website is a place where you can go to access the most current information about classes, academic programs, and instructor contact information. Because it is easy to update information on a website, you are more likely to receive the most accurate information.

In addition to general information about degrees and departments, your college's website may also give you access to professors' syllabi and assignments. Use this information to investigate which courses you want to take based on what the course objectives are and what papers are assigned.

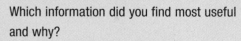

EXERCISE 1.9   *Critical Thinking*

Name three ways you received information on campus so far this semester. Did you read a bulletin board flyer? Did you pick up a student newspaper? Describe the information you received and how it was presented. Which information did you find most useful and why?

Companion
Website

Learning Styles Application

This chart lists the four learning styles and tips based on the chapter's main ideas. Locate your learning style and read the corresponding tips to maximize your success in college.

REVIEW

Visual learners will enjoy the new sights and meeting new people in college. You may think the campus is attractive and inviting. Where your classes are, where you hang out, and who you meet will affect your experience in college.

The new sounds at a college campus—whether the silence of the library study rooms or the noise in the student center—will pique aural learners' interest and imagination. You will enjoy talking with new people and listening to lectures.

Read/write learners will find many things on a college campus to interest you. There will be plenty to read for class, but there will also be a student newspaper or newsletter, literary magazine, and flyers that will grab your attention.

Those whose learning style preference is kinesthetic will find a variety of programs that will satisfy the need to be active. Whether it is welding, dental assisting, or office technology, you will be able to do more than listen to lectures, read textbooks, and write papers.

Path of Discovery

Journal Entry

What is your experience so far with the college culture? What is the biggest difference you have experienced so far between high school or work and college?

FROM COLLEGE TO UNIVERSITY

The changes in culture and college services

If you are moving from your community college to a larger, more diverse university, you may experience a slight culture shock despite the semesters you already have under your belt. In addition to a bigger campus with more buildings to find and more students to meet, you may also find that a university seems more impersonal. Many students who transfer from a smaller community college complain that professors do not seem to care about them personally and that they lack the support and guidance they received at their previous school. Transfer students also note that expectations are higher— and their grades are lower—especially as they move into their majors and begin working toward a career.

Culturally, you should expect that your new university will offer more activities and groups than your smaller community college. You also should expect some kind of adjustment period as you get used to what your new professors expect of you. Statistically, transfer students do experience a slight drop in their GPA. This drop, however, is not necessarily an indication that they were not properly prepared by their community college.

All in all, the culture shock you experience when transferring to a four-year university will depend on how much bigger than and how different the school is from your community college. Just remember that whatever differences you notice, you will have similar resources at your disposal. Seek out counselors, advisors, faculty, and students who can help make your transition smoother. There are people at the four-year school to help you. Take your campus map and faculty and administrator list and find them.

FROM COLLEGE TO CAREER

How the culture will change again

Just as you adjusted to the college culture, you will have to make a new adjustment to the workforce if you have never held a full-time job. When starting your first job after college, you will experience a period of getting used to the way the office or business works. You will encounter new terms, new methods of doing things, and new people. In addition, you will experience working in groups or teams to accomplish tasks, and you will be expected to communicate orally and in a written format. You may also rely more heavily on e-mail and computers to get your work finished. Integrity will be an important part of your working experience. There will be less supervision and more expectation that you do the work you say you will do.

Any anxiety you may feel can be alleviated by paying attention to how others act on the job. Just as you made friends and found mentors in college, you should look for others who can offer guidance and help as you learn the ropes of a new career. Also, think about how you adjusted to college and use the same strategies to make the new environment seems less foreign and more comfortable.

Chapter in Review

1. Name and describe five different characteristics that professors will expect from you as a college student.

2. How will you use what you learned about grades to prepare yourself for earning grades in college?

3. What differences exist between high school and college or a full-time job and college?

4. Grades are limited because an A cannot fully express what was achieved. Describe other ways that students can mark their success in a class.

Case Scenarios

Read the following case scenarios and determine what each person should do. Refer to the information in this chapter as you write a description and plan of action for each student.

1. In Jennifer's literature class, she is reading Tim O'Brien's *The Things They Carried*. Although she understands the book is about the Vietnam War, she doesn't know why she has to read a book that contains so much profanity and graphic images of death. She made an appointment to speak to her professor about the reading assignment because she wants to avoid reading a book that is so depressing and discomforting. What advice would you give Jennifer before she speaks to her professor? Predict the outcome of the talk and what the consequence of the discussion will be on Jennifer's college career.

2. Ja-Ling is taking a biology class, and one of her assignments is to create a group presentation on an assigned topic. Her group's topic is the theory of evolution, a theory that Ja-Ling finds fascinating; however, when she meets with her group to prepare for the presentation, two of her group members express deep concern they are being asked to study something they don't believe in. They refuse to help with the project even though they know their lack of participation will lower the whole group's grade. What should Ja-Ling do?

Research It Further

1. Find the University of South Carolina's (USC's) Carolinian Creed on the Internet. Try the website www.sa.sc.edu/creed/index.htm. Using USC's creed as a basis, write your own creed that fits your college's values. Is there anything you would revise or add to USC's creed?

2. Find a map of your college and determine what building or landmark is the geographical center of the campus. Then, write a short paper on how that building is an appropriate "center" of your college. Questions you may want to consider include the following: What does the building house—a library, a classroom for the engineering department, a student center? What does the building symbolize? If you were to design a display or piece of art that reflects the college's "center," what would it look like?

3. Choose one of the job descriptions listed in Exhibit 1.3. Find out who on your campus fulfills that role. Interview that person about his job and how it fits into the college's structure. Present the information you obtained to your class.

4. Working in groups or individually, choose a campus building to research. As part of the research, learn as much as possible about the building, including the square footage, operating hours, points/rooms of interest, history, interesting or unusual stories about the building, what departments or areas it houses, and which college officials occupy the building. Then, make a presentation, complete with visual aids, about the building.

References

American Association of Community Colleges. "Community Colleges Past to Present." Retrieved July 26, 2005, from http://www.aacc.nche.edu/Content/NavigationMenu/AboutCommunityColleges/HistoricalInformation/PasttoPresent/Past_to_Present.htm.

Banner, J. M., & Cannon, H. C. (1999). *The elements of learning*. New Haven, CT: Yale University Press.

2 Who Are You?

arry learned as he took courses and planned for his degree that considering values and evaluating goals are important first steps to being a successful college student. To assist you with this process, the chapter provides information to help you understand yourself better. This chapter also answers questions you may have right now:

- What is "self-awareness" and why is it important?

- What will I gain from college? How will I understand myself better?

- What are mission statements, goals, and values?

- Why is goal setting so important?

- What are learning styles and personality types?

COMMUNITY · COLLEGE ·

Student Profile

NAME: *Larry Lemmons*   AGE: *33*

MAJOR: *Physical Therapy*

1. What are your values?

   I value helping others, honesty, education, and being true to myself.

2. What are your long-term career goals?

   I want to be a physical therapist who helps low-income patients. I also would like to be a philanthropist.

3. What are your short-term goals?

   I want to do well in all my classes and learn as much as possible. Making As and Bs is a short-term goal as well.

4. What is your VARK learning style?

   Kinesthetic.

Who Are You?

The question "Who are you?" sounds easy to answer. You may start by listing a variety of characteristics: male, age 25, married, father of a son, electrician, and a Native American. Or, you are a single female, age 19, part-time sales assistant, full-time student, and mountain climber. But what are you beyond those labels? Where have you been? What are you doing now? Where are you going and where do you want to be? Now the questions get a little more difficult to answer, and they take more time and thought. The point is that you need to have some idea of who you are, or at least an idea of where you want to be, when you begin college.

Maybe you don't know who you are yet, but you hope that enrolling in classes and pursuing a degree will help you come to a better understanding. Don't worry, though, if you cannot immediately articulate the essence of you. This question and the possible answers have intrigued human beings for thousands of years. In his book *Who Are You? 101 Ways of Seeing Yourself*, Malcolm Godwin (2000) explores the ways people try to answer the question "Who am I?" From body types, to ancient Indian mysticism, to workplace dynamics, there are numerous ways you can learn more about what and how you think. Understanding yourself is called self-awareness and its purpose— or the reason you should be concerned with self-awareness—is to know yourself and your environment well enough to reach your goals.

Of course, who you are will change, maybe even dramatically, as you take classes, encounter new subjects, and research interesting topics. But taking the time to think and reflect on yourself will help you map a course throughout your community college experience and beyond—back to work, to raising a family, to another college, or to a satisfying career. This chapter helps you to understand who you are by identifying where you have been, what you know, what you want to become, and how you learn. This book will also help you make decisions about who and what you want to be. Think of the information in the chapters that follow as road maps for understanding where you came from and for directing you to where you want to go. Remember that enrolling in college means you have taken the first step on a journey to knowledge and self-discovery. And each journey, as the Chinese philosopher Lao-Tzu said, begins with that first step.

IN BOX

Keys to Self-Awareness and Personal Fulfillment

- Background: Where you come from, what you have experienced
- Values: What you believe in
- Priorities: What is important to you at a given moment
- Motivation: What makes you do what you do, what keeps you on track to reach your goals
- Mission: What you say about what you believe in and what you want to do
- Goals: Where you want to go, what you want to achieve
- Personality Types and Learning Styles: What you are like and how you like to learn

Where Have You Been?

Before you answer the question "Where are you going?" you should consider the question "Where have you been?" How, you ask, will your past experiences help you understand where you want to be in the future? Without acknowledging where you have been and what you have learned along the way, you will have a difficult time understanding yourself completely. Although the old adage "Those who do not know their history are doomed to repeat it" may seem trite, not acknowledging that your past helped shape who you are today may stand in your way of eliminating bad habits and negative behavior and continuing positive behavior. Take, for instance, one student's statement about where she has been:

> I couldn't understand why I thought I would never go to college and earn a degree until I realized that my father used to tell me that I wasn't very smart and would never amount to anything. I learned in one of my classes that I was internalizing his expectation of me rather than listening to myself as to what I think I am capable of. Once I realized this, I could put those thoughts behind me and think positively. Sometimes when I am stressed, I start doubting myself, but I have learned some techniques to help me stay focused on my goals.

As this student points out, she acknowledges why she felt insecure about her abilities in the past, but she uses that knowledge to keep herself on track to reach her goals.

What Do You Value?

Understanding and accepting your past allows you to honestly explore your values. Values are part of your belief system and are what make you unique—your values will not be exactly the same as someone else's. A value of yours may be honesty, which means you try to be truthful and straightforward in most situations and you expect others to be honest with you. If you value hard work, then you strive to do your best in life. Values can be learned from your parents, or they can come from what your culture, religion, or ethnicity regard as important. For example, your family may value loyalty, which is shown when your father sticks by his sister no matter the bad choices she made in the past. Or, your family may value the elderly, which is shown by listening to the advice of parents and grandparents.

Values can also be formed in reaction to a negative experience. If you were discriminated against in the past, you may strive to be open-minded and value that in others. Likewise, if you grew up with family members who did not value their health and did not take care of themselves, then you may have watched them go through painful illnesses or even death. Your determination to take care of yourself and stay healthy was shaped by the negative experience of living with those who did not have the same value. Whether developed through positive or negative experiences, your values make up the belief system that underlies any decision you make even if you don't consciously realize it.

The importance of understanding your values is that this knowledge can help you set realistic goals. If you value a satisfying career, for instance, you

Your Values Do Affect Your Everyday Life

IN BOX

VALUES	REFLECTIONS OF THESE VALUES IN EVERYDAY LIFE
Honesty	Telling your best friend the truth even if it hurts her
Loyalty	Sticking up for your brother even if he made a bad choice
Family	Making time to visit relatives even if it means spending less time with friends or participating in a hobby
Financial stability	Forgoing weekend trips with friends to save money for a special purchase or retirement
Spirituality	Setting aside time to attend religious services or meditate even if it takes time away from other activities

will set goals that support that value. Therefore, you will probably investigate challenging and interesting careers and fields. If you value a stable financial future, you will set goals that enable you to earn enough money to provide for your needs and wants. If you value your family, you will make spending time with them a priority. The box above lists examples of values reflected in everyday life.

Regardless of what ultimately shapes what is important to you, your values should be a true reflection of who you are and what you believe. If they are not, you will have trouble attaining your goals because your real values will conflict.

For example, a student's parents want her to be a doctor because they value financial success and career prestige or perhaps because they are doctors. What if the student values, instead, meeting new people and traveling? What if she wants to study ancient cultures? If she decides to adopt her parents' values and ignore her own, what kind of future can you envision for her? Although her parents' intentions may be well meaning, she will have to compromise herself in order to meet their goals for her, and she will probably suffer some regret in the future.

Does this example mean that you should ignore others who try to help you figure out what you want to be? Certainly not. But you should pay attention to what you want when you do get help with your educational and career goals. Be open to others' suggestions, but make sure you feel comfortable with your final decision. Those who truly want you to succeed will be proud when they know you have achieved your heart's desire, not theirs.

Practice

EXERCISE 2.1

Write down five things that you value in yourself (e.g., honesty, work ethic, appreciation). Then, briefly answer these questions: Where did the values come from? Who or what influenced the development of these values?

Companion
Website

What Are Your Priorities?

As you reflect on your values, also consider what your priorities are as you begin college. Simply stated, a priority is something that is important at a particular moment. Although priorities, by their very nature, can change weekly if not daily or even hourly, you also have "big picture" priorities that remain fairly constant. For example, before you enrolled in college, your priorities may have been something like the following:

STUDENT 1

1. *My job.* I have to get to work on time, work effectively during the day, and leave when my work is finished.
2. *My family.* I need to arrive home early each evening to help with child-care duties and housework.
3. *My health.* I quit smoking two years ago after a health scare, and now I regularly exercise and watch what I eat.

STUDENT 2

1. *High school.* I have to study and complete my work so I can graduate and get into college.
2. *My family.* I need to help my parents care for my grandmother after school so they can tend to their other priorities.
3. *My friends.* Because I won't see some of my high-school friends until they return home from college next summer, I want to spend time relaxing and having fun with them.

Now that you are enrolled in college, your priorities may have changed order or you may have replaced one of your top priorities with college. If you have not replaced one of your top priorities with college yet, then you should seriously consider how you will handle the demands of higher education if you have other, more important activities demanding your attention. This bears repeating: In order to meet your educational goals (which you will learn more about later in the chapter), you have to make college a top priority most of the time. Yes, there will be times that you have to put in extra time at work or take care of an ill family member, taking time away from studying, but if you consistently place your college education at the top of the list, you will more likely be successful in your educational pursuit. Here are one student's changed priorities:

STUDENT 3

1. *My education.* I waited a long time to get a degree, and it is my top priority. The majority of my energy and time will go toward making my dream a reality.
2. *My family.* I waited until my family can handle my change in priorities. I worked out a plan with my spouse so we can both take care of our children and our household. There may be times when I need to rely on other family members and friends to take care of errands.

3. *My job.* I moved from a full-time to a part-time job so I can spend more time taking classes. My employer is supportive of my educational goals and promised to work with me as my priorities change.

What Motivates You?

Determining your values and priorities are essential first steps to learning more about yourself so you can set realistic, achievable goals. The next step is to reflect on what motivates you. Motivation is often defined as the driving force that helps you achieve a goal. What is your driving force? What motivated you to enroll in college? What motivated you to consider completing a certificate or degree? What will motivate you to enroll next semester and the next? For some students, the driving force is knowing that to get a better job, they have to get a degree. Seeing their family and friends successfully complete a degree may motivate others. Still others are motivated by the fact that they are learning more about the world around them and how they fit into it.

Reflection

EXERCISE 2.2

How have your values changed over the years? Compare what you valued 10 years ago with what you value now and discuss why that change occurred.

Companion
Website

Motivating Factors for Enrolling in College

- Pride
- Increased income, better job
- Opportunity for self-improvement
- More respect at home, at work
- Meet new, diverse people
- Become independent
- Experience change
- Intellectual stimulation
- Personal challenge
- New career
- Friends/family are going to college
- Certification/degree requirements for current job

Not all motivating factors are positive, and negative motivators often result in undesirable outcomes. Consider, for instance, a student who enrolls in college classes because her father informs her that he won't support her if she doesn't get a degree. If the student doesn't have any motivating factors other than her father's threat to "cut her off" financially, then she has little to keep her in college if her financial situation changes. She may also feel pressured to choose a degree or major to please him. Now consider a student who enrolls in college only to receive grant money or a scholarship in order to pay bills and purchase a new stereo and has no intention of completing a degree. This may be an extreme example of a student being motivated by the wrong reasons, but you can well imagine that once the money is deposited, there is no other motivation to attend classes and complete the work.

Before you get to the next step, goal setting, consider what motivates you. What motivated you to apply to this college? What motivated you to register for classes, choose a degree plan? What motivated you to take this class? You may have been motivated by many factors, some positive and some negative. Does this mean that even though you enrolled in this class, for example, for the wrong reasons (e.g., it sounded like an easy A; I won't have to study at all) that your action cannot have a positive outcome? Definitely not. Some of us make choices for the wrong reason, but in the middle of the action or experience, we realize the importance and worth of the choice and become motivated by something positive.

Take the example about enrolling in this class again. What if you were negatively motivated to enroll in the class, but when you bought your book and started reading about how to succeed in college, you realized that what you are learning is exactly what you needed to know? Or what if your instructor really impressed you the first day as a caring, giving, encouraging individual? It would then be likely that you would experience a positive outcome from your action, even if your initial motivating factor was not positive. The key, then, is to look for positive motivators along the way to replace the negative ones because there may be times that you need those positive motivators to get you through a class, degree, or other life experience.

What Is Your Mission Statement?

Your past experiences, values, priorities, and motivators all work together to form your mission, or purpose, in life. Considering your purpose in life, especially for those who have never thought about the reason they exist, can be a very powerful experience. All it takes is some time to think about what you have done in the past and what you believe is the right journey for you to take now.

Once you have determined what your mission is, you can write your mission statement. A mission statement is a declaration of what a person or institution believes in and what she or it hopes to accomplish. A mission statement, then, usually contains the broad strokes of the overall picture of what you want to accomplish. Values are the foundation of a mission statement. If you are unsure of your values, your mission statement will not be easy to understand and follow. You also need to have a good understanding of your priorities and motivators.

Critical Thinking PLUS*

Consider how understanding your personality style or learning preference can help you through challenging situations.

You strongly believe that abortion is wrong. You were raised with the value that all life, at any stage, is precious. While studying the human life cycle in a biology class, your professor spends a class period discussing the biological effects of abortion. You are outspoken about your beliefs and you learn best by debating ideas, so you challenge the professor during class. When he asks to talk to you after class, you worry that you made a wrong move. You didn't intend to come across as disrespectful, but you do feel strongly about your viewpoint. What do you think your professor will say? What should you tell him about your actions in class?

NOTES

*PERSONALITY + LEARNING STYLE = UNDERSTANDING SITUATIONS

In order to better understand and articulate your values, take a look at your college's mission statement, which reflects what it intends to do for its students. Likewise, your mission statement will reflect your intentions. As you meet your goals and learn new things, your mission may change and your mission statement should be revised.

SAMPLE COLLEGE MISSION STATEMENT

Northern County College provides high quality, accessible educational opportunities at the freshman and sophomore level in associate degree and technical certificate programs, a college-transfer curriculum, continuing education, and industry-specific training to support individual and community needs in the state. The College's mission is to enable individuals to develop to their fullest potential and to support the economic development of the state.

Practice

Using your values as a guide, write a mission statement you can use during your college experience.

Companion
Website

Keeping in mind your values, complete Practice Exercise 2.4. More than likely, you will need to revise it as your values and goals change and become more specific. Here is a sample mission statement you can use as a model.

SAMPLE PERSONAL MISSION STATEMENT

My mission is to have a fulfilling personal and professional life that allows me to meet new people, take on new challenges, and have flexibility in my schedule. As a mother and wife, I want to have a close relationship with my family, acting both as a caregiver and a role model. As a teacher, I am dedicated to providing students with an education that will prepare them for a four-year university curriculum and the demands of the world of work.

What Are Your Goals?

To fulfill your mission in life, you must have a plan. Setting goals and achieving them puts you on the path to fulfilling your mission. If you are not used to writing down daily tasks or voicing your future plans, then start making lists and talking about what you want to be and do.

Using your list of values and your mission statement, you can formulate goals that support both what you believe in and what you want for yourself. The fact that you are reading this book is evidence that you are someone who has set a goal and is working toward achieving it. Also, the fact that you are in college says that you value education as a means of improving your life. You may have overcome many obstacles to get where you are today. You may have faced pressure from your family and friends to go straight to work from high school rather than go to college, or you may have gotten negative feedback from others when you decided to stop working, or stop working as much, to get a degree.

Nonetheless, realize that setting and achieving goals is not as easy as writing them down and crossing them off. You will encounter obstacles, some of which may threaten to knock you off course. Flexibility and determination, then, are the keys to achieving your goals despite setbacks.

Writing Down Your Goals

Even with the loudest cheerleaders and most supportive friends and family, you still need some well-defined goals to give you direction as you chart your course in college. A goal is something you work toward—it may be to learn how to cook macaroni and cheese, to quit a bad habit, or to write a novel. Whatever your goals, they should be reasonable and attainable in the time frame you assign. For instance, if you want to lose 10 pounds in one week, you may have to rethink the time in which you want to achieve your goal. A more reasonable goal for losing weight might be to lose 10 pounds in four months. Just like a slow weight loss, a reasonable goal is more likely to be met.

As you begin to think about your goals, consider dividing them into long-term and short-term goals. Certainly, one of your long-term goals is to get an education. This goal may take a year or more, depending on how many degree requirements you need to complete and how many other responsibilities you may have. A short-term goal that contributes to achieving the long-term goal of earning a degree is to complete your classes successfully.

When making a list of your goals, consider the following guidelines:

- Make your goals attainable and reasonable.
- Break larger goals into smaller goals that will lead to fulfillment.
- Think of setting goals in these time frames: one week, one month, one semester, one year, five years, and ten years.
- Review your goals regularly and make changes as necessary.

Take time to reflect on your goals and write them down.

Because it is difficult to plan 10 years into the future, make a list of goals tied to the near future. For instance, if you want to own your own business in ten years, think about structuring your short-term and long-term goals this way:

LONG-TERM GOALS (10 YEARS)

Run a successful landscape design firm

Provide landscaping for low-income properties

LONG-TERM GOALS (5 YEARS)

Work for a landscape design firm

Continue community service and encourage coworkers to participate

LONG-TERM GOALS (3 YEARS)

Complete my associate's degree in landscape design and management

Continue community service work

SHORT-TERM GOALS (9 MONTHS)

Complete two semesters of landscape design classes

Continue working at the garden center

Plant and maintain my own flower and vegetable garden

Participate in community service project landscaping low-income properties

SHORT-TERM GOALS (1 SEMESTER)

Complete classes that count toward my degree

Look for community service project landscaping low-income properties

SHORT-TERM GOALS (1 MONTH)

Help friend plant new trees

Attend local lecture on seasonal planting

Begin research for final paper on plant diseases

SHORT-TERM GOALS (1 WEEK)

Study for classes

Apply for job at a garden center

Weed and fertilize yard

Take a hike in the park

No matter what you want to achieve, write down all of your goals and review them every few months to assess your progress. Henriette Anne Klauser (2001) made a career of helping people write their dreams and goals on paper so they can finally realize them. In her book, *Write It Down, Make It Happen: Knowing What You Want and Getting It!*, she states, "Writing down your dreams and aspirations is like hanging up a sign that says 'Open for Business.' . . . Putting it on paper alerts the part in your brain known as the reticular activating system to join you in the play" (p. 33). According to Klauser, the process of writing down your goals tells your brain to start paying attention to your ambitions and makes you aware of opportunities to achieve them.

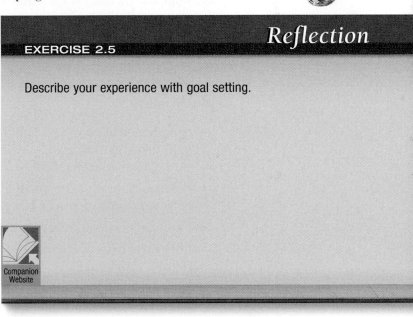

Reflection

EXERCISE 2.5

Describe your experience with goal setting.

Companion
Website

Being Realistic About Goals

Some of us set goals that sound great on paper, goals we sincerely want to achieve, but we don't always consider the whole picture. We get excited about the end result, but we don't consider the challenges we will have to overcome to reach a goal. A world-class athlete who dreams of a gold medal around his neck also envisions the countless practices, the changes in his lifestyle, which may restrict his other interests and time spent hanging out with friends and family. He may also have to travel extensively, which will leave him little time at home. He may have to sacrifice an enormous amount of time, effort, and other personal interests to reach his goal. It would be foolish of him to assume that he can reach his goal of athletic glory without changing his priorities, without monitoring his goals closely, and without pushing himself to his limit, both physically and mentally. Eating chocolate bars on the couch every day does not contribute to an athlete's goals.

Although you won't be asked to put your body through the paces a world-class athlete does to train for an event, you will have to be realistic about your expectations as you work toward a certificate or degree. The following is an extreme example of a student with a realistic goal but unrealistic expectations.

- *Student A's goal:* I want to get a degree in psychology and become a high-school counselor.
- *Student A's expectations:* I don't like to read anything that doesn't interest me, so I skip any chapters in my textbooks that are boring. I don't like to write and I am not familiar with the library, so I will avoid any professor who assigns a research paper. I don't have a lot of time to devote to studying, so I am going to take classes that are easy and require very little outside work.

Do you think Student A will successfully reach her goal if she maintains these expectations? Although Student A demonstrates excessively unrealistic expectations, it is worth noting that we all have moments when we do not consider all the hard work required and possible challenges when faced with a large goal. Sometimes we get so excited about the end result we forget to think about what it takes to get there. What can Student A do to change her expectations and reach her goal? What can you do if you feel you have unrealistic expectations?

The following is a checklist to keep your expectations realistic and keep you on track.

- Visualize, write down, or talk through the possible steps to achieving your goal, including those that may be unpleasant (e.g., staying up late to finish a paper, saying "no" to social activities because you need to study).
- Acknowledge that there may be unforeseen obstacles that will stand between you and your goal.
- Determine a plan of action if you encounter an obstacle to your goal.
- Enlist the help of friends and family as backup support as you work toward your goal.
- Talk to an advisor or professor if you feel your expectations are not realistic or if you have any difficulty reaching your educational goals.

As these steps suggest, a little planning and a review of your expectations will help you set realistic goals you can attain.

Reaching Your Goals and Considering New Ones

In addition to writing your goals down on paper, make sure you do at least two activities a week that contribute to your long-term goals. For example, if you want to get a job writing for a newspaper, then read a newspaper or magazine each day, or write in a journal for 10 minutes a day. Once you have accomplished some of the short-term goals that contribute to a long-term goal, keep adding new short-term goals. If you successfully read newspapers and write in your journal for a month, then add another part of your long-term goal; for instance, check your career counseling center for internships at newspapers or publishing houses. Each time you achieve a short-term goal, create a new one or move to the next one on your list. Before you know it, you will reach your long-term goals and will be ready to create new ones.

When making lists of goals, remember that your free time is just as important as the time you spend working on your goals. Downtime to rest and relax is essential to refueling your energy reserves. A car stops running if you don't refuel and take care of it, and you will too if you don't give yourself the care that is needed to keep you healthy. One method of making sure you get the relaxation and rest you need is to make it a goal. Just as you have work and college goals, you should write down when you plan to do nothing and be committed to meeting that goal.

Eliminating Negative Influences

As you work toward your goals, make an effort to eliminate anything that keeps you from focusing on them. If you think you don't have time to accomplish two short-term goals during the week, then examine where you have spent your time and get rid of any activity that does not contribute to your goals or that does not reflect your values.

If you watch seven hours of TV a week, and you aren't achieving a short-term goal of becoming more informed, then replace the hours spent watching TV with something that does contribute to your goal. In addition to activities that don't contribute toward your goals, anyone or anything that distracts you and is unnecessary in your life should be eliminated: a gossipy neighbor or a destructive or dangerous habit.

If you are unsure of whether or not your activities contribute to your goals, take a few minutes to list what you did this week and determine how each activity supported or did not support one of your goals.

ACTIVITIES THAT CONTRIBUTE TO YOUR GOALS

- *Car maintenance:* Allows you to get to school and work safely
- *Exercise:* Allows you to remain healthy and reduces stress
- *Eating and sleeping:* Keep you healthy and reduce stress
- *Reading the newspaper:* Keeps you informed, helps you improve reading skills, contributes to learning

ACTIVITIES THAT MAY DISTRACT YOU FROM YOUR GOALS

- *Excessive socializing:* Takes away time and energy from other goals
- *Mindless TV watching:* May not contribute to learning
- *Using drugs and alcohol:* Keeps you from focusing on goals, is dangerous
- *Irregular sleeping and eating:* Creates stress that inhibits your ability to reach goals habits

Although you cannot remove all of the people in your life who don't support your goals, you do have the power to reduce the effect of their negativity. If you have someone in your life, a friend or a family member, who belittles your efforts to go back to school and earn a degree, try to limit your time with that person or try to focus on conversation topics that are not related to you. Lillian Glass (1997), in her book *Toxic People: 10 Ways of*

Dealing with People Who Make Your Life Miserable, recommends limiting contact with people who make you feel hurt, stressed, dumb, or unworthy. Dr. Glass refers to people who stand in the way of being your best as "toxic" because they "are hazardous to others' mental, emotional, and physical health" (p. 12). Dealing with toxic people reduces the time and energy you have to work on your goals and to benefit from the positive influence of those who support you.

Collaboration

EXERCISE 2.6

Working within a group, create your own list of activities that may distract you from reaching your goals. Then, determine what can be done to eliminate these activities or to turn them into more productive pursuits (e.g., watching TV can become an activity that supports a goal if you limit what and how much is watched).

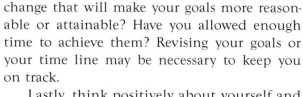

Companion
Website

Staying Motivated to Achieve Your Goals

One of the hardest parts of reaching goals is maintaining the momentum necessary to achieve them. There will be times in your academic career when you will feel overwhelmed by the responsibilities you have and unsure of your ability to handle it all. When you feel weighed down by all you have to accomplish that week or that day, take the time to calm yourself first. If you can, talk with a friend, an instructor, or counselor and explain your frustration and stress.

Sometimes, if an instructor knows you are feeling overwhelmed by the expectations of a course, he will help you by giving you more time to complete an assignment. A friend may also volunteer to help out by studying with you.

To stay motivated and to resist the temptation to give up because of the stress, review your short-term and long-term goals. Is there anything you can change that will make your goals more reasonable or attainable? Have you allowed enough time to achieve them? Revising your goals or your time line may be necessary to keep you on track.

Lastly, think positively about yourself and your progress. Many students before you successfully juggled a job, classes, and a family. That is not to say that they did not doubt themselves along the way or suffer small setbacks. The difference between them and those who were not successful is that they persevered because they believed in themselves. Tell yourself that you can get through stressful times.

Critical Thinking

EXERCISE 2.7

In what ways will goal setting affect your college experience?

Companion
Website

Personality Types and Learning Styles

o far in this chapter, you have been asked "Who are you?" and "What do you value?" but there is still a question that remains: "What are you like?" What is your personality type? Do you like to sing karaoke in front of a group of strangers? Do you like to participate in group sports? Do you enjoy bungee jumping or mountain climbing? Would you rather read a book than go shopping? Do you believe in love at first sight?

Describing personality types has been an activity for thousands of years, and all cultures have some way to describe different types of people. One example from hundreds of years ago is known as the four "humors" or "tempers": sanguine, choleric, melancholic, and phlegmatic. Malcolm Godwin, in his book *Who Are You? 101 Ways of Seeing Yourself* (2000), describes the four personalities:

1. *Sanguine:* "Carefree, easy-going, extrovert, lively, sociable . . . ."
2. *Choleric:* "Tends to react very quickly to situations and becomes easily over-excited, impulsive . . . ."
3. *Melancholic:* "Quiet and often withdrawn, pessimistic, sad, reserved . . . ."
4. *Phlegmatic:* "Detached, aloof, nonchalant, thoughtful, careful . . . "
   (pp. 46–47).

Our tendency to classify personalities is likewise seen in the descriptions of the zodiac signs. The person who asks, "Hey, baby, what is your sign?" is not just interested in knowing what month another person celebrates her birthday. He wants to know if her personality will be compatible with his. Finding potential mates is not the only reason we want to learn more about ourselves and others. Body types (pear or apple, endomorph or mesomorph) and the body mass index (BMI) system are two examples that give us information about how healthy we are or should be depending on our height and weight. We classify all aspects of our lives in order to better understand them, to improve *self-awareness* and, ultimately, to improve ourselves.

Being aware of yourself and knowing your personality type are ways to better understand how you learn. Most personality tests provide feedback on what motivates you and how you best work with others. Learning styles inventories, likewise, provide feedback on how you learn best depending on your personal preferences or strengths. Information about what you like and dislike, how you relate to others, and how to work productively will help you achieve your goals and, as Gordon Lawrence (1995) states in his book *People Types and Tiger Stripes,* help you make "dramatic improvements in the effectiveness of [your] work" (p. 5).

There are many different personality tests and learning styles inventories. Although this chapter discusses the Left-Brain/Right-Brain, Neil Fleming's VARK, Howard Gardner's Multiple Intelligences, and the Myers-Briggs Type Indicator, it is worthwhile to know there are others out there you may want to investigate on your own.

Left-Brain/Right-Brain

Based on scientific research done in the 1960s and made popular in the classroom by Betty Edwards' book *Drawing on the Right Side of the Brain* (1979), descriptions of left-brain and right-brain processes help teachers adapt their teaching styles to different types of learners and help students adapt their note-taking and study habits. Nancy Lightfoot Matte and Susan

Hilary Green Henderson (1995), in their book *Success, Your Style! Right- & Left-Brain Techniques for Learning*, describe left-brained people as "analytical, taking things and ideas apart to comprehend something" and right-brained people as "holistic, looking for patterns and relationships" (p. 3). Matte and Henderson further state that left-brained people "respond to facts while right-brained people respond to feelings" (p. 3). The purpose of determining which side of the brain you rely on most when processing information is to help you determine which learning methods you prefer and recognize which teaching types work best for you and which will be a good workout for the other side of your brain.

Left-Brain/Right-Brain Learning Style Inventory

Matte and Green Henderson (1995) provide the following learning style inventory.* To get a sense of your preferred learning style, for each of the following statements, circle the letter corresponding to the response that describes you best. Scoring instructions are provided at the end of the exercise.

1. I prefer to spend my weekends and free time:

    a. Doing what I want to do whenever I want to do it.

    b. Making a list of what I have to do and checking things off as I do them.

2. When an instructor gives an assignment, I prefer:

    a. To know the exact requirements for completing the assignment—when it is due, how long it should be, how to format it, and so on.

    b. To have some freedom to set the standards, figure out different ways to do it and turn it in when I please.

3. When planning a party, I:

    a. Make lists of whom I'll invite, what food and drink to serve, and what I need to do before the party.

    b. Think about the type of party mood I want and then invite the right people to create it.

4. When I move into a new place, I:

    a. Mentally visualize how the furniture can be arranged.

    b. Draw a floorplan before arranging the furniture.

5. When talking with a friend, I:

    a. Understand what my friend is telling me mostly from the words spoken.

    b. Get the message from my friend's facial expressions and gestures (i.e., nonverbals) as well as his words.

6. When thinking about how I talk and write, the statement that describes me best is:

    a. I use very precise language to describe and explain what I am talking about. I am very conscious of and careful with grammar and the meaning of words.

---

*From *Success, Your Style! Right and Left Brain Techniques for Learning*, 1st Ed., by Matte/Henderson. © 1995. Reprinted with permission of Wadsworth, a division of Thomson Learning: www. thompsonrights.com. Fax 800-730-2215.

    b. When talking or writing, I use metaphors, similes, and other figurative language. My communication style is descriptive, and maybe even poetic or emotional.

7. When solving a problem or learning a new concept or process, I:

    a. Prefer to look at the parts and put things in step-by-step order.

    b. Prefer to get a sense of the whole problem or concept first.

8. When I try to determine how I feel about an issue, I:

    a. Look at the facts, think about the issue logically and rationally, and then come to my conclusion.

    b. Often make up my mind based on emotion or intuition.

9. It is easy for me to see how things fit in a pattern or relationship.

    a. Yes.

    b. No.

10. Generally, I know what time it is.

    a. Yes.

    b. No.

SCORING

Assigning the following number values for each of the responses for items 1–10, total up your score and divide by 10.

  1. a=7   b=1
  2. a=1   b=5
  3. a=1   b=5
  4. a=5   b=3
  5. a=3   b=5
  6. a=1   b=7
  7. a=3   b=5
  8. a=1   b=7
  9. a=7   b=1
10. a=3   b=5

A score between 1 and 3.4 indicates you function primarily in a left-brained mode, while a score between 3.5 and 4.9 suggests you use a combination of left- and right-brain functions. A score between 5 and 7 indicates you are more of a right-brained processor.

VARK

Although the left-brain/right-brain learning styles inventory gives you only two descriptions of how you may learn best, there are other learning styles inventories that provide more choices. VARK, which stands for Visual, Aural, Read/Write, and Kinesthetic, is a system developed by Neil D. Fleming that helps you determine what type of learner you are and provides study strategies based on your strengths. If you have strong preferences in more than one mode, you are considered MM, or multimodal. You can determine what your learning style is by answering questions similar to the following.

1. When getting directions to someone's house, what do you need to do to remember them?
   a. Write them down.
   b. Recite them.
   c. Look at a map.
   d. Drive or walk to the person's house.

If you answer A, you fall into the read/write (R) category. If you answer B, you are an aural (A) learner. If you answer C, you learn better with visual (V) information. And if you answer D, then you are a kinesthetic (K) learner. Fleming developed a focused learning styles questionnaire that helps you understand how you may respond in certain situations. However, as Fleming states on his website:

> VARK deals with only one dimension of the complex amalgam of preferences that make up a learning style. The VARK questions and results focus on the ways in which people like information to come to them and the ways in which they like to deliver their communication. The questions are based on situations where there are choices about how that communication might take place. It is important to say what VARK is not, so that other components are not perceived as being a part of it. VARK has little to say about personality, motivation, social preferences, physical environments, intraversion–extraversion.

VARK Learning Styles Inventory

The following information comes from Neil Fleming's website, www. vark-learn.com.*

This questionnaire aims to find out something about your preferences for the way you work with information. You will have a preferred learning style, and one part of that learning style is your preference for the intake and output of ideas and information.

Choose the answer that best explains your preference and circle the letter. Please select more than one response if a single answer does not match your perception.

Leave blank any question that does not apply.

1. You are about to give directions to a person who is standing with you. She is staying in a hotel in town and wants to visit your house later. She has a rental car. You would:
   a. Draw a map on paper.
   b. Tell her the directions.
   c. Write down the directions (without a map).
   d. Collect her from the hotel in your car.

2. You are not sure whether a word should be spelled "dependent" or "dependant." You would:
   a. Look it up in the dictionary.

*Used with permission.

    b. See the word in your mind and choose based on the way it looks.

    c. Sound it out in your mind.

    d. Write both versions down on paper and choose one.

3. You have just received a copy of your itinerary for a world trip. This is of interest to a friend. You would:

    a. Phone her immediately and tell her about it.

    b. Send her a copy of the printed itinerary.

    c. Show her a map of the world.

    d. Share what you plan to do at each place you visit.

4. You are going to cook something as a special treat for your family. You would:

    a. Cook something familiar without the need for instructions.

    b. Thumb through the cookbook looking for ideas from the pictures.

    c. Refer to a specific cookbook where there is a good recipe.

5. A group of tourists has been assigned to you to find out about wildlife reserves or parks. You would:

    a. Drive them to a wildlife park.

    b. Show them slides and photographs.

    c. Give them pamphlets or a book on wildlife reserves or parks.

    d. Give them a talk on wildlife reserves or parks.

6. You are about to purchase a new stereo. Other than price, what would most influence your decision?

    a. The salesperson telling you what you want to know.

    b. Reading the details about it.

    c. Playing with the controls and listening to it.

    d. It looks really smart and fashionable.

7. Recall a time in your life when you learned how to do something like playing a new board game. Try to avoid choosing a very physical activity (e.g., riding a bike). You learned best by:

    a. Visual clues—pictures, diagrams, charts.

    b. Written instructions.

    c. Listening to somebody explaining it.

    d. Doing it or trying it.

8. You have an eye problem. You would prefer the doctor to:

    a. Tell you what is wrong.

    b. Show you a diagram of what is wrong.

    c. Use a model to show you what is wrong.

9. You are about to learn to use a new program on a computer. You would:

    a. Sit down at the keyboard and begin to experiment with the program's features.

    b. Read the manual that comes with the program.

    c. Telephone a friend and ask questions about it.

10. You are staying in a hotel and have a rental car. You would like to visit friends whose address/location you do not know. You would like them to:

    a. Draw a map on paper.

    b. Tell you the directions.

    c. Write down the directions (without a map).

    d. Collect you from the hotel in their car.

11. Apart from the price, what would influence your decision to buy an optional textbook?

    a. You have used a copy before.

    b. A friend was talking about it.

    c. Quickly reading parts of it.

    d. The way it looks is appealing.

12. A new movie has arrived in town. What would most influence your decision to go (or not to go)?

    a. You heard a radio review about it.

    b. You read a review about it.

    c. You saw a preview of it.

13. Do you prefer a lecturer or teacher who likes to use:

    a. A textbook, handouts, and readings.

    b. Flow diagrams, charts, and graphs.

    c. Field trips, labs, and practical sessions.

    d. Discussion and guest speakers.

SCORING

QUESTION	A CATEGORY	B CATEGORY	C CATEGORY	D CATEGORY
1	V	A	R	K
2	R	V	A	K
3	A	R	V	K
4	K	V	R	
5	K	V	R	A
6	A	R	K	V
7	V	R	A	K
8	A	V	K	
9	K	R	A	
10	V	A	R	K
11	K	A	R	V
12	A	R	V	
13	R	V	K	A

CALCULATING YOUR SCORE

Total number of Vs circled _____

Total number of As circled _____

Total number of Rs circled _____

Total number of Ks circled _____

Multiple Intelligences

Harvard psychologist Howard Gardner is well known for his theory of multiple intelligences, which is another term for "what we know, understand, and learn about our world" (Lazear, 1991, p. xiv). Gardner identified eight intelligences that describe how we know and learn. *Verbal/linguistic* intelligence is evident in people who use language with ease. People who demonstrate the verbal/linguistic intelligence enjoy reading and writing and may be journalists, novelists, playwrights, and comedians. The *logical/mathematical* intelligence is demonstrated by an ease and enjoyment with numbers and logic problems. People who have a strong leaning in the logical/mathematical intelligence like to solve problems, find patterns, discover relationships between objects, and follow steps. Career choices for logical/mathematical people include science, computer technology, math, and engineering.

Collaboration

EXERCISE 2.8

Complete the VARK inventory individually. Then, form small groups in which someone with each learning style is represented (at the least, include one other learning style in the group). Discuss the different ways each person likes to learn and determine if there are similarities or differences among the different learning style strengths.

Companion Website

Your career choice should take into account your personality type, your intelligences, and many other factors.

Visual/spatial is an intelligence characterized by anything visual—paintings, photographs, maps, and architecture. People who have a strong visual/spatial sense are usually good at design, architecture, painting and sculpture, and map making. *Body/kinesthetic* is an intelligence that focuses on body movement. Body/kinesthetic people enjoy using their bodies to express themselves. Obvious career choices for this intelligence include dancing, sports, and dramatic arts. *Musical/rhythmic* intelligence encompasses the mind's proficiency with the rhythms of music and hearing tones and beats. People who have strong musical/rhythmic intelligence may use musical instruments or the human voice to express themselves. Career choices for this intelligence include all types of musical performers.

How you relate to others and yourself is part of the interpersonal and intrapersonal intelligences. People with strong *interpersonal* intelligence relate well with others. They read others' feelings well and act with others in mind. *Intrapersonal* intelligence centers around the ability to understand oneself. People who possess intrapersonal intelligence know how and why they do what they do. *Naturalistic*, the eighth intelligence, refers to people who enjoy and work well in an outdoor environment. Naturalistic people find peace in nature and enjoy having natural elements around them.

Myers-Briggs Type Indicator

The Myers-Briggs Type Indicator, or MBTI®, is a popular personality test that was developed in the 1970s by Isabel Briggs Myers and Katharine Briggs. The "four dimensions of type" the MBTI uses are:

Extraversion (E) / Introversion (I)
Sensing (S) / Intuition (N)
Thinking (T) / Feeling (F)
Judgment (J) / Perception (P)

- *Extraversion:* Likes to focus on people, is active in the world
- *Introversion:* Reflective, thinks before acting, attuned to inner world
- *Sensing:* Observes using all five senses, in touch with physical realities
- *Intuition:* Imagining, thinking about possibilities
- *Thinking:* Using logic, being objective and skeptical
- *Feeling:* Employs personal feeling, sensitive to people's needs, dislikes conflict
- *Judgment:* Goal-oriented, planning, controlling
- *Perception:* Curious and open-minded, taking in information

Sixteen personality types can be identified using combinations of the four dimensions; for example, ENFJ, ISTP, ESTJ, and INTJ.

Knowing your MBTI type is one way to understand who you are and what your strengths and weaknesses are. However, there

Critical Thinking

EXERCISE 2.9

If a friend wants to be a nurse because he thinks he can make a good living but has no interest in the field other than financial, what would you tell him? What if you know his true dream is to write?

Companion
Website

are many more ways of understanding you, and no test can accurately measure exactly what you want out of life and how you will get it.

Many other learning styles and personality types questionnaires will allow you to explore what ways of receiving and giving information work best for you. The goal is to realize your personality and learning style strengths and use them when you are studying new or difficult material or considering a career. However, don't forget your weaker areas. You can improve them with a little work, but you may want to wait until the material you are learning is easier before you begin experimenting with different learning styles.

What Else Do You Want to Know?

Now that you realize that you know much more than you thought, take some time to make a list of what you want to know more about. No doubt, you are in college because you want to learn more about a particular topic or field, which may be your major and your career goal.

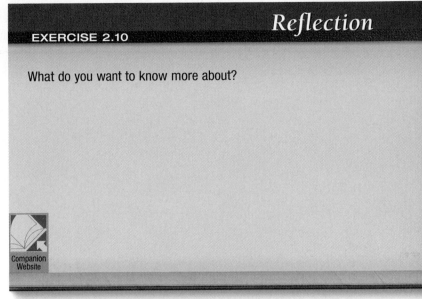

Reflection

EXERCISE 2.10

What do you want to know more about?

Companion
Website

Learning Styles Application

This chart lists the four learning styles and tips based on the chapter's main ideas. Locate your learning style and read the corresponding tips to maximize your success in college.

VISUAL

Visual learners find meeting goals easier if they can see a visual representation of the goal. If you want a degree so you can start your dream job, cut out a picture of someone in your dream job role and place it in a prominent place. Whenever you need some extra motivation, look at the picture for inspiration.

AURAL

Those who learn better by hearing may need to talk to a close friend or mentor to keep the momentum going to reach their goals. You may even want to record your own motivational words to play when you need reassurance that you can make it.

READ/WRITE

Writing down goals is a comfortable activity for read/write learners. Spending some time each day or every other day checking off to-do lists and rearranging daily priorities will keep you on track to reaching your goals.

KINESTHETIC

Kinesthetic learners feel best when they are engaged in activity. You will achieve short-term goals more easily if you limit your list to items you can do within a couple of days. The act of completion will keep you motivated to add to your short-term goals list and to achieve them.

Path of Discovery

Journal Entry

Name and describe three people or situations that changed your life. What did these people or situations teach you about your values, priorities, motivators, or goals? How have they changed you?

FROM COLLEGE TO UNIVERSITY

What you know and how you learn will change

If your beliefs, goals, and values remain relatively unchanged during your community college experience, then your move to a four-year university should be easy, right? The transition can be relatively smooth if you are willing to apply some of the ideas in this chapter to your new environment. Chances are good that your new school will present a variety of challenges that will require you to adapt.

First, your definition of who you are may have changed, perhaps dramatically. You will be more confident in your abilities and better able to handle the stress of juggling numerous responsibilities. Your values may also change after your semesters at a community college; if you were unsure of what you valued before, you may finally have a clearer picture of your belief system. On the other hand, you may be more confused than ever about what you believe after studying different religions, psychological theories, and social ideas. Because higher education values inquiry and research, no matter what shape your values are in when you transfer, you will find support as you struggle to make sense of it all at the four-year university.

Just as your knowledge of yourself and your values will change, your goals will go through a transformation. Although your main goal of graduating with a four-year degree will still be in sight, you will notice that you have already met some of your smaller goals. Perhaps you successfully completed an associate's degree, or you just became more organized. Just the fact that you are ready to transfer credits means you accomplished some necessary steps to fulfilling the rest of your goals.

In addition, you can revise your list of what you know because what you know changes after taking classes at a community college. You may even be able to include in your "What I Know" list a career choice. Also, you may know yourself better, through the application of the learning styles. However, you have to be prepared to adapt to different teaching styles and new pressures after you transfer.

Now, to prepare for the next step, revise, preferably on paper, your list of what you know. Recognize that the learning styles you felt most comfortable with may have to be adapted—or new styles explored and used—at your four-year school.

FROM COLLEGE TO CAREER

Goals and a mission will help you succeed

Many businesses rely on creating mission statements, strategic plans (long-term goals), and operational plans (short-term goals) to chart a course for their success. Because you have experience writing your own mission statement and goals, you are able to contribute to your company's planning. You can do this because you understand how the company's values underlie its mission and how its goals create its road map to success. Your experience in goal setting will help you write departmental or personal goals. Because you understand how values, mission, and goals fit together, you can create goals that are explicitly linked to the focus of your workplace.

Chapter in Review

1. Create a list of your values and priorities at this time in your life.
2. Using what you learned from this chapter, explain why you think some people have difficulty reaching their long-term goals.
3. Design a plan to help you reach three short-term goals.
4. Evaluate two of the personality tests/learning styles inventories and determine which one is more helpful for college students to know. Explain why you think the personality test/learning styles inventory is the best one for students.

Case Scenarios

Read the following case scenarios and determine what each person should do. Refer to the information in this chapter as you write a description and plan of action for each student.

1. Ahmed has started college, but he is not sure what he wants to do. In fact, he is afraid to tell his parents that he wants to be a dental hygienist because his parents want him to take over the family business. Neither of his parents went to college, and they don't understand why any of their children would want to work outside the family business. Ahmed values loyalty to his family—he has been through many challenges that strengthened his relationship with his parents—but he also has a strong interest in the health field. Ahmed's ultimate goal is to be a dentist, but he thinks that working as a hygienist first is a way to make sure that he has what it takes. What advice would you give Ahmed? What should he do to make sure his goals are met?

2. Serena, a single parent, has started her first semester in college, but she also works full-time in a law office. Her sister keeps her twin boys while she works, but she sometimes has to miss work when her sister is unavailable. Serena wants to get a four-year degree and eventually go to law school, but she feels it will take too long if she doesn't start now. She is motivated by time and money. She wants to hurry and get her degree, and she wants to be financially independent so she can take care of her boys. She works very hard, but she doesn't have any other family or friends who can help her. To add to her obstacles, her sister is not supportive of her desire to get a degree and improve her life. Serena's sister thinks that she has all she needs and shouldn't "mess it up by going to college and getting all kinds of crazy ideas."

What advice would you give Serena? What have you learned about setting goals and managing priorities that would help Serena? What have you learned about overcoming challenges that would help Serena?

Research It Further

1. During the Middle Ages (500–1500 A.D.), the terms *sanguine, phlegmatic, choleric,* and *melancholic* were used to describe people. Research these descriptions further and have the class determine which category each student falls into.

2. Choose a long-term career goal and research what qualifications are necessary to accomplish it. For example, if you would like to be a network administrator, check your college catalog for degree requirements and look on the Internet for job descriptions that include the kind of degree and work experience required. List any other skills necessary for the career.

3. Using the keywords "mission statements," search the Internet for college and business mission statements. Print out at least three different mission statements and identify the similarities and differences. Report your findings to the class.

References

Edwards, B. (1979). *Drawing on the right side of the brain.* Tarcher.

Fleming, N. D. "VARK: a guide to learning." Retrieved 20 Sept. 2003, from www.vark-learn.com/english/index.asp.

Glass, L. (1997). *Toxic people: 10 ways of dealing with people who make your life miserable.* New York: St. Martin's.

Godwin, M. (2000) *Who are you? 101 ways of seeing yourself.* New York: Penguin.

Klauser, H. A. (2001). *Write it down, make it happen: Knowing what you want and getting it!* New York: Simon & Schuster.

Lawrence, G. (1995). *People types and tiger stripes* (3rd ed.). Gainesville, FL: CAPT.

Lazear, D. (1991). *Seven ways of teaching: The artistry of teaching with multiple intelligences.* Palatine, IL: Skylight.

Matte, N. L., & Green Henderson, S. H. (1995). *Success, your style: Right- & left-brain techniques for learning.* Belmont, CA: Wadsworth.

3 Managing Your Time and Stress

Stuart's time management practices are similar to many college students'—they write down only the important activities. In this chapter, your goal is to find the method that works best for you to help you keep time and stress under control. This chapter presents you with different methods and ideas for increasing your chances of success. Specifically, you will be able to answer the following questions once you have completed the chapter:

- *What is time management and how will it help me in my life?*

- *How do I manage my goals and priorities?*

- *How do I get organized?*

- *How do my energy levels relate to time management?*

- *What can I do to stop procrastinating?*

- *How can I minimize negative stress at work, home, and college?*

COMMUNITY · COLLEGE ·

Student Profile

NAME: **Stuart Dixon**   AGE: **24**

MAJOR: **Criminal Justice**

1. How do you manage your time?

    I actually manage my time pretty well. I don't really write down what I need to do; I keep up with it mentally.

2. What do you do as a stress reliever?

    To relieve stress, I write, draw, listen to music, and box.

3. What have you learned about your ability to handle stress?

    I have learned that I handle most things better than the people I work with.

4. What is your VARK?

    Kinesthetic.

The Next Step

Now that you have a better understanding of college culture and have read and thought about values, goals, and priorities, it is time to figure out how to make it all fit together. In order to connect your educational objectives with your college's demands of you as a student, you must develop good time and stress management skills. Without them, your goals will be harder to achieve; with them, you will find the path to realizing your dreams a little easier and your steps along the journey more stable. This is not to say that attaining your educational goals will be simple—there is no way to predict what obstacles lie in your path—but the ability to plan your time and reduce stress effectively will keep those goals in focus and give you the confidence to meet them.

Managing Your Time

Despite our many differences, we all have the same number of hours each day and the same number of days each week. Why, then, does it seem as though some people are more accomplished than others? Are they able to magically extend the day by a few hours or sneak eight days into a week? Do they forgo all sleep, meals, and personal needs just to get things done? Although we would like to believe that high achievers have superhuman strength, the truth is they usually do not do anything to achieve their goals that we cannot do as well. When you talk to very productive people, they usually tell you that the secret to their success is that they learned to manage their time efficiently. Effective time management is not a talent; it is a skill, one that gets better as you practice over time.

Analyzing Your Time

If the first step is recognizing that we all have the same amount of time to work with, then analyzing your time is the second step to effective time management. Tim Hindle (1998), in his book *Manage Your Time*, suggests keeping a time log of your day that is divided into 30-minute increments (p. 9). The purpose of a 30-minute time log is to raise your awareness of what you are doing throughout the day. Make your own time log like the one in Exhibit 3.1 for one day's worth of activities. Keeping an eye on how you spend your time helps you make realistic time management goals and keeps you from wasting too much time or miscalculating how much time it takes to complete tasks.

Asking the questions "Where did the time go?" and "What do I do with my time?" is a start to analyzing your time. You should also analyze your time management skills—or how well you use your time wisely to meet your goals and stay healthy in the process. The following assessment asks 10 questions about time management abilities.

Practice

EXERCISE 3.1

Complete the Personal Time Assessment worksheet to determine how well you manage your time.

Companion
Website

EXHIBIT 3.1 *Time log example.*

TIME	WEDNESDAY'S ACTIVITIES
7:00 A.M.	Get ready for classes; eat breakfast
7:30 A.M.	Review notes for business class
8:00 A.M.	En route to school
8:30 A.M.	Business Communications
9:00 A.M.	Class, continued
9:30 A.M.	Class, continued
10:00 A.M.	See advisor to plan next semester's classes

You may already be a good manager of time. Certainly, if you are able to work, take care of your family, and attend your college classes without getting confused or overwhelmed, then you can already manage your time. Nonetheless, what causes students the most stress is trying to schedule enough time to prepare for classes, study for exams, write papers, and

ACTIVITY   *Personal Time Assessment*

Circle the number (1-Never, 2-Sometimes, 3-Usually, 4-Always) that best describes your experience.

STATEMENT	NEVER	SOMETIMES	USUALLY	ALWAYS
1. I arrive to class prepared.	1	2	3	4
2. I review my notes within 24 hours of class.	1	2	3	4
3. I spend my time on campus taking care of personal business, talking with professors, studying, or doing research.	1	2	3	4
4. I have study goals, and I achieve them each week.	1	2	3	4
5. I feel prepared for tests.	1	2	3	4
6. I spend enough time on writing assignments.	1	2	3	4
7. I get enough sleep each night.	1	2	3	4
8. I spend some time each week doing something I enjoy.	1	2	3	4
9. I have enough time to take care of most of my personal needs.	1	2	3	4
10. I get support from others to help me meet my educational goals.	1	2	3	4
Score each column.				
Add each column's total.	**Total**			

(continued)

SCORE RANGE	MEANING
32–40	You do a good job managing your time. For the most part, you are satisfied with how you manage your time and what you accomplish each week.
26–31	You do a good job managing your time for most activities. Identify your weaker areas and create a plan to improve time management in those areas.
19–25	You may be dissatisfied with your time management and find only a few goals are met each week. Review what you are doing right with some of your time and make a plan that will draw upon your time management strengths.
Below 18	You may feel as though you are not meeting most of your goals during the week. An honest look at your goals, necessary activities, and priorities is needed.

participate in various extracurricular activities. Good time management skills include knowing your goals and priorities, being aware of how much time you have and how you are spending it, and making adjustments along the way. We all are given the same number of hours in a day, but how we use those hours differs greatly because of the way we manage our time.

Multitasking

One way you can manage your time more effectively is by multitasking or doing more than one activity at once. If you have the ability to focus on more than one activity at a time, then multitasking may be a good way to manage your time wisely. If, for example, you're talking on the phone, you may be able to fold clothes or sweep the floor at the same time. There may be times when you can take your reading material with you while waiting at the doctor's office or getting your car's oil changed, generate ideas for a paper as you listen to the news on the radio, or listen to lecture recordings while riding a bicycle at the gym. You can multitask most effectively if both tasks do not require your complete attention. For instance, you shouldn't read a textbook while driving or chopping vegetables! Be prepared for multitasking opportunities by carrying along reading material, notes, and paper and pen for writing ideas down. Then, take advantage of those times when you can complete two or more tasks at once.

Getting Creative

You cannot create more time, but you can get creative with how you use it and manage it.

- If you have children, consider setting up a "babysitting co-op" where classmates, friends, or neighbors watch each other's children while you study or take care of personal errands.

- Use the Internet to automate tasks that take considerable time to do. Your bank may provide automatic bill payments that will save you time and stamps each month. Consider browsing and shopping online for items that may take several trips to different stores to find.

- If you need to save time running errands, find out whether local businesses offer deliveries—some do for free—and take advantage of them. Think about the time you will save having your cleaning, groceries, and medicine delivered.

- Create a monthly newsletter for family and friends to replace hours on the phone talking to individuals and on the computer sending e-mail.

Managing Your Priorities

Managing your time and priorities when you are in college can be a game of strategy, action, and patience. In the activity on the following page, consider what should be top priority; what can be completed if there is time; and what can be delegated, modified, or rescheduled for another day. It is Monday morning, and you have 10 items on your to-do list to accomplish today, but you don't have time to complete them all. Determine which activities are top priorities and which are not. Then, list those you eliminated and explain why you decided to make them low-priority items. Finally, describe how you will accomplish the low-priority items the next day.

Before you can begin to manage your time and monitor your stress levels, you have to make sure that your goals and priorities are clear. As you learned in Chapter 2, writing down your goals and setting your priorities, which may change frequently, are the first steps to realizing your dreams; they are also the first steps to figuring out how much time you need to spend on each goal. Before thinking about time management, take time to review what you have written down as your short-term goals and priorities.

If you listed your priorities right now, college would be near the top. Certainly, enrolling in college and reading this book mean you are committed to furthering your education. Nevertheless, you have to figure out where the priority of going to college fits in with your other priorities. Perhaps attending classes is your only priority because you live alone and do not work; more likely, however, college competes with other priorities. If you are going to succeed in college, your education must be a top priority most of the time.

In addition to college, you have to consider your family as a priority. Depending on your situation, you may have family members who need you for emotional, physical, and financial support. You may even be the only one they can rely on. Because family is often a first priority for many students, it is important to manage your time with them wisely and effectively.

If you have not yet done so, talk to your family about the new responsibilities you have. Be honest in your descriptions of what you are doing and what you need from them. If you think time will be limited for family trips and weekend activities, let them know. If you think you will need to cut out some basic duties such as planning meals, cleaning the house, and running errands, be sure to communicate this to your family. The more they know about what to expect, the better able they will be to support your decision to enroll in college.

MONDAY'S TO-DO LIST—FOURTH WEEK OF CLASSES

- Pick up sister at airport at 7:30 P.M. (Airport is 15 minutes away.)
- Attend two classes, one at 2:00 P.M. and one at 4:00 P.M. (You have a one-hour break in between.)
- Complete paper for 4:00 class. (You will need an hour to finish.)
- Prepare dinner for family at 6:30 P.M. (It will take at least 30 minutes.)
- Study for Tuesday's psychology exam. (You would like to spend two hours.)
- Take children to school at 7:45 A.M. (School is 10 minutes from your house.)
- Get up at 6:00 A.M. and go to gym for an hour workout.
- Call your cousin who had surgery last week. (Spend 20 minutes.)
- Help children with homework. (Spend 1 hour.)
- Meet study group at noon to start working on final project for business communications class.

From the list above, identify which three items should be top priority.

Top priority _____

Top priority _____

Top priority _____

Why did you identify these to be the most important? _____

_____

With the time remaining, determine what else you can accomplish in the same day.

Additional activity _____

Additional activity _____

Additional activity _____

Additional activity _____

Why did you decide that those activities could be completed if time allowed? _____

_____

What items can be low priority, modified, or rescheduled?

Low priority _____

Low priority _____

Low priority _____

Why did you choose these items as low priority? _____

_____

How might you modify the low-priority items so that they can be completed in the same day? _____

_____

Another priority you may have is your job. Most community college students work as well as attend classes. For some, their jobs supplement their household income and are not necessary for survival; for many others, their jobs are more important than college because they provide the primary or sole income for the family. If your job is your top priority, then you should know where the other priorities must fall, and you should be prepared to make sacrifices in other areas to ensure that your job remains at the top.

With all the other responsibilities you have, it is easy to overlook the priority of relaxing; without it, the other priorities can run you down. Don't forget that you can have fun while in college, and you certainly should participate in activities you enjoy. Without them, your college career will seem stressful and dull. Scheduling downtime to play and rejuvenate is an important part of effective time management. Get outside, read for pleasure, or participate in those activities you enjoy. Relaxing and having fun will recharge your body and mind to concentrate on the demands of your other priorities.

EXERCISE 3.2

Collaboration

Working with another classmate or within a group, describe the different priorities a student may have while balancing work, family, and college. Which ones will conflict with one another? What advice would you give someone having difficulty managing her priorities?

Companion Website

Managing Your Goals

You will see this suggestion throughout this book: In order to accomplish anything, you must set goals and write them down. Even something as simple as spending two hours preparing for class should be written down as a goal for the day or week. The goals must be manageable, however. Having too many goals for the week may make you feel overwhelmed at the thought of meeting them all or like a failure for not accomplishing them all. Avoid the temptation to over-schedule, and be realistic about how long it will take to complete your goals for the day or week. Setting too few goals for the week may make you feel like a rudderless ship, which makes it easier to get off track.

Once you have them written down, communicate the goals to your coworkers, family, and friends. Enlist their help to meet your goals, especially if you need to schedule time to study and complete assignments. Tell them that you must have the evenings free of distractions, or make arrangements with them to have a weekend or weekday to yourself to study. Don't assume that because they *know* you are in school that they will also *know* you need extra time and personal space to get your work finished. Managing time is much easier if your priorities and goals are concrete, realistic, and communicated to those around you.

Managing Your Energy

Just as important as managing your time is managing your energy. Think about this scenario: You have all weekend off from work and your spouse took the kids to visit the grandparents. Therefore, you have 48 hours of complete solitude to write a research paper that is due on Monday. Sounds ideal, doesn't it? But what if you have the flu for those two

Time is valuable only if you plan and use it well.

days? Does the time mean anything when you don't have the energy to do any work? What if, instead of having the flu, you worked two double shifts and haven't slept more than five hours in two days? Will you be able to use your free 48 hours productively or will you need to take care of yourself?

Time is only valuable if you have the energy to use it well. Thus, you need to be aware of how you feel, how energetic you are, and how willing you are to use your time wisely. To determine which times of the day you feel the most energetic, complete the activity on page 71. In the first section, place an X in the appropriate column for each time of day. If you work nights and sleep during most of the day, create your own chart with the times you are awake.

Critical Thinking
EXERCISE 3.3

Looking at the third section, which shows Carla's energy levels, what times are best to schedule classes? What times are best to study? What times are best to take care of simple tasks such as organizing her notes or cleaning her study space? Why did you make your decisions?

Companion
Website

Second, assess your energy levels in another way: in addition to the time of day, your energy levels rise and fall during the week. Do you find yourself tired on Monday mornings, but full of energy on Fridays? Or do you feel worn out by Thursday evenings, but rejuvenated on Sundays? Depending on your work, school, and personal schedules, you will find that you have regular bursts of energy at certain times of the week. Use the second section to determine which days of the week you feel most energetic. Place an X in the appropriate columns.

Finally, complete Exercise 3.3 by referring to the third section.

TIME OF DAY	HIGH ENERGY	NEUTRAL	LOW ENERGY
6:00 A.M.			
8:00 A.M.			
10:00 A.M.			
12 noon			
2:00 P.M.			
4:00 P.M.			
6:00 P.M.			
8:00 P.M.			
10:00 P.M.			
12 midnight			

WEEKDAY	HIGH ENERGY	NEUTRAL	LOW ENERGY
Sunday			
Monday			
Tuesday			
Wednesday			
Thursday			
Friday			
Saturday			

Carla's Energy Levels

TIME OF DAY	HIGH ENERGY	NEUTRAL	LOW ENERGY
6:00 A.M.			X
8:00 A.M.	X		
10:00 A.M.	X		
12 noon		X	
2:00 P.M.			X
4:00 P.M.			X
6:00 P.M.	X		
8:00 P.M.		X	
10:00 P.M.			X
12 midnight			X

Along with managing your energy you must maintain your health. You cannot expect to experience high levels of energy and productivity without taking care of yourself. Sleeping regularly and eating small meals often help you maintain your energy levels, as does moderate exercise; sugar, caffeine, and a sedentary lifestyle zap energy reserves, making it difficult to manage energy and time efficiently. As always, though, check with your doctor first before changing your dietary and exercise habits. At the least, avoid fad diets, rigorous exercise plans, and late-night activities during the semester, all of which drain your energy reserves.

Reflection

EXERCISE 3.4

Describe a situation in which you had the time to complete a task but had a low level of energy. How did you feel? Were you able to complete the task or did you have to reschedule it?

Companion
Website

Identifying Time and Energy Zappers

Despite your best efforts to manage your time and energy, there will be times that your plans are interrupted by people and last-minute changes. A few distractions during the day can be a nice break from the mundane tasks of going to school and working or caring for a family. However, if they take so much time away from your studies that you can't seem to keep up with the pace of your classes or that you are stressed out, you will need to find ways to lessen the frequency of or eliminate the intrusions.

Although you may be able to create your own list of time and energy zappers, here are a few common ones:

Reflection

EXERCISE 3.5

If you need to visit the library to find sources for a paper, which day of the week is best for you? If you need to study for a math exam, which day of the week is best? What class work can you do on the days when your energy is the lowest? What class work can you do on the days when your energy is the highest?

- People who want your attention and time, but don't need it
- Interruptions such as unnecessary phone calls
- Fatigue and illness
- Personal problems
- Mindless television watching
- Internet surfing that serves no purpose
- Continuous "chatting" online
- Playing video or computer games
- Inability to say "no"
- Procrastination
- Poor organization

Companion
Website

- Inability to concentrate because of learning difficulty, medication, or stress

Now is the time to block out the zappers. You can't afford the time they waste, and you must be proactive in getting rid of them. Some will be easy to eliminate, such as playing video games or hanging out all day with friends, while others will be more difficult, such as learning to say "no" to people or eliminating procrastination. The key to getting rid of the energy and time wasters is to take on the easiest ones and work on, through goal setting, the others.

One way to help yourself manage your energy is by becoming aware of which activities relax you when you are stressed and which activities allow you to refill your energy reserves. Complete the activity below.

ACTIVITY   *What Relaxes You?*

In the table below, place an X in the appropriate column next to each activity. If the activity both relaxes and energizes, place an X in both columns. If the activity does neither, leave both columns blank.

ACTIVITY	RELAXING	ENERGIZING
Watching television		
Spending time with family/friends		
Pleasure reading		
Doing housework		
Exercising (light to moderate)		
Gardening		
Talking on the phone		
Writing		
Cooking		
Shopping		
Napping		
Participating in a hobby		
Surfing the Internet		
Organizing closets, drawers, files		
Enjoying a nice meal		

Getting Organized

Personal Space and Supplies

If your personal space is cluttered and disorganized, it is hard to keep your life straight. To manage your time effectively and efficiently, you must organize. First, find a place in your house or apartment that you can call your own. Make sure it is comfortable and quiet and has adequate space for books, notebooks, and other supplies. It has to be a place you *want* to be or it will be difficult to go there to stay on task. Consider starting or ending your day with straightening or cleaning your work space. Leaving it until it gets too messy may make working difficult, as you are likely to lose items and waste time looking for what you need.

To stay organized, buy two calendars, preferably one to hang on a wall and one to carry with you. How they are organized, by month or week, is up to you. Both calendars, however, should allow you to look ahead easily. Make it a habit to write your daily and weekly tasks on both calendars. Make it part of your routine every evening to write down your goals for the next day and to review each morning what you need to do during the day. As you complete each task, scratch it out. Here is an example of a typical day's activities:

Collaboration

EXERCISE 3.6

Working within a group or with another classmate, describe the types of activities that can zap students' time and energy, then create solutions for eliminating them.

Companion Website

THURSDAY

- Make appointment to have oil changed
- Pick up dry cleaning
- Take kids to baseball
- Study for history quiz on Friday
- Read 30 pages for English
- Get book from library

Using a Calendar

In order to juggle all your family, work, and college responsibilities, use a calendar. Which one you choose depends on how you can best visualize your time. Once you get a calendar, write down all your planned activities and tasks. Because you have quite a few things to do for college, consider getting a separate calendar or planner just for your classes.

Exhibit 3.2 shows a typical wall or large desk calendar. The benefits of using a monthly calendar are that you can visualize the whole month at one time and can anticipate busy days or weeks. Drawbacks to using a monthly calendar are that it is usually not very portable and it does not provide much space to write details about your duties. They are good, however, for major activities and appointments.

Another type of calendar is weekly, whereby you can glance at each week at a time (see Exhibit 3.3). A benefit to a weekly calendar is that you have room

EXHIBIT 3.2 *Monthly calendar.*

SUNDAY	MONDAY	TUESDAY	WEDNESDAY	THURSDAY	FRIDAY	SATURDAY
					1	2
3	4	5 library w/ B.W., 2:00	6	7	8	9 picnic, noon
10	11 work late	12	13 Dr. appt., 2:00	14 play rehearsal 7:00	15 pay bills	16
17	18	19 library w/ B.W., 2:00	20 lunch w/ Rhea	21 play rehearsal 7:00	22	23
24	25 nutrition exam 10:00	26	27	28 English paper due	29	30 birthday party 2:00

EXHIBIT 3.3 *Weekly calendar.*

MONDAY	TUESDAY	WEDNESDAY	THURSDAY	FRIDAY	SATURDAY	SUNDAY
8:30 Work 2:00 Geology 3:00 Trig 5:00 Pick up dinner 7:00 Study for Accounting	9:00 English 11:00 Acct. 6:00 Help sister with painting	8:30 Work 2:00 Geology 3:00 Trig	9:00 English 11:00 Acct.	8:30 Work 2:00 Geology 3:00 Trig 7:00 Movie with friend	8–10 Clean house 3–4 Exercise 6–11 Study	3–8 Work on paper

EXHIBIT 3.4 *Daily calendar.*

TIME	FRIDAY, MARCH 10, 2006
7:00 A.M.	Get ready for school
8:00 A.M.	Arrive to school early and study in the library
9:00 A.M.	Algebra
10:00 A.M.	English 2
11:00 A.M.	Study for biology exam
12:00 A.M.	Eat lunch; review notes for algebra
1:00 P.M.	Biology—EXAM!!
2:00 P.M.	Drive to work; errand to return book
3:00 P.M.	Work
4:00 P.M.	
5:00 P.M.	

to note the details of each activity; a drawback is that because you can only view one week at a time, it is difficult to anticipate what you must do the next week.

A daily calendar (see Exhibit 3.4) works well if you are very busy during the day. However, this kind of calendar is the most difficult to work with if you need to plan ahead. Because you cannot visually see the rest of the week or month, you may overlook important events or be surprised by them. Use a daily calendar only if you are extremely organized and can plan ahead effectively, or use it in conjunction with a longer-term calendar.

Whichever type of calendar you choose, be sure that it is used every day. Write down your daily and weekly tasks and scratch them off as you complete them. Also, check your calendar each morning before you leave for work or school. Knowing what to expect for the day makes surprises less likely.

Keeping It Clean

With new calendars and a designated space at home to schedule and review your tasks, you shouldn't need much more, right? There is one last suggestion for keeping your life organized: Keep your area clean. As stated before, you will lose valuable time looking for important papers if your work area and bookbag are cluttered. Make it a point each day or week to straighten up your personal space. Get rid of unnecessary slips of paper and other items. The better you can see your calendar and your workspace, the easier it will be to reach your goals. Think about your personal space as if it were the path to your goals. If you purposely put obstacles in your way (e.g., clutter) as you work toward your goal, it will be more difficult to get to your destination. If, however, you clear the path of clutter, then your footing will be more secure, and your path will be safer, making it easier to reach your goal.

Running Low on Time and Energy

There will be times when you find yourself with daily or weekly goals still left on your list, but you don't have the time and energy reserves that you hoped to have. Sometimes life throws us a curveball, and our beautiful plans are mangled if not completely destroyed. If you find yourself in such a situation, you will benefit from changing your goals and priorities quickly and eliminating unnecessary items from your to-do list. For example, you planned to bake a friend a birthday cake from scratch, but you don't have two hours to do it. What can you do? How about buy a cake on the way to your friend's house? The outcome is still the same: your friend has a cake for his birthday. You hoped to get all the bills paid by the end of the day, but you don't have the time and energy left? Pay the bills that are due the soonest and complete the task the next day.

There will be some days that you just can't do it all. You may find that you cannot read the assigned chapter in your sociology class the night before. If this happens to you—and it will at some time in your college career—then create a back-up plan. Avoid giving up completely if you run out of time or energy; do something, even if it is just a little bit. Can't get to the library to start looking for sources for your research paper? Create an outline or a task list instead and go to the library the next day. Do something that keeps you moving forward, but don't give up. You will have more energy and time the next day to complete new tasks.

Procrastination

An example of time and goal management at its worst is procrastination, an activity that seems to be an integral part of going to college. One would think that all college students routinely participate in cramming and "pulling all-nighters." Putting off studying and completing projects certainly adds to your stress, but procrastination does not have to be a necessary part of going to college. Realistically, community college students delay starting projects and studying because they are pressed for time, not because they are wasting time hanging out with their friends or having fun.

There are many humorous sayings about procrastination:

If it weren't for the last minute, nothing would get done. —Anonymous

I never put off till tomorrow what I can possibly do . . . the day after. —Oscar Wilde

Kidding aside, procrastination can be, American author Elbert Hubbard remarked, "the father of failure." Postponing an activity or task because you do not want to do it or can find more interesting activities to do can have serious consequences. For example, if you put off researching your legal terminology paper until the night before, you might find that the library closed early or access to online databases is down. You may even discover that your computer won't work and your printer is out of ink.

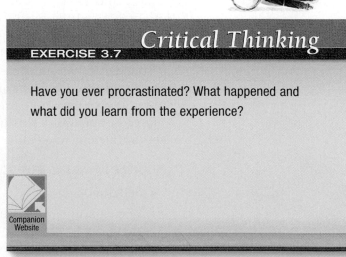

Critical Thinking

EXERCISE 3.7

Have you ever procrastinated? What happened and what did you learn from the experience?

Companion Website

Procrastination can, then, be a barrier between you and your goals and cause you undue stress. Managing your time and planning ahead will, however, minimize your desire to procrastinate. Writing down your tasks and goals, too, will make them visible and instill the need to cross them off your list.

FIGHTING PROCRASTINATION

- Divide the project into smaller parts. If you have a paper to write, break the task into generating ideas, drafting the paper, and completing the final draft. Do only one part at a time.

- Create a time line for when you want to complete each part. Make adjustments if needed, but try to stick to the schedule.

- Give yourself enough time to complete each part. It is easy to assume that you can find all the resources you need for a paper in one day. A more realistic goal is to find two sources during one trip to the library.

- Just do it. Start right here, right now, and don't think about finding a better time to begin.

- Recognize that behind every procrastinator is someone who fears—the unknown or failure. Acknowledge that fear by writing down what the fear is. Once you recognize your fear, you are more likely to move past it.

- Reward yourself for completing a particularly difficult or boring project.

- Write a list of consequences of *not* doing the project on time and a list of consequences for doing the project on time. Decide which list you can live with.

- Remind yourself of the reason you are in college and think about how this project supports that reason.

Managing Stress

Stress is a physical and psychological response to outside stimuli. In other words, just about anything that stimulates you can cause stress. Not all stress, however, is bad for you. For example, the stress you feel when you see someone get seriously hurt enables you to spring into action to help. For some students, the stress of an upcoming exam gives them the energy and focus to study. Without feeling a little stressed, these students might not feel the need to study at all.

Not everyone, however, handles stress the same way, and what is a stressful situation for you may not be for someone else. How we handle stress depends on our genetic makeup, past experiences, and the stress-reducing techniques we know and practice. There are ways to reduce stress or change our reaction, both physically and psychologically. First, though, it is important to be able to identify causes of stress. This list is not exhaustive, but it can start you thinking about different ways you experience stress.

POSSIBLE CAUSES OF STRESS

- Self-doubt
- Fear of failure or the unknown
- Speaking in public
- Uncomfortable situations

Taking care of your body (and mind), including taking time to relax, will help you alleviate the negative effects of stress.

- Pressure to succeed (from yourself or others)
- Lack of support—financial, physical, or psychological
- The demands of a job such as a promotion/demotion, deadlines, and evaluations
- Life experiences such as the death of a loved one, having a child, getting married, and moving
- Too many activities and not enough time to complete them
- Congested traffic
- Waiting in lines

Stress Patterns

Each of us has certain triggers, such as the ones listed previously, that stress us. Usually, however, the same situation doesn't stress us the same way each time we are in it. Take, for example, waiting in line at the bank. One day, you might be extremely angry about waiting 15 minutes in line to cash a check because you are late for a job interview. The next time, though, you are in the same line waiting the same amount of time, you may be calm and relaxed because you are enjoying a little quiet time to think while your mother waits in the car. Thus, it is not necessarily the situation or action that causes negative stress, but more likely other factors that are involved.

When you suffer from lack of sleep, you may be more likely to react negatively to people and situations that usually do not bother you. When you feel unsure of your ability to be successful in college, you may take constructive criticism as a personal attack. Being aware of times and situations that cause you the most stress is one step to managing your stress better. For example, if you realize that you are sensitive to others' feedback because you feel insecure, then you may be less likely to react negatively. Complete the activity below.

Minimizing Stress in College

Because there is stress in college, at work, and at home, it is important to identify the different stressors in each environment and work toward minimizing negative stress in each area. Some weeks, you will have to contend

ACTIVITY   *Assessing Your Stressors*

Identify which situations are stressful and which are not. Consider other situations, or people, that cause you to react negatively and add them to this list. The goal is to recognize a pattern of stress and then work to overcome it. When you can tell your professor or coworker that you experience negative stress when assigned a big project, then they can help you create a plan to complete it.

SITUATION	STRESSES ME	DOES NOT STRESS ME
Starting a big project		
Paying bills		
Being in a messy environment		
Receiving graded papers and exams		
Not getting enough sleep		
Taking a personal or professional risk		
Getting out of bed		
Not getting feedback on my work		
Being distracted by other people		
Thinking about the future		
Taking tests		

with negative stress in only one area, but there will be times when it seems as though each part of your life is making you miserable. The more you know about what you can and cannot control, the more likely you will work through stressful times and stay on track with your goals.

Stress in college is inevitable, but it doesn't have to be overwhelming if you know what you can do to minimize negative stress. There are several ways students unknowingly cause stress:

- Failing to read the catalog for course prerequisites and descriptions as well as degree program requirements.
- Registering for more hours than they can handle.
- Trying to do too much at work and home.
- Missing deadlines.
- Arriving late for class or appointments.
- Keeping the same social schedule.

The information in this chapter, and others, should help you minimize stress in college by providing you with information and strategies for accomplishing your goals. Even if you avoid the listed behaviors, you may still find that things don't go your way in college. If you realize that there will be times that you or others make mistakes, then you will be more likely to bounce back from problems. Following are some suggestions for minimizing negative stress at school:

- Read all information you receive from the college.
- Pay attention to flyers on doors, bulletin boards, and tables.
- Talk to your advisor, instructor, and counselor on a regular basis.
- Check out the college's website.
- Read publications such as newspapers and newsletters the college sends to the community.
- Ask questions.
- Get involved with campus organizations and clubs.

Minimizing Stress at Home

Reducing stress at home will, no doubt, be the first step to minimize your overall stress. Because your family and friends are your most important supporters, what they think of you and the demands they place on you must be

INTEGRITY MATTERS

One way to eliminate stress and anxiety is to make integrity a top priority. Even though it may seem less stressful to take the easier path, in the long run, your negative stress will be less when you maintain integrity.

discussed. Some family members may be unsure of what you are doing or worried that your schoolwork will leave little time for them. Your friends may feel the same way, especially if they are used to hanging out with you after work and on the weekends. The key to minimizing stress at home is to communicate your needs. Talk to your loved ones about what you and they can expect when you are taking classes. Here are some other tips for making your home life a sanctuary rather than an asylum:

- Tell your family when you have exams or major projects due.
- Inform them of your breaks and vacation time. They may be excited to count down the days until you are finished with the semester.
- Explain how your responsibilities will change when you are in college.
- Be aware that you are a role model for your family. You may be inspiring other members to go to college.

Minimizing Stress at Work

For some, stress on the job can be the most difficult because of the fear of performing poorly and being fired. It can also be particularly tough to manage because you may feel uncomfortable confronting coworkers and being honest about your feelings. There are ways, though, to cope with the negative effects of stress at work. To help minimize the amount of stress you have about your job, you should do one or more of the following:

- Talk to your employer about your educational goals. Your boss may be very excited that you are increasing your knowledge and improving your skills.
- See if your employer will allow flextime to take classes. You may be able to arrive at work early, skip a lunch break, or stay late in order to take classes during the day.
- Let your boss know when you have finals or other activities that may interfere with your regular workday.
- Unless you ask permission, avoid studying on the job.
- Handle any conflict that may arise with your schedule as soon as possible. Coworkers may be jealous of your success or they may misunderstand the arrangements you made to work and go to school. Address any concerns you have about your workplace environment to the appropriate person.

There is no cure-all for stress. It is an integral and important part of life and can actually be thrilling and exciting. Nonetheless, preventing or reducing it in the first place can keep you happier and healthier, which will make you better able to achieve your goals.

Reducing the Negative Effects of Stress

Because you cannot eliminate all stress, develop methods for reducing the negative effects your body and mind experience when stressed. One of the quickest, easiest ways to reduce the negative effects of stress is to take a deep breath. You may have even told someone who was upset to breathe deeply in order to calm down. The breath is, as many cultures have known for thousands of years, an important part of life; for example, in yoga, the ability to control it is essential to controlling the mind and body and to bringing in fresh air to the lungs and other organs.

Visualization is another method for reducing the effect stress has on the mind and body. In order to visualize a more relaxed time and place, find a quiet, comfortable spot, sit down, and close your eyes. Relaxation experts suggest that you visualize a place that makes you feel warm and relaxed. Many people think about a beach because the mood there is often relaxed and the sound of the ocean is comforting. You should find your own special place.

Once you decide where you want to go mentally, start noticing the details in your place. If you are at the beach, then you should feel the sunshine's heat. Next, listen to the waves crashing on the surf and smell the salty air. Depending on how long you need to visualize this special place, you may want to stick your toe in the water or lie down on the beach and soak up the rays—leave your stress in those designated beach trash cans. The goal of this method of relaxation is to stay there as long as you need to; when you come back to your present location, mentally that is, you should feel refreshed and renewed.

Sometimes physical activity can be a better stress reliever than mental exercises. Getting outside or to the gym to work out your frustrations and stress is an excellent way of maintaining your health. Exercising eliminates the physical side effects of stress while taking your mind off your troubles. If you do not usually exercise, start slowly. Begin, for instance, with a 15-minute walk around the block or do some simple stretching exercises on the floor. Overdoing exercise can lead to more stress, so start small and increase the time you spend as you get stronger.

If you happen to exercise too much, you can look toward massage therapy to reduce all your stress. Although it is a little less conventional than other methods of reducing stress, a massage can improve circulation and alleviate muscle soreness. Seek professional massage therapy or ask a family member to rub your neck, shoulders, or feet. Massage therapy can give you the rejuvenation you need to tackle the rest of the week.

You have heard that cliché that "Laughter is the best medicine," and it is also an ideal way to eliminate stress. Have you ever been in a very stressful situation when someone made you laugh, and you thought, "Boy, I needed that." You probably felt all the tension melt away as you doubled over giggling. Surrounding yourself with people who make you laugh is one way to keep stress at a minimum. Other ways include renting comedies or reading funny books. Of course, good, old-fashioned acting silly can relieve stress and anxiety as well.

Lastly, comfort yourself with familiar favorites to eliminate the negative effects of stress. A special meal or a visit with your best friend will put you at ease. Looking at old photographs, reminiscing about family trips, and watching your favorite movies are great stress relievers. If you are in college in a new town or have moved out on your own for the first time, you may find comfort in the familiar, whether it be an old pillow or stuffed animal. Make sure, though, that your methods of reducing negative stress are healthy; drugs and alcohol may temporarily relieve stress, but they cause more problems in the long run.

Practice

EXERCISE 3.8

Complete the following sentences.

When I feel stressed, I like to . . .

Three activities that make me feel better after a hard day are:

1. _____

2. _____

3. _____

Companion
Website

Staying Flexible

An important method of managing stress is to remain flexible. If you try to control too many aspects of your life, you will quickly discover you can't do it all. Although it is important to manage your time and mark your progress toward your goals, you must still plan for the unexpected and be willing to make adjustments. Good time managers plan for problems by keeping their schedules loose enough to make room for adjustments. For example, if you have a doctor's appointment at 2:00, you shouldn't schedule a job interview at 3:00. Delays in the doctor's office or traffic problems could keep you from your 3:00 appointment. Instead, give yourself plenty of time in between scheduled tasks, especially if you have to rely on others' time management skills.

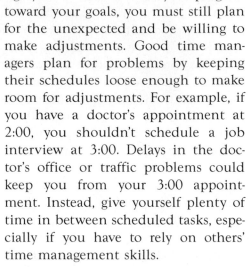

Reflection

EXERCISE 3.9

What stresses you? In what ways can you eliminate or reduce the amount of stress you have?

Companion
Website

Knowing When to Get Help with Stress

If you ever feel as though you cannot cope with the amount of work and responsibility you have—despite attempts to reduce your stress—seek professional help. Excessive crying, difficulty breathing, inability to get out of bed, and suicidal thoughts are severe reactions to stress. Knowing when to reach out to other people is crucial to your recovery.

When asking for help, find someone you trust who will be objective about your experiences. Sometimes, close friends and family members can be your best allies to combat stress, but other times an outside party, who will listen to what you have to say without judging, can be extremely helpful. When you talk to someone, be honest about what you are feeling. Don't try to minimize any fear or anxiety. The more they know about what you are experiencing, the better able they will be to help.

Critical Thinking PLUS*

You are working 40 hours a week, taking 12 credit hours for the semester, and have two children under the age of 5. You are stressed because you are having trouble managing all of your responsibilities. Although you don't have any family members who live nearby, you do have a few good friends, one of whom has children as well, and another who is also in college. When you approach them about making a plan to help you juggle all of your responsibilities, both your friends have very different ideas. The one with children thinks you all should go out to a park and let the kids play while you talk. The other offers to pick you up sometime to go out to dinner. You would prefer time alone to study and take care of errands, but you don't know how to voice your opinion without offending your friends. What do you do?

Consider how understanding your personality style or learning preference can help you through challenging situations.

NOTES

*PERSONALITY + LEARNING STYLE = UNDERSTANDING SITUATIONS

Learning Styles Application

This chart lists the four learning styles and tips based on the chapter's main ideas. Locate your learning style and read the corresponding tips to maximize your success in college.

VISUAL

Visual learners find using calendars an effective time and task management tool because they visually represent upcoming events and activities. You also benefit from visualization techniques for stress management and can reduce stress by watching TV, reading magazines, or going through old photographs.

AURAL

Aural learners usually benefit from talking about their priorities and goals and how they will accomplish tasks. Talking through stressful situations is also advisable for this type of learner. You can also relax by listening to their favorite music.

READ/WRITE

Read/write learners find the act of writing down a to-do list or a goals list an effective way to manage their time and efforts. Pleasure reading, journaling, or writing to friends and family is an effective way to deal with stress.

KINESTHETIC

Kinesthetic learners deal with stress most effectively by getting out and participating in a physical activity. Exercise, even moderate activity, is a good stress reliever.

Path of Discovery

How do you feel when you have a day or a week when it seems as though you cannot achieve your goals because of unexpected challenges? What have you done in the past to get back on track after such a day? How have you used those experiences to prepare each day or week?

FROM COLLEGE TO UNIVERSITY

How your stress will change and how to handle the new pressures

There are many possible stressors awaiting you when you make that move from your community college to university. Increased tuition, higher expectations, more difficult workload, impending graduation, and goal realization are all reasons to feel anxious about the transition, but remember that you have already succeeded in college by getting this far.

To meet the challenges that await you, be honest about them. For example, your professors will be asking more from you academically. In addition, recognize the fact that you will be graduating in just a few semesters and that you should plan for life after school. These realities, while daunting, do not have to be defeating if you are honest about them. With some work—and the good habits you form at your community college—you can overcome them with the same success.

Regardless of the new challenges, once you transfer, it will be even more important to have a solid support structure at work and at home. In addition, you will be making connections with people who will hopefully help you get a job after college. All of these relationships can provide you with a system for handling the demands of a four-year university. Be mindful of the stress-reducing strategies that work best for you. Practice them regularly and seek out help with achieving your goals; you then will be more relaxed and more confident in your abilities.

FROM COLLEGE TO CAREER

Decreasing stress and improving time management on the job

If you decide to go directly from college to work, or back to work, your time and stress management skills can make the difference between a dreaded job and a life-fulfilling career. Time management is even more important on the job because your actions affect more people. Likewise, if you have difficulty managing your stress, then people will find working with you stressful. Practice makes perfect, and the more you practice good time management skills, the less stress you should have. You won't, however, be able to eliminate stress altogether. On the job, the stakes are much higher than in college.

One way to decrease stress on the job is to cultivate relationships with coworkers who can provide support. It is important to turn to colleagues for help when times get rough. A good relationship with a coworker can mean the difference between wanting to throw up your hands and getting through the challenges. Another way to reduce the stress you feel on the job is to keep the lines of communication open with your supervisor as well as your family. The more they know about what you are facing, and how you feel, the more sensitive they can be.

In addition to managing your stress on the job, be vigilant about managing your time. No doubt, you will have more tasks and responsibilities to juggle, and how well you can manage all the balls in the air will determine your future in your job. Using a calendar and writing down daily tasks will help you keep up with your work. Also, being honest about *not* meeting deadlines will keep you on top (and help minimize stress). There may be times when you won't be able to manage your time as effectively as you wish, but if you can be honest, and speak up quickly, you may be able to save others time and reduce their stress.

Chapter in Review

1. What should you consider when you begin drafting a time management plan for a semester?

2. What stresses you? In what ways can you eliminate or reduce the amount of stress you have?

3. What activities zap your time and what can you do to eliminate the amount of time they take from you?

4. Use your work from Practice Exercise 3.1 to answer the following questions: What did you spend the most time on? What did you spend the least time on? Are you spending the most time on activities that contribute to your goals? If not, why? What surprised you about how you spent your time?

5. Remember the last time you procrastinated. What did you learn from the situation? What would you do differently now?

Case Scenarios

Read the following case scenarios and determine what each person should do. Refer to the information in this chapter as you write a description and plan of action for each student.

1. Chaya is doing very well in her classes. She manages her time wisely and adjusts her schedule any time something unexpected comes up. However, Chaya has had a hectic week. Her boss expects her to stay late to finish a special project; she has an important exam Thursday evening; her daughter is sick with a stomach virus; and her husband has been out of town for the last two weeks. Her goal is to take care of each problem without jeopardizing her job, her grade, or her daughter's welfare. What do you recommend she do? Is it realistic to expect that she can take care of each of her problems?

2. George has a 20-page research paper for his Abnormal Psychology class due at the end of the semester. The professor asked that an annotated bibliography, an outline, and a rough draft be turned in at the same time as the

final draft. George is feeling overwhelmed. Help him map out a plan of action so he can fulfill the requirements without unnecessary stress.

3. Barbara was sick for two weeks and fell behind in her classes. She is worried that she won't be able to catch up or make up her work. What should she do?

4. Glenn's coworkers do not understand why he is going back to school to get a degree. They think he is wasting his time, and they have started leaving him out of social functions because he has canceled so many times before, saying he has to study. Glenn is usually good-natured, but his coworkers' daily negative comments are starting to take a toll, and he is contemplating quitting school after the semester is over. What advice do you have for Glenn? Can he manage his college classes and his job? What should he do about his coworkers' attitudes and actions?

Research It Further

1. Keep a journal of how you spend your time for the next seven days. Write down how long you spend on each activity. Make sure you are honest and that you write in your journal every few hours. Then, create a report for your class as to how you spend the majority of your time.

2. Create a survey that asks your classmates how they cope with stress. Once you collect your data, report the results to your class and determine which stress relievers are healthy and which are unhealthy.

3. Brainstorm the different ways students can relieve stress in unhealthy ways. Then, search the Internet or library resources for information about the effects of these unhealthy activities.

4. Create a "toolbox" for students who are plagued by procrastination. Make the toolbox creative and fun.

References

Hindle, T. (1998). *Manage your time.* New York: DK Publishing.

4 Navigating Technology

Navigating the sea of technology available today is a definite challenge for a college student. There is so much to know and so much expected of you when you step into a classroom or log in to your online course. Apryl expresses the experience of many community college students: They know how to use some of the communication technology out there, but when it comes to using computers and software to complete assignments, they are not as experienced as college professors want them to be. If you find yourself in a similar situation, there is really no better place to be than in college where you have learning opportunities all around to help you enhance your computer skills. Although not intended as an introduction to computers, this chapter will help you learn the fundamentals of using a computer in college. More specifically, you will find answers to these questions:

- What are the basic parts of a computer I should know?

- What computer skills will college professors expect me to have?

- How should I use the Internet as a college student?

- What should I know about using e-mail, discussion boards, and chat rooms?

- How should I evaluate my ability to be successful in an online course?

COMMUNITY • COLLEGE •

Student Profile

NAME: **Apryl Cullum**   AGE: **21**

MAJOR: **Psychology**

1. How do you use technology in college?

   I have a cell phone that I use all the time to talk to my friends and my mom. I also use the computer lab when I need to write a paper.

2. Do you think students should know how to use technology effectively in order to succeed?

   Definitely. I am not really good with computers, and I have learned a lot since being here, but most professors expect that you know how to send an e-mail or post a discussion message.

3. What are the challenges to using technology in college?

   There are rules in class about cell phones and pagers. It's hard to remember to turn them off or not have them sitting out during tests. It is also hard to use a computer if you don't have one at home. You have to think about when you will need one and make sure you have plenty of time to use it.

4. What is your VARK?

   Aural.

Technology in College

I t really wasn't that long ago that college classroom technology consisted of a chalkboard, desks, and a wastepaper basket. There may have been the occasional filmstrip or slide presentation, but students still used paper and pencil to take notes. In just a short time, technology in the classroom has changed drastically.

Despite some exciting improvements in classroom technology, not everyone is convinced that computers and the Internet are good for education. Would you believe that at one time the pencil and eraser were considered controversial because, it was argued, students might be encouraged to make mistakes, something that pen and ink did not permit? Some people still view advances in technology the same way: technology potentially encourages the worst in us. Thankfully, many professors realize the incredible potential technology has for improving and enhancing learning even for those students who find it difficult to learn using traditional methods.

If you want to learn more about using a computer or navigating the Internet, consider signing up for a computer skills workshop, registering for a college-credit computer class, or asking for help in the computer lab. The library staff will also assist you with the growing number of electronic resources used for research. Take advantage of the opportunities you have while in college!

Basic Computer Terms

E ven those with the least computer knowledge are familiar with some of the basic parts. A monitor, keyboard, and mouse may need no explanation, but do you know what RAM means? Or what a computer processor does? Or who your ISP is? Knowing the answers to these questions will make using a computer easier for you.

A computer consists of several parts, besides those that are obvious. The hard drive holds your files and folders of information. A central processing unit (CPU) processes all of the instructions sent when you create a document or save a file. Other important parts include the random access memory (RAM) and the motherboard, which makes all the parts work together.

To connect to the Internet, you need a modem, a device that connects one computer to another; a phone line or cable connection; and an Internet service provider (ISP). People who have "dial-up" connect to the Internet through a phone line, which requires that the computer dial the ISP's number. A digital subscriber line (DSL) uses a phone line as well, but the transmission of text and graphics is much faster than with a dial-up connection. Another method of connecting to the Internet is through cable. If you have cable television available in your neighborhood, you may also be able to subscribe to cable Internet.

Computer Software

K nowing how to use word-processing software is essential to your success in college. Most computers come with some kind of program that allows you to type and print your work. Microsoft Word, Microsoft Works, and WordPerfect are three very common word-processing programs. Each program has its advantages and disadvantages, but they all function about the same. Some specific skills necessary to use word-processing software include opening

EXHIBIT 4.1   *Types of files.*

FILE TYPE/EXTENSION	DESCRIPTION
.doc	Microsoft Word file
.wps	WordPerfect file
.rtf	rich text format; allows users with different word-processing software to view and edit file
.pdf	portable document format; allows users to view document the way it was created, including images, colors, and fonts; requires Adobe Reader (free) to view
.xls	Microsoft Excel file
.jpeg, .jpg	joint photographic experts group image file; used for graphics and photos
.gif	graphical interchange format; used for graphics
.html	hypertext markup language; is the computer language used to create Web pages
.ppt	Microsoft PowerPoint file; used to create and watch slides

a new document, creating a header/footer, adding page numbers, changing the font size and style, inserting pictures and page breaks, creating a table, and saving your work. Other programs you may need to learn include a spreadsheet program such as Microsoft Excel (for accounting and business classes) and a slide presentation program such as Microsoft PowerPoint.

Once you become comfortable creating documents or files, you have to store them for later use or for submission to your instructor. Exhibit 4.1 lists various types of files; Exhibit 4.2 lists and describes the various methods of storing files and data.

EXHIBIT 4.2   *Methods of storing files.*

STORAGE DEVICES	DESCRIPTIONS
Hard drive	A disk that stores and reads stored data; storing a file on your hard drive is the same as storing it in your computer
3.5" diskette	Portable storage device; cannot hold a large amount; can be carried and used in different computers; allows you to alter files after you save them; place in the disk drive to access files
CD-ROM	Portable storage device that can store a large amount of files and programs; can be carried and used in different computers; can be used to save files if using a writable CD-ROM; does not allow you to alter files after you "burn" them; place in the CD drive to access files
Thumb drive, pin drive, memory stick	Small portable storage device that holds a large amount of files and programs; can be carried and used in different computers; allows you to alter files after you save them; connect to a USB port to access files

Keeping Your Computer Healthy

In order to use a computer and the Internet responsibly, it is important to be familiar with terms that signal a potential problem. One such term that you will encounter when using e-mail and the Internet is "spam," which refers to unwanted messages sent to your e-mail account. Although you can receive spam from someone you know, it's more likely the spam is coming from someone sending the same message to hundreds of thousands of people at the same time. Some e-mail programs have "spam filters" that allow you to move spam into a designated folder; others allow you to report the unwanted message to your Internet service provider. Usually, spam will not harm your computer if you do not open the message, but it can clog up your inbox and make it difficult to tell which messages are legitimate and which are not.

A virus is a computer program or written script that attacks your computer, causing it to run poorly or not at all. Your computer can "contract" a virus in a variety of ways, but a typical avenue is through infected e-mail messages that contain attachments. Arming your computer with the latest virus protection program and arming yourself with information about how a virus is spread are two necessities in today's technologically advanced world. A computer that has no virus protection and is connected to the Internet is more vulnerable to attack.

You can also protect your computer by regularly searching for operating system and virus protection updates and installing them. You can usually find updates by going to your operating system's website and looking for an "updates" link. You can also use a search engine to locate those websites that offer system updates. If you are not familiar with this process, but are interested in keeping your computer safe, talk to someone at the college computing lab for advice and help.

Worms and Trojans are virus types that are particularly menacing. Keeping your system up to date and running only those programs you know are legitimate are two ways to keep worms and Trojans out of your computer. Running frequent scans with your virus protection program should also detect and delete any viruses. Spyware, programs that "spy" on your Internet habits and information, can cause major computer problems. Most spyware is contained in downloaded programs. Often, you will not know the spyware is there. As with viruses, you can download free software (e.g., Ad-Aware or Spybot) that will check your computer for spyware and remove it.

A final term that you should know is "virus hoax." Smart, well-meaning friends and family who do not confirm information they receive often transmit a virus hoax through e-mail. For example, you receive an e-mail that warns you about a virus that may be on your computer. It lists steps for

Reflection

EXERCISE 4.1

What do you already know about computers? What do you want to learn more about?

Companion
Website

removing the potential problem and asks you to send the message to all your friends and family. Usually, the result is that you have removed a file or program from your computer that is necessary for its operation. When in doubt about information, research it before proceeding. Numerous websites provide legitimate information about viruses and virus hoaxes.

Computer Skills Needed for College

Your college professors expect many things of you, including that you use a computer and the Internet effectively. Some of the activities that you will participate in while taking classes include:

- accessing a computer regularly to complete work and communicate.
- using a computer program such as word processing.
- saving a file to a disk.
- saving a file in different formats (e.g., rich text format).
- printing a file from a hard drive, disk, CD-ROM, or memory stick.
- e-mailing a clear, concise message and using e-mail responsibly.
- attaching a file to an e-mail.
- navigating the Internet efficiently to find appropriate material for course work.
- using an online learning system, such as Blackboard or WebCT, to access course materials, participate in electronic discussions, submit assignments, and take quizzes.

Reflection

EXERCISE 4.2

From this previous list of computer skills, which can you do well and which do you need to learn?

Companion
Website

Computer Equipment Necessary for College

- Computer, monitor, keyboard, and mouse
- Operating system with at least the basic software for connecting to the Internet and word processing
- Speakers
- Printer, ink cartridges, paper
- Headphones
- Storage devices such as diskettes, writable CD-ROMs, or a memory stick

Using the Internet

The Internet can be used to research, shop, communicate, apply for jobs, play games, study, and learn—just to name a few activities. As a student, you will use the Internet to connect to the college's website for information, access the library's collection of resources, log into an online learning system, research topics, and find supplemental study material for your classes. Knowing how to find pertinent information is crucial to using the Internet effectively. We all could spend countless hours just going from page to page indiscriminately and achieve nothing, but with the right search engine and a few search techniques, you can narrow your topic and find what you need quickly.

Search engines and meta-search engines (see the lists below) are just two methods of finding information on the Internet. A search engine searches webpages based on the terms typed in. Not all search engines are alike; some do a better job of searching for the exact information you want, while others look for combinations of the terms. If you are unfamiliar with search engines, consider testing a few with a single topic and then noting which engines provide a list of the most helpful or relevant sites.

SEARCH ENGINES

www.altavista.com

www.excite.com

www.google.com

www.lycos.com

www.webcrawler.com

Another way to surf the Internet is to use a meta-search engine. Meta-search engines search other search engines based on the terms typed in. Again, try several meta-search engines to determine which are the most useful and user friendly. You may also ask a librarian to teach you how to use both search and meta-search engines effectively.

META-SEARCH ENGINES

www.allonesearch.com

www.beaucoup.com

www.dogpile.com

www.mamma.com

www.surfwax.com

Evaluating Websites

A part of using the Internet responsibly is learning to evaluate what you find before you rely on it for information or research. Chapter 11 provides detailed information for assessing websites, but it is worth introducing the evaluation criteria here as well. When you find a website that you think will be useful, consider the following aspects:

- *Authority.* Who is the author of the information? Is it a person or an organization? Is the site commercial (.com) or is it maintained by an educational institution (.edu) or organization (.org)? Is the person or organization reliable?
- *Accuracy.* Does the site provide truthful information? Are there any obvious errors or omissions?
- *Objectivity.* Is it obvious there is an agenda as evidenced by the language or topic? Does the site seem to present information as "black and white"?
- *Timeliness.* Is the information current? When was it last updated?

This simple checklist will help you determine which sites are legitimate and useful and which are not. When in doubt, especially when no author or responsible party is listed, avoid using the site's information in your class work. Practice your critical thinking skills by questioning everything you read online.

Study Guide and Papermill Websites

The Internet is a great place to find information and help when studying for a class or researching a topic for a paper. Dozens of sites offer study guides for almost all subjects and plot summaries for literary works. Many of the sites are fine sources to reinforce what you have already learned and read, but be careful about using them as a replacement for doing the class work or using them as resources in essays or research papers. As a research resource, study guide sites are not considered authoritative.

Be wary, too, of sites that offer essays and research papers for free or for sale. These sites replace the papermills of yesterday that were often found in student apartments or dorm rooms: files of papers that earned students good grades and were then recycled to new students taking the same class. The Internet has made selling papers a big business and one that is easily accessible to college students. Most of the papers for sale on these websites are of questionable quality; despite claims that they are A papers, many are poorly written and researched. Aside from that, purchasing a paper is a form of cheating and a clear ethical violation. Your instructor has the same access to the site as you do, and it takes only seconds to find the same paper online. If (when) your cheating is discovered, you will be disciplined for an academic integrity violation according to your school's policy.

Electronic Library Resources

Don't overlook the online resources the library offers as a place to get valid, reliable information. (Chapter 11 provides more information on accessing and navigating online catalogs, databases, and other electronic resources.) Your college's library webpage should provide links to resources such as virtual library tours, information literacy interactive tutorials, and direct access to an e-librarian who can help you find what you need using e-mail.

College Computing Policies

A discussion of technology and computer skills is not complete without talking about college policies regarding the use of computers, the Internet, and e-mail. Most colleges now have an acceptable use policy that they expect students to follow. It is important to remember that on-campus computers are the property of the college; when you use them, you are responsible for following the college's computing policies. These computing policies also cover college servers that provide access to the college e-mail account or online learning system. As a general rule, do not expect any privacy when using a college computer or accessing a server. Colleges may monitor what you view, what you write, and what you send.

Using computers and networks responsibly includes learning to surf the Internet cautiously, avoiding sites that contain pornography; whether you stumble across or willingly visit these sites, you can be held responsible for accessing them. Of course, colleges are strongly opposed to people who use the Internet or e-mail to verbally harass faculty, administrators, or fellow students. Some colleges have specific policies about using the Internet to intimidate or "stalk" others (see the box below for a sample policy).

If you are harassed via e-mail or an online learning system, report the incident immediately to the appropriate person, such as a faculty member. Last but not least, as a general rule, do not open attachments from unknown senders; delete them and do not reply or send personal information over the Internet.

Critical Thinking
EXERCISE 4.3

Why would a college have an acceptable use policy? Who are they protecting, the college or the student?

Companion
Website

Example of a College's Acceptable Use Policy

IN BOX

Users of the College's computers and networks should not expect privacy. Violations of the Acceptable Use Policy include, but are not limited to, the following:

- Accessing, downloading, uploading, saving, receiving, or sending material that includes sexually explicit content or other material using vulgar, sexist, racist, threatening, violent, or defamatory language
- Disclosing College information without prior authorization
- Gambling and illegal activities
- Sending fraudulent or forged e-mail messages using the account of another person

Communicating with Technology

Technology on campus means more than a computer terminal and Internet access. Just look around and you will see students and faculty alike using cell phones and pagers to keep connected while on campus. With these advances in technology come a few new classroom rules. To eliminate interruptions and distractions, some instructors have policies about using cell phones and pagers during class; they may ask students to turn them off or turn them to a silent setting. If you must use a phone or pager because of your job or a special circumstance, let your instructor know before class begins.

Another type of technology cropping up on campuses—one that is actually given to students by professors to use in class—is the clicker. A clicker is a handheld device that allows students to respond to multiple-choice questions by clicking a button to answer. The instructor can then instantaneously post the class's responses, usually through a projection device. This technology provides instant feedback to the instructor about the students' comprehension and application of the material; it also allows students to see what they get right and wrong and how the rest of the class understands the concepts.

E-Mail

Communication technology that is as ever-present as the cell phone and pager is e-mail. Learning to use e-mail effectively will help you communicate better with classmates, instructors, and administrators. Some of the basics of communicating well through e-mail include choosing an appropriate e-mail address, writing effective messages, observing basic e-mail etiquette, and successfully sending assignments via e-mail.

Choosing an appropriate e-mail address. If you do not have an e-mail account yet, now is a good time to set one up. You can get an e-mail account through an ISP when you purchase Internet access, through your college if they provide free e-mail accounts, or through a website such as www.yahoo.com or www.hotmail.com. Except for an account through your college, you can choose your account name. When creating an account

INTEGRITY MATTERS

Many instructors now forbid the use of cell phones, especially picture phones, and pagers in the classroom during exams because students may be able to transmit exam answers using text messaging or by taking a picture of the exam. As you can see, technology advances have taken cheating to new heights even in the on-campus class. Online test integrity is also a concern for instructors. You may encounter policies about technology restrictions during exams, such as surfing the Internet during an online test. If you are ever unsure of what you can and cannot have or do during an exam, be sure to ask your instructor. At the very least, avoid sharing information about the test with anyone taking the class.

Learning to use e-mail effectively is an important communication skill in college.

name, select something appropriate for sending e-mail to your professors or potential employers. Although e-mail addresses such as sweetkitten@inkspot.com or handsomedude@xyz.net may be suitable for e-mails to your friends, they are not the best way to make a good impression on your instructors or potential employers.

Writing effective e-mail messages.

Learning to write effective e-mail messages need not be a difficult task, and it becomes easier with a little practice. As a general rule, keep e-mail messages short, professional, and to the point. More specifically, follow the guidelines below for good e-mail etiquette.

E-MAIL ETIQUETTE FOR COMPOSING MESSAGES

- Type a specific subject heading in your message. Do not leave the subject line blank.
- Include a salutation such as "Dear Prof. Hurley" or "Dear Mr. Taylor."
- Write short messages.
- Ask questions early in the message so they don't get "lost" in the bottom of the message.
- If you are sending a file with the e-mail, ensure that the correct file is attached.
- Proofread your message before you send it.
- Remember that e-mails are not private and are easily transmitted to anyone, anywhere.
- Close the message with your full name.

E-MAIL ETIQUETTE FOR READING AND SAVING MESSAGES

- Assume that all messages are written in a compassionate, kind tone.
- Ask the sender for permission before forwarding e-mail to another person.
- Download attachments only from people you know and only when you expect to receive an attachment.
- Track all of your e-mails, sent and received, by placing them in a designated folder.

Exhibit 4.3 offers examples of clear, brief messages on which you can model your own.

EXHIBIT 4.3 *Sample e-mail messages.*

E-MAIL MESSAGE 1

From: Phillip Gergin (pgergin@technet.com)

Sent: Friday, February 1, 2008

To: Amy Baldwin

Subject: Missed Class

Dear Ms. Baldwin,

I am Phil Gergin and am in your college seminar class at noon on MWF. I want to let you know that I missed Monday's class because I was sick. I got notes from a classmate, but I want to make sure I didn't miss anything else. Could you let me know if I did miss something?

Sincerely,

Phil Gergin

E-MAIL MESSAGE 2

From: Cindy Levine (cindylevine@smartmoves.com)

Sent: Monday, March 4, 2008

To: Amy Baldwin

Subject: Appointment

Ms. Baldwin,

I'd like to make an appointment to see you during your office hours next week. Is Monday at 2 P.M. a good time?

Thanks,

Cindy Levine

We have discussed Internet searches and e-mail, two of the most common uses of computers. Exhibit 4.4 lists several other forms of electronic communication made possible by computers and the Internet, some of which are discussed next.

Discussion Boards

Another method of communicating with classmates and instructors is an electronic discussion board or forum, which works very similarly to a bulletin board where people post their messages for everyone to read. Real-life bulletin boards often get cluttered, obscuring others' postings. Electronically, discussion boards are generally more organized. Like e-mail, discussion boards are *asynchronous,* meaning that you don't have to be online at a certain time to communicate with your classmates; unlike e-mail, however,

Practice

EXERCISE 4.4

Write a brief sample e-mail message to a professor about making up a missed exam (try to make at least two errors in the message). Trade your sample message with another student and critique each other's message, pointing out what can be improved.

Companion Website

EXHIBIT 4.4   *Forms of electronic communication.*

ELECTRONIC COMMUNICATION

TERMS	DEFINITIONS
E-mail	Electronic mail, send and receive messages using an e-mail address
Discussion board, bulletin board	An electronic message board that allows you to leave and read messages
Chat	An electronic communication forum that allows you to talk to others via your computer in real time
Weblog	An online journal, also called a "blog," that is posted for public access; may contain daily or weekly entries and pictures
Text messaging	Sending messages via your cell phone to another phone using the phone keys as a keyboard
Instant messaging	Sending real-time messages to selected users; creates a private chat

discussion boards are often used to promote discussion outside class. Instructors are increasingly using discussion boards to provide access to discussions "after hours" and to continue spirited in-class discussion; some are even requiring out-of-class asynchronous communication among classmates. The more you know about how to use this type of electronic communication, the more actively you can participate in the online requirements for your classes.

One tip to remember when using a discussion board is that everyone who has access to the board can see what you write once you post the message. Instructors often provide guidelines for student posts. For example, an instructor may ask for formal discussion postings that analyze a course topic, or she may encourage you to be casual in your posts so you feel comfortable contributing to the online discussion. If your instructor uses a discussion board as part of the class, be sure to take advantage of it by posting and reading your classmates' responses. You have the opportunity to learn what others think in a way that you cannot in the face-to-face classroom.

As with e-mail messages, there are some basic etiquette rules for using a discussion board.

ETIQUETTE FOR POSTING DISCUSSION MESSAGES

- Use a subject heading for your posting.
- Follow the instructor's posting requirements.
- Avoid "flaming," or posting a remark intended to anger other students or the professor.

Reflection

EXERCISE 4.5

Describe three different ways you could use a discussion board to learn more about class topics and fellow students.

Companion Website

- Credit sources you use in a post.
- Use language carefully.
- Proofread your message before posting it.

Chat Rooms

Although less often used to supplement learning in the classroom, a chat room, or an electronic "area" in which two or more people communicate with one another, provides an opportunity for you to interact with fellow students and your professor. Unlike e-mail and discussion boards, chat rooms require *synchronous* communication, which means two people must be online at the same time in the chat room to communicate. Chat rooms are used to talk to others across the country (or around the world) or across the campus about issues ranging from studying for classes to career planning. Some colleges use a chat function, more like AOL's Instant Messenger, to communicate with prospective and current students. Chat rooms are also popular with students who participate in learning communities—they stay connected despite different schedules outside class.

Here are a few guidelines to help you get the most out of chat rooms.

ETIQUETTE FOR PARTICIPATING IN CHATS

- Keep sentences short and simple.
- Refrain from making any statement or using any phrases that might be offensive or misinterpreted.
- Stick to class topics.
- Proofread messages before sending them.

Critical Thinking

EXERCISE 4.6

What are the advantages of using online communication to express your confusion about course topics to your instructor? What are the disadvantages of writing an e-mail message or discussion post to your instructor explaining your difficulties?

Companion Website

Weblogs

An increasingly common method for communicating online is called a "weblog," or "blog." Weblogs are online journals or diaries that are updated frequently by the person who posted it. Weblogs are popular with journalists as they provide a personal means of recording events and impressions. They are also popular with those who want to share their life experiences. For students, they are a great way to share the challenges and triumphs of attending college. Some community colleges provide space on their websites for student blogs so that prospective students can read about what it is like to be a student there. Blogs on college websites may be monitored for content, but most provide an honest look into the lives of their creators.

Electronic Communication and Privacy

Whether you communicate primarily in person or through e-mail, always be conscious of your privacy and the privacy of others. In Chapter 1, you read about the Family Educational Rights and Privacy Act (FERPA) and the rules that

college employees must follow to ensure that your academic record remains private. When communicating with your instructor, especially through an electronic medium, be sure that no one else has access to your account. If you are concerned that someone may read e-mail messages you receive, print a hard copy of the message and then delete it.

Finally, when communicating through e-mail or voice mail, be sure to give your instructor enough time to read your message, think about it, and respond. We are all guilty of expecting a quick response because the methods of communicating are fast, but people still need time to read the message carefully and respond thoughtfully.

Critical Thinking

EXERCISE 4.7

What are some potential problems that can arise when communicating with other students online?

Companion
Website

Online Learning Systems

More and more colleges are turning to online learning systems, sometimes called course management systems, to provide students with a platform to access course materials, use a discussion board, submit assignments, and take tests. Some of the online learning systems used by colleges and universities include:

- Blackboard
- WebCT
- E-college
- Angel
- Moodle

Students and instructors alike are enjoying the many benefits of an online learning system, such as Blackboard or WebCT, because it allows learning to take place anytime, anywhere. No longer are you confined to the place and limited time of an on-campus class. With an online learning system, you can access course materials, ask your instructor questions, and receive feedback on assignments before the next class meeting. Online learning systems have many advantages that enhance your learning while in college.

Although online learning systems are typically used to deliver distance learning courses, many colleges use them for all kinds of learning activities because of the versatility. Your professors may use the system to supplement your classes by posting course syllabi and lecture notes; you may also find that your college offers "hybrid" courses, in which a class meets part of the time online and part on campus. Your college may also offer completely online classes as well for those students who need classes offered at convenient and flexible times.

Online Classes

When the topic of taking a class online is discussed, the usual questions arise. Do students really learn anything in an online class? Will online classes replace the need for campuses and classrooms? The answer to the first

Many Web-based surveys exist to help you determine if you are a candidate to take online courses. You may complete this brief questionnaire to see if online courses will be a good fit with your learning style and personality type. Make a check underneath "Yes" if the answer to the question is "yes" and "No" if the answer is "no."

QUESTION	YES	NO
1. Are you comfortable using a computer?		
2. Do you enjoy learning something new on your own?		
3. Do you manage your time well?		
4. Do you handle personal crises well?		
5. Do you make a Plan B in case problems arise?		
6. Do you express yourself clearly in writing?		
7. Can you understand instructions just by reading them?		
8. Do you need face-to-face interaction in order to learn?		

If you answered "Yes" to all questions but the last one, then taking online courses may be good for you.

question is "Yes"—students really can learn in an online environment if the course is adapted properly and the student is comfortable with the technology. The answer to the second question is "No." Online courses will not eliminate the need for face-to-face contact despite what people may report; instead, online learning enhances traditional education methods and allows more people to pursue a degree.

The key to being a successful online student is to be attuned to your comfort level and work through or eliminate any obstacles you face while taking a class online. Determining whether or not you are prepared to take an online class is the first step. If, however, you are unsure about taking an online class, a hybrid course may be a good compromise—you get the feel of an online class by doing your work via the Internet, but you also have the safety of seeing the instructor and your classmates regularly in case you get lost or overwhelmed with the material. Even if you believe that neither online nor hybrid courses fit your learning style and personality type, you may still be required to take an online course for some degree programs at the community college or university level. Prepare for such a possibility by looking for ways to learn more about technology and by embracing any technology experiences that are part of your face-to-face classes.

What online classes does your college offer? Once you determine you are prepared to take an online class, find out what your college offers via the Internet; as mentioned earlier, your college may offer supplemented and hybrid courses in addition to truly online classes. Look through a class schedule and

Critical Thinking PLUS*

Consider how understanding your personality style or learning preference can help you through challenging situations.

NOTES

You consider yourself right-brained because you are highly creative and do not manage your time as rigidly as some of your more left-brained classmates. Your learning style strength is aural and kinesthetic—you want to use both to become a musician or a music director after completing your associate's degree. You discover that two of the classes required to complete your degree are not offered at times that are convenient to you, but one is offered online and one as a hybrid. One class is Psychology and the Human Experience and the other is Biological Science (with an on-campus lab). Although the courses are necessary, you are unsure if you will be successful. What can you do to be successful in these classes?

*PERSONALITY + LEARNING STYLE = UNDERSTANDING SITUATIONS

on the website for a list of online courses, and check the catalog to see if your college offers entire degree programs online. Talk with administrators about what classes will be offered in the future. If you plan on completing your degree online, you need assurance that there will be online classes that will satisfy the degree requirements.

What online services does your college offer? In addition to online courses and degrees, you should also investigate what services will be available if you decide to take an online course. For example, will you have access to tutoring services online? Will you be able to search the library's databases off campus? The following is a list of student services that your college may make available online. Determine which ones you can access off campus and which ones you must be on campus to receive:

LIBRARY

- Can you access the card catalog and databases?
- Can you e-mail a librarian?
- Can you get books and documents delivered to you?
- Can you renew library books online?

TUTORING

- Can you access an online tutor?
- If not, what arrangements are in place for online students to get help with math, writing, and science?

COUNSELING

- Do you have access to a counselor for disability services and career services?
- How do you contact them?
- How is confidentiality maintained?

BURSAR

- Can you make tuition and fee payments online?
- How will you be informed of changes to your account?

REGISTRAR

- Can you access your transcript and schedule through the Internet?
- Can you request transcripts online?

ADVISING

- Can you access advising material online?
- Can you complete a degree plan online?
- Do you have access to an advisor through the Internet?

Making the Decision

Before registering for an online course, get as much information as possible about how it will work. Check the college's website for information; it may even have a link to the course where you can learn more about the course requirements. Talk to an advisor, preferably one who understands how online classes work. Also, seek out an instructor who teaches online and a student who takes courses online. Talking with both will give you a good idea of how the courses work and what you will need to be successful in them. Finally, look for orientation sessions and college material that will help you navigate an online course successfully.

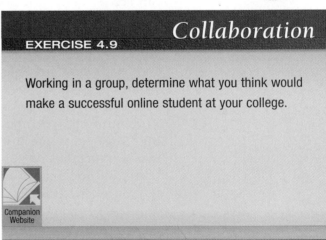

Collaboration

EXERCISE 4.9

Working in a group, determine what you think would make a successful online student at your college.

Companion Website

Special Considerations

The following are questions you should ask when considering taking an online class:

- What are the hardware and software requirements for my computer?
- What Internet connection speed do I need? Is there a preference for a dial-up, cable, or broadband connection?
- How much time is involved in taking an online class? Will I need to spend more time reading and working for this class?
- What are the communication expectations? Will my instructor respond to my questions within a certain time frame?

- What will I be required to do? Participate in a bulletin board or chat room? Download video clips? Take exams online? Complete group projects?
- How often will I need to log into the class? What do I do if I cannot log in for a few days?
- Are there alternative methods for submitting assignments?
- Is the instructor available on campus in case I have questions? Can I call or fax the instructor?
- What do I do if I have technical problems? What do I do if the college has technical problems?

Other online students can provide even more information to consider, but if you can get these questions answered, then you will have a good understanding of what is expected of you in an online class and what you can expect to experience.

Navigating the Course

Although each online learning system may differ, there should be some common functions and materials. Either there will be a syllabus available online or it will be sent to you through the mail. If you do not receive a syllabus, you can access the instructor's name, contact information, and course objectives once you log into the online learning system.

Another common feature of online classes is a place to communicate with the other students and with the instructor. Discussion boards, e-mail, and chat rooms are common in online courses. Discussion boards and chat rooms often take the place of in-class discussion, so look for those tools to be used extensively in an online course.

Online courses often use an online exam tool to assess student learning. Although some instructors may require that you come to campus to take a proctored exam, others test completely online. If the exams are taken online, then you should take some precautions to ensure you do your best. First, read all instructions from your professor regarding online testing and note any special requirements such as special software or Internet connection. Determine how the exam will be structured (multiple-choice, essay questions, etc.) and how long you will have once you open the test. If the instructor forbids the use of notes, textbooks, and Internet sites, then abide by the restrictions—take special precautions to make sure you do not receive any unapproved assistance while taking the exam. Also, if you can double check your answers before submitting the exam, be sure to do so.

Communicating with Instructors

After deciding to take an online class, consider how you will communicate with the instructor. You should at least be able to e-mail the instructor when you have questions, but you should also determine whether other methods are available. For example, does the instructor allow you to call, fax, or come by her office? If so, make use of these alternative methods if e-mail does not satisfy your needs.

Communicating with Classmates

An integral part of many online classes is the interaction you have with your classmates. Although you are communicating in cyberspace, you can still enjoy getting to know others, perhaps better than you might in a traditional classroom setting. Because of this freedom, there are some guidelines you should follow to maximize the benefits of getting to know your classmates and keep miscommunication at a minimum.

First, as stated earlier in the chapter, read the communication guidelines for interacting with classmates provided by your instructor. You can use the electronic tools, such as the discussion board and e-mail, to communicate. If appropriate, introduce yourself to the class during the first week and tell the others a little bit about yourself. As you begin to get to know others, you might ask to join an electronic study group or offer to help people review for an exam.

Maintaining Integrity

As with any course, make sure you are doing the work with integrity. In order to maintain integrity in your online course, read all material provided by the instructor and the college about the expectations for online students. Note any special requirements for online students with regard to academic honesty. Because the line between what is appropriate in an online class and what is not is sometimes blurred, the following is a list of common ways to maintain integrity in an online environment:

- Do your own work. If you must get help with assignments, get approval from the instructor first.
- Do not allow anyone to take a class for you, and don't take a class for anyone else.
- Keep the log in information and password safe; don't allow anyone else access to your course user-name and password.
- Ask the instructor for permission before sharing information about course requirements and assignments.
- Do not print and distribute online exams without express permission from your instructor.
- Ask if you have any questions about the material or use of the material.

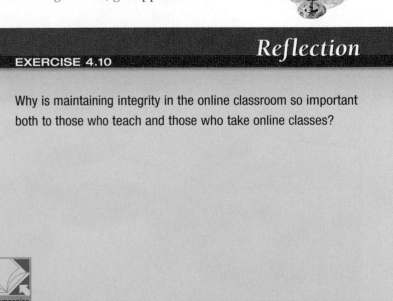

Reflection

EXERCISE 4.10

Why is maintaining integrity in the online classroom so important both to those who teach and those who take online classes?

Companion
Website

What If Online Courses Are Not Right for You?

- Do you feel overwhelmed by the demands of the class?
- Do you find it difficult to make time to do your work and log into the course?
- Do you find yourself confused by the technology?

Even if you feel online courses are not right for you, you may choose to take a class that incorporates some Internet-based instruction.

If you answer "Yes" to two of these questions, then it may be a signal that the online course is not right for you, but that doesn't mean that online classes will never be a good fit for you. There could be other reasons—that have nothing to do with technology—that keep you from doing well in an online class. For example, online courses in math and science may be more difficult because they rely on problem solving and application, while the history and psychology courses may be less difficult because they rely on reading and discussing. Your strategy should be to choose online courses wisely and avoid those courses that make you feel uncomfortable.

A Final Note about Online Courses

Even if you think that online classes are not right for you, remain open-minded about taking one or taking a class that incorporates some Internet-based instruction. Although online classes will not be the death of traditional, face-to-face instruction, they will soon become an integral part of the future of education and the future of the workplace. The more comfortable you are with alternative methods of communicating and learning, the more adept you will be at using that technology in your career and for lifelong learning.

Learning Styles Application

This chart lists the four learning styles and tips based on the chapter's main ideas. Locate your learning style and read the corresponding tips to maximize your success in college.

VISUAL

Most technology is geared toward visual learners. Computer programs and games with realistic graphics and "eye friendly" colors and texts are particularly stimulating. However, online classes or even word-processed handouts that lack visual appeal are more difficult to navigate and read.

AURAL

Aural learners enjoy the "noisy" technology such as cell phones and pagers and computer programs that incorporate music or sounds to enhance the appeal. You will learn best when an aural component is added to the material. For example, if you are studying poetry, look for CDs or websites that provide recorded poetry readings.

READ/WRITE

E-mail, discussion boards, chat rooms, text messaging, and AOL's Instant Messenger are popular with read/write learners. To enhance your learning, look for ways that technology can be used to take notes, work with others, and study for exams.

KINESTHETIC

Kinesthetic learners are not overlooked by advances in technology. Many websites that provide instructional materials will also allow you to simulate processes, such as dissecting a frog, with a mouse or keyboard. Take advantage of opportunities to engage in activities through technology.

Path of Discovery

Journal Entry

How has technology changed the way in which you communicate with others? Has it brought you closer or has it made it easier to remain distant? How has technology changed the way you learn? Does it satisfy your curiosity or overwhelm you?

FROM COLLEGE TO UNIVERSITY

Strong technology skills will spell success for you

There is no time like the present to improve your comfort level with technology. When you transfer to a four-year university, for example, you may be required to create an electronic slide presentation and publish it on the Web. You may also find yourself in a class that uses webconferencing or compressed video to connect to another class across the country—or world—or to bring in an expert in the field. Your confidence with using a wide variety of technologies will make the transition easier as you juggle the new demands of upper-level classes. Being adept at using technology will help you work more efficiently and effectively.

FROM COLLEGE TO CAREER

Online communication is essential to paving your professional path

If your college professors encourage you to communicate with them using electronic means, be sure to take advantage of it. The more you practice sending messages electronically, the easier this method of communication will be when you are employed. Most companies, no matter how small, now expect employees to communicate electronically—with each other, with vendors, and with clients.

Communicating electronically requires great responsibility on your part. Familiarize yourself with your company's e-mail etiquette and communication policies. Also, err on the side of caution if you are ever unsure about the appropriateness of what you are sending through cyberspace. At the very least, refrain from forwarding jokes, chain letters, and pictures (especially ones that could be considered offensive), and watch the tone of your messages. If you are sending messages for business purposes, such as communicating with a client, proofread them for errors. Also, include contact information in case the recipient wants to call you to clarify information in the message.

Because of the permanence of these messages (and the ease with which they can be saved, forwarded, and printed), businesses have a vested interest in requiring that employees' messages are professional and appropriate.

Chapter in Review

1. List and describe the different ways you can use technology to communicate with classmates and professors.

2. Choose two types of technology discussed in this chapter and list the possible educational benefits.

3. How has the Internet changed your life?

4. Using the criteria to evaluate websites, evaluate a study strategies website (type "study strategies" in a search engine and explore the options).

Case Scenarios

Read the following case scenarios and determine what each person should do. Refer to the information in this chapter as you write a description and plan of action for each student.

1. Prema had a difficult time in the beginning of the semester, and she is not passing two of her classes because of work and family distractions. She wrote her professor the following e-mail message, but has not sent it yet.

> To: Leslie McGuire
>
> From: Sister Girl
>
> Date: April 15, 2007
>
> Subject: Hi!
>
> *i know i am not doing good in your class but i was hoping that you will let me turn in an assingmint that is late I really, really need to pass this class or else.*
>
> *I will lose my scholarship can you help.*

What advice would you give her before she sends this message?

2. Heather is uncomfortable with computers. She would never take an online class, and any time she has a paper due, she asks her brother to type it for her. When she walks into the first day of a literature class, she discovers that the professor expects the students to log into a website each week to participate in a discussion and turn in assignments. She is very upset because she doesn't want to go online to complete any work. Before class is over, she storms out and walks over to the registrar's office to drop the class. Before she drops the class, what advice would you give her?

3. Julie and Rob started a website that rates the professors at their college. They listed all of the professors and the classes they teach. In order to provide ratings, they encouraged all of their friends and classmates to post what they

think of each professor. The site is very popular, and most of the instructors are rated. When you log in, you notice that one of the professors who you will have next semester received low ratings for being too demanding, mean, and unrealistic about students' abilities. One rater calls the professor "crazy" and warns students not to take his classes. What do you think about the website? What would you do about taking the "undesirable" professor's course? Would you drop? Why or why not?

Research It Further

1. Type "papermill" or "free college essays" into a search engine or meta-search engine. From the list of papermill websites, choose two that allow you to download papers for free. Take some time to look at the way the websites are arranged and what steps a person has to take to retrieve a paper. Read at least one paper from the site, and report your findings to the class. Consider how the sites market the products and what the quality is.

2. What is your college's acceptable use policy for using college-owned computers and networks? Talk to the Chief Information Officer or a networking administrator on your campus about common policy violations. Report your findings to your classmates.

3. If your college offers online courses or an online degree program, research what the requirements for taking a class online and what resources are available for online students.

5 Diversity and Relationships

One of the easiest parts of college can be the hardest for busy students. The easy part of making friends and forging relationships is that people are everywhere—in class, computer labs, and the library. As Elnora discovered, getting to know those around you is essential to your well-being and happiness while working on your degree. The hard part, however, is making the time to cultivate relationships. As a community college student, you most likely have other activities outside of class: work, family, hobbies, church or synagogue, and friends. This chapter's purpose is to show you the benefits of starting and maintaining strong relationships with people on campus. More specifically, this chapter answers these questions:

- *What is diversity and how is it important in college?*

- *How are stereotyping, prejudice, and discrimination related?*

- *What are the benefits of cultivating relationships in college?*

- *What kinds of professors will I encounter and how will I learn from them?*

- *How do I handle any conflict that might arise?*

- *What is constructive criticism and what is its purpose?*

COMMUNITY • COLLEGE •

Student Profile

NAME: **Elnora Wesley**   AGE: **21**

MAJOR: **English**

1. What is the most rewarding part of making friends at college?

   I have people to talk to—I can discuss instructors, courses, and the stress of college life.

2. What is the most challenging part of cultivating relationships at college?

   The hardest part is meeting people from various backgrounds and cultures. There are not as many diverse groups of people as I would like. I think a "true college" experience is about meeting people from different cultures.

3. What advice would you give other students regarding relationships with instructors?

   Talk to your instructors, interact with them—make it a point to communicate and get to know them and have them get to know you. The better you know the instructor, the more likely you are to get lenient treatment if you have an emergency.

4. What is your VARK?

   Kinesthetic.

Knowing Yourself Before You Relate to Others

One underlying theme of the first few chapters is self-awareness—knowing who you are and how you relate to the world around you. Knowing yourself is essential to learning about and appreciating others. You learned in Chapter 2 how to define and describe yourself. That information will be helpful as you read about the many ways we categorize others—it provides you with the insight that although labels are sometimes helpful, they do not completely tell the world who we are. Self-awareness is also critical to handling conflict with others because it helps us understand why we do and say the things we do. Understanding others, as this chapter helps you do, enables you to resolve conflict more successfully. The goal is to know yourself well enough to work with others effectively and have meaningful, healthy relationships.

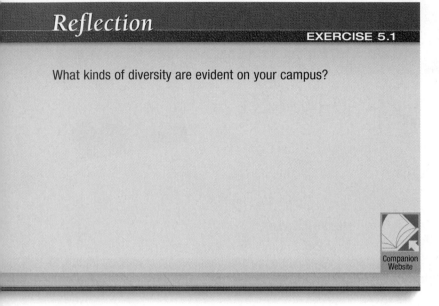

Reflection

EXERCISE 5.1

What kinds of diversity are evident on your campus?

Companion
Website

Exploring Diversity

An exciting part of college is meeting and working with people of all ages with different backgrounds. At your community college your classmates may include a grandparent, a home-schooled teenager, a veteran, an administrative assistant to a dean, a full-time detective, and a minister. It is crucial, then, to be sensitive to others' values and perspectives.

A simple definition of diversity is "difference" or "variety." Another term that often floats around when diversity is discussed in a college setting is "multiculturalism." Although diversity and multiculturalism have different implications, their use is often for the same reason—to expose the community to a variety of ideas, cultures, viewpoints, beliefs, and backgrounds.

When people talk about diversity, they usually mean race, gender, ethnicity, age, and religion. Colleges that want to promote diversity on campus often look for opportunities to hire and enroll people from different backgrounds. They do this with the belief that diversity enriches the educational experience for all because it exposes students to new ideas and challenges their preconceived notions of the world around them.

TYPES OF DIVERSITY

- racial, ethnic, cultural
- religious
- political

- sexual orientation
- generational
- socioeconomic
- physical and intellectual
- motivations
- comfort level/orientation to college/readiness
- learning styles/personality types
- teaching styles

Stereotypes

Stereotyping is an oversimplified opinion of someone or something. We use stereotypes to make quick decisions every day. For example, when choosing a checkout line, we may make a quick decision as to which is fastest based on the people in line and what is in their carts. When playing outfield on a softball team, we may stereotype the smaller players as weaker hitters, which causes us to move closer to the infield. Parents also encourage children who have difficulty making complex decisions to stereotype about "strangers" in order to protect the children. Although such stereotypes are not necessarily harmful, they can create problems for

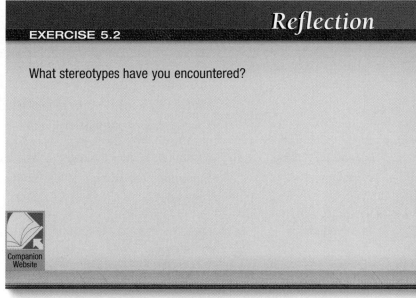

Reflection

EXERCISE 5.2

What stereotypes have you encountered?

Companion Website

us and others. We may end up standing in our grocery line for a longer time; we may move so close to the infield that the smaller player hits the ball over our heads; and we may confuse children about the characteristics of a stranger, making it difficult for them to trust adults.

Stereotypes may serve a purpose in the short run, but as the three examples illustrate, stereotypes do not take into consideration all of the facts. For the most part, stereotypes prevent us from having to think about the complexity of issues, and as a result, we may be unable to appreciate the beauty of diversity. Even though stereotypes can be both positive and negative, in essence, stereotypes are a shorthand method of evaluating situations and making decisions. If used repeatedly, such shortcuts can become prejudice and discrimination (see Exhibit 5.1).

Prejudice

Prejudice is literally "pre-judging" a person or situation without knowing the facts. Prejudice is often based on stereotyping, which is one of the dangers of stereotyping in the first place. Let's use a seemingly harmless example of stereotyping that can result in prejudice: If you assume that all smaller softball players are weak hitters, then you may extend that stereotype to include refusing to play with smaller players because they don't make the game very challenging.

EXHIBIT 5.1   *Diversity factors and common stereotypes.*

DIVERSITY FACTORS	COMMON POSITIVE AND NEGATIVE STEREOTYPES
Gender	*Women:* maternal, caring, passive, weak *Men:* strong, brave, stoic, active
Sexual orientation	*Heterosexuals:* politically conservative, want children, intolerant, moral *Gays and lesbians:* creative, politically liberal, not interested in having a family, tolerant, immoral
Race, ethnicity, and culture	*Asian Americans:* intelligent, hard-working, overly concerned with achievement *Southerners:* polite, old-fashioned, religious, poorly educated
Generation	*Generation Xers and Nexters:* realistic, computer literate, achievers, unfocused, disrespectful *Veterans and Baby Boomers:* idealistic, respectful, out of touch, computer illiterate
Socioeconomic	*Upper class:* successful, leisure-focused, charitable, greedy, pampered *Middle class:* hard-working, family-focused, dissatisfied with government *Lower class:* strive for better, efficient, lazy, unemployed
Personality types/ learning styles	*Left-brain:* always logical, rational, in control, unfeeling *Right-brain:* always creative, disorganized, emotional *Extrovert:* always prefers being with people
Teaching styles	*Lecture:* easy to understand, boring, passive learning *Discussion:* active learning, disorganized, difficult to take notes

Like stereotyping, prejudice is a judgment based on little or no information or misinformation about a person or thing. In other words, it is based on ignorance or a lack of correct information. That is why education is so important—you can avoid prejudging people and things by learning about them and making decisions about them based on *knowledge*, not ignorance. Although we cannot always avoid stereotyping, we can eliminate prejudice and subsequently eradicate discrimination by deciding to learn about others.

There are a variety of ways we can categorize and classify ourselves and others, as you will see later in this chapter. When used as one way of understanding ourselves better, these types of diversity are helpful tools. However, if they are used to stereotype and then prejudge people, the categories become a means to discriminate.

Critical Thinking
EXERCISE 5.3

When are stereotypes helpful or even necessary for survival? (Think about how we stereotype situations, ideas, and objects.)

Companion
Website

Discrimination

Discrimination occurs when an action is taken on the basis of a prejudice. If, for instance, you decide that you do not want to play softball with smaller players because you believe they

From Stereotype to Discrimination

Sometimes it is difficult to see how stereotypes, prejudice, and discrimination all fit together. Here are two examples of how a stereotype evolves into discrimination:

EXAMPLE 1

Stereotype: 18-year-old college students are immature and irresponsible.

Prejudice: I do not like to talk to 18-year-old college students.

Discrimination: I refuse to be placed in a study group with 18-year-old college students.

EXAMPLE 2

Stereotype: Biology professors are atheists.

Prejudice: I don't think that atheists should be allowed to teach biology.

Discrimination: I am giving my biology professor a poor evaluation because she is an atheist.

are not as fun as bigger players, then you are discriminating against smaller players. Because of recently enacted laws and the resulting lawsuits, colleges and businesses are sensitive to discrimination issues. Sexism, racism, and ageism are the discrimination types most commonly found in the workplace. It is an important part of your education to understand how and why people discriminate so that you can avoid similar problems.

Even though most workplaces strive hard to eliminate sexual, racial, and age discrimination, there are still other types that can creep into everyday situations. For example, a coworker may declare that she won't hire anyone from a certain college because she believes that all its graduates are more interested in partying than working. Your boss may indicate his disdain for people from a certain part of the country and then refuse to promote an employee who is originally from the same area. Although you may not be able to change everyone's mind, be aware of these more subtle forms of discrimination and make an effort to eliminate them.

Understanding Diversity: Eliminating Stereotypes and Prejudice

You will have an opportunity to work with others in class when you are assigned a group project or presentation. Even if all of the group members are of the same gender, race, religion, and age, you will still find that each person is different and has different expectations and opinions. The ability to work with others, regardless of their learning and work styles, is a skill. The more you experience diversity, the more you will appreciate the differences between you and everyone you meet. The following sections provide an overview of just a few types of diversity as well as examples of the

The more you experience diversity, the more you will be able appreciate the differences between you and others.

prejudice and discrimination that can occur because of ignorance and intolerance. As you read about each type of diversity, consider how learning more about others helps you improve your relationships with others.

Gender and Sexual Orientation Diversity

It may seem strange to think that several decades ago, the presence of women in college, especially in law and medical schools, was considered unusual. According to the American Association of Community College's website, at the Fast Facts link, in 2000, almost 58 percent of students in college were women. Unless you attend a same-sex institution, you will encounter gender diversity at college. What this means is that you will have many opportunities to work with both men and women and explore any preconceptions you have about the differences between the sexes. You may have to pay more attention to society's assumptions about gender and be more attuned to how various disciplines define gender differences.

Sexual orientation is another type of diversity that you will likely encounter in college, if you have not already. Homosexuality and bisexuality are just two categories of sexual orientation diversity. Organizations such as the Human Rights Campaign (www.hrc.org) strive to educate others about discrimination that can—and does—occur because of the stereotypes and prejudices that exist regarding sexual orientation. Why should you know more about sexual orientation as a part of diversity? Sexuality is part of the human experience, and one purpose of higher education is to help you better understand and appreciate your and others' experiences. Recognizing sexual orientation as a category of diversity gives you a more complete picture of humankind.

Sexist Attitudes

Although the increased number of women in college caused the American culture to become more sensitive and inclusive of women, stereotypes and prejudices about females still exist. Unfortunately, sexism is not limited to prejudice against women. Men, too, suffer from sexist attitudes based on stereotypes. The following are two examples of sexist attitudes found in college:

- My welding instructor is a woman! What does she know about welding? I can't possibly learn what I need to know for a job.
- My male psychology professor is so much more demanding than the female professor. I should have taken her class instead. Plus, she would understand that I am a parent who has to juggle raising kids and going to school.

Homophobia

Sexual orientation prejudice often takes the form of homophobia, or a fear of homosexuals. Homophobia sometimes results from ignorance and sometimes it comes from a person's background and values. Some examples of homophobic attitudes in college include:

- My algebra instructor is gay. I don't approve of homosexuality, so I'm very uncomfortable being in his class.
- I am not taking composition this semester because the only class I can take is taught by the lesbian instructor. She won't grade me fairly because I am a male.

Sexual Harassment

Sexual harassment is a form of sex discrimination that violates Title VII of the Civil Rights Act of 1964. Although Title VII applies only to employers with 15 or more employees (including federal, state, and local governments), employment agencies, and labor organizations, many states have enacted legislation that broadens the sexual harassment prohibition coverage. According to U.S. Equal Employment Opportunity Commission, 2005:

> Unwelcome sexual advances, requests for sexual favors, and other verbal or physical conduct of a sexual nature constitute sexual harassment when this conduct explicitly or implicitly affects an individual's employment, unreasonably interferes with an individual's work performance, or creates an intimidating, hostile, or offensive work environment. Sexual harassment can occur in a variety of circumstances, including but not limited to the following:
>
> - The victim as well as the harasser may be a woman or a man. The victim does not have to be of the opposite sex.
> - The harasser can be the victim's supervisor, an agent of the employer, a supervisor in another area, a coworker, or a nonemployee.

- The victim does not have to be the person harassed but could be anyone affected by the offensive conduct.
- Unlawful sexual harassment may occur without economic injury to or discharge of the victim.
- The harasser's conduct must be unwelcome.

Despite education programs for new students and required seminars for employees, colleges are not immune from instances of sexual harassment. According to Katz (2005), the American Psychological Association surveyed female graduate students about their experiences in college. The survey results show that 12.7 percent of female students experienced sexual harassment and 21 percent avoided taking certain classes for fear of being sexually harassed. Surveys concerning sexual harassment in the workplace paint a dimmer picture—31 percent of female employees and 7 percent of male employees claim to be sexually harassed at work.

Educating yourself about the seriousness of sexual harassment, your college's policy on sexual harassment, and those behaviors commonly considered sexual harassment are steps in the right direction to minimizing incidents. Sexual harassment is no laughing matter, and a review of your college's policy will reveal the lengths the college will go to to discipline those who sexually harass others. Some college policies list the following behaviors as sexual harassment:

- Offensive jokes or comments of a sexual nature
- Requests or demands for sexual favors in return for favorable treatment or rewards (e.g., a good grade)
- Unwanted physical contact or assault
- Showing or distributing sexually explicit materials to others
- Posting sexually explicit images or websites on college-owned online course management systems or e-mailing those images or websites using college-owned computers

Although not considered sexual harassment because it's not distributed to others, accessing sexually explicit websites using a college-owned computer is usually prohibited and may result in disciplinary action by the college.

Remember, be sensitive to others, treat everyone you meet on campus with respect, and be honest with others if you feel uncomfortable in a situation or with certain conversation topics.

Racial, Ethnic, and Cultural Diversity

Over the last 20 years, colleges embraced and developed multicultural studies in response to past emphasis on "white, male, Western" history, ideas, and culture. In 2001, we began to deal with our feelings and attitudes toward Middle Eastern culture and religion as the world's spotlight focused on our country's relationship with Afghanistan and Iraq. Cultural and racial ignorance at its worst has led to the deaths of millions of people all over the world. Having an understanding of and appreciation for cultural and ethnic diversity creates connections between people who have much to learn from each other.

Tips for Appreciating Racial, Ethnic, and Cultural Diversity

- Racial, ethnic, and cultural jokes, images, and cartoons are insensitive and may constitute harassment. Avoid making fun of others' heritage. Be sensitive to others' backgrounds.
- Learn more about your heritage and culture.
- Strive to learn more about cultures that are new and different to you.
- Participate in college and community cultural celebrations.
- Attend seminars, lectures, and artistic performances about different cultures and countries.
- Do not tolerate others who exhibit racial and cultural insensitivity. If you don't feel comfortable saying something to them, then avoid them and similar situations in the future.

Racist Attitudes

Racist attitudes are either obvious or subtle. Like all other prejudices, people may hold racist views and not realize they are being intolerant of others. Asking people of other races what kinds of racism they experience is one way to understand what they perceive as prejudice. Monitoring your own words, actions, and attitudes is another way to be more sensitive to other races and cultures. You may think you don't mean any harm by what you say or do, but others don't always agree. Examples of racist attitudes in college include:

- I am going to study with the two Asian Americans in my physics class. They are very smart and maybe that will rub off on me.
- My professor's name is Gonzalez. I am sure he is Hispanic, which means I won't be able to understand a word he says.

Generational Diversity

The idea that your parents' generation is vastly different from yours, which will be greatly different from your children's generation, is considered a fact of life. It's almost a requirement for adults to bemoan the younger generation's habits and attitudes just as it is common for teenagers to roll their eyes when their parents start singing the popular songs of their generation. One unifying viewpoint among the generations is that different generations view the world differently.

You will, no doubt, encounter generational diversity at college and in the world of work—more so than other generations. The American Association of Community Colleges (2004) cites the following statistics from the National Center for Education Statistics: A 1999 study found that 46 percent of community college students are over the age of 25, and 15 percent are over 40. These statistics mean that almost half of the students on a community college campus are not the traditional college age of 18 to 22. In other words, you will be attending classes and working with other students who come from a different generational cohort.

EXHIBIT 5.2 *Generations and their core values.*

GENERATION	BIRTH YEARS	CORE VALUES
Veterans	1922–1943	Dedication, sacrifice, patience, respect for authority
Baby Boomers	1943–1960	Health and wellness, optimism, personal growth
Generation Xers	1960–1980	Diversity, fun, self-reliance, global thinking
Nexters	1980–present	Civic duty, morality, street smarts

What is a "generational cohort" and what does it mean for your college and work experience? According to Zemke, Raines, and Filipczak (2000), a generational cohort is a group of the population born within a certain period of time, that marks as important some of the same world events and holds certain common values. Zemke et al. recognize and describe four generations that can be found in the workplace (and college for that matter) (see Exhibit 5.2).

Each of the generational groups, according to Zemke et al. (2000), holds certain values that influence how they work with others and how they achieve personal success. The diverse core values and attitudes can either create enriching experiences for all those generations that work together or cause conflict for those who do not understand and appreciate fellow students and coworkers from a different generation. Misunderstanding generational differences may develop into ageism, which is discriminating against someone because of his or her age. The key with generational diversity—as with all types of diversity—is to learn more about yourself and others and appreciate the differences.

Ageist Attitudes

As discussed earlier in the chapter, different generations have different values and viewpoints. An environment in which people from different generations work closely together can be exciting or tense, depending on how much people are willing to recognize, understand, and appreciate their generational differences. Problems arise, though, when people have prejudicial attitudes about a certain age group. Although we usually think of ageist attitudes as ones that stereotype older people, people can hold prejudicial views against those younger than they. The following are two examples of ageist attitudes found in college:

- I don't want to be in a study group with him. He could be my grandfather, and I am sure he doesn't know one thing about computer networks.
- I can't relate to the young women in my project group. All they talk about is dating. They have no real responsibilities, and they don't take this class seriously.

Reflection

EXERCISE 5.4

What generational cohort do you belong to? What do you consider the historical events that define your generation?

Companion
Website

Personality Types and Learning Styles Diversity

As you learned in Chapter 2, there are a variety of ways to describe what we are like and even how we learn. This information is certainly important to understanding ourselves; it is also helpful as we work with others in the classroom and on the job.

Take for example a couple that is trying to decide what to do on Saturday night. Person A suggests they go out with friends to a club to dance. Person B suggests they stay home and watch a movie. It's not hard to imagine that the subsequent conversation contains the question "Why do you always want to . . . ?" Either one person gives in and does what the other wants or each engages in a separate activity. Now, consider that the couple took a personality test and knows that one is an extrovert (the E in the MBTI inventory) and the other is an introvert (the I in the MBTI inventory). Knowing that each has a different preference when enjoying free time may not eliminate the conflict completely, but it does provide information and insight into the other's likes and dislikes. That information makes it easier for both to appreciate their differences and opens the door to compromise.

Now, consider personality types and diversity in the classroom or workplace. Here is an example of how personality diversity can affect group work:

EXAMPLE OF PERSONALITIES AT PLAY

Jackie, Mark, and Yolanda are working in a group to complete a task. Jackie wants to list all the possible ideas before making a decision on which they should pursue. Yolanda wants to consider only one or two ideas; she feels that going through more would waste valuable time. When Jackie and Yolanda ask Mark which action they should take, he shrugs his shoulders and says, "I don't care. Whatever you want." Yolanda and Jackie are frustrated by Mark's reaction because they assume he doesn't care about the project. Although Mark thinks both Yolanda and Jackie are wrong in their approach, he doesn't think it is worth telling them what he really thinks because they are so domineering.

Do you think this group will successfully complete their task? Even if they do complete it, they will not understand each other's work personality, which may cause problems again if they receive another group project. They certainly do not understand themselves sufficiently to work well with other personality types on future projects.

What if, instead of trying to work together without an appreciation for the diversity of personalities, they first discuss what they are like and how they like to work? If Mark tells Jackie and Yolanda that he avoids conflict and would rather listen to others than offer an opinion, then they will both understand his response to what he thinks is impending conflict. If Jackie tells the others that she loves generating ideas and needs constructive criticism to help her shape her ideas, she may find that both Mark and Yolanda are willing to give her feedback without being afraid of hurting her feelings. If Yolanda tells Jackie and Mark that she would rather support others toward a common goal instead of identifying the goal herself, the group can change how they are approaching the project in order to take advantage of each other's personality types and strengths.

Teaching Styles Diversity

You will encounter many different personality types on campus—in and out of the classroom. You will also encounter a variety of teaching styles. Even though most professors teach according to their own learning style, there are instructors who use a variety of teaching methods to encourage student learning. You will be more successful if you can identify each teaching style and what you should do to adapt to it. Gone are the days of saying, "I just can't learn in her class. She doesn't teach the way I need her to." Like people who must work together in groups and be sensitive to each other's personalities, you, too, have to recognize what your learning style is and how it fits into your professor's teaching style. Ideally, your instructor recognizes that his or her students have different learning style strengths and adapts the material to those learning styles, but not everyone will vary his or her teaching style to meet your needs. Your best bet is to be ready to learn no matter what the teaching style. To help you recognize the different methods of teaching, Exhibit 5.3 includes a description of each and tips for for successful learning.

EXHIBIT 5.3 *Teaching styles.*

TEACHING STYLE	DESCRIPTION	TIPS FOR SUCCESS	VARK CATEGORY
Lecture	Professor talks for most of the class; a brief outline may be included; questions are limited or discouraged; usually very structured	Practice good listening skills; record lectures with permission; take good notes during class and review them frequently	Aural, Read/Write
Discussion	Professor poses a question and requires students to answer and build upon an idea or theme	Practice good listening skills; record theme or question for the discussion; note repeated ideas; record essence of each person's contribution; participate in discussion	Aural, Read/Write
Project	Professor bases student learning on projects; provides instruction for assignment; assigns roles; monitors progress	Make connection between project assignment and course objectives; ask for feedback during project to ensure you are progressing; refer to course materials for extra help	Aural, Kinesthetic
Problem solving	Professor poses a problem; walks through solving the problem	Break process down into steps; identify any step that is unclear; ask for extra practice and feedback if needed	Visual, Read/Write, Kinesthetic

College Relationships

As stated earlier in this chapter, in college, you will encounter a variety of people with diverse backgrounds. Learning to get along and work effectively with different people is an integral part of your education. If you have trouble relating well to others, you will not realize your dreams and meet your goals. Thus, it is important to understand the types of people you will meet and learn how to relate to them.

Classmates

The most obvious people you should get to know better are your classmates. Why? These relationships provide you with a built-in support group. Who can better relate to the challenges of studying for a chemistry final than the students in the class with you? You can also rely on classmates as study partners or emergency note takers if you can't be in class. Another benefit to making friends with fellow students is that you can learn about other classes, instructors, and degree programs—this firsthand knowledge can help you choose the best classes and the most promising programs.

Getting to know your classmates is relatively simple. Here are a few tips for creating lasting relationships with fellow students:

- Introduce yourself to those sitting around you. Arrive at class early and start conversations with other students.
- Exchange phone numbers or e-mail addresses with classmates who seem reliable and trustworthy. You may need to call someone if you miss a class.
- Offer to study with someone. Not only will you help a classmate, but you will learn the material too.
- Maintain contact with friends even after the semester is over. Although you may not share classes anymore, you may still be able to study together and offer support to one another.

Professors

It is important to remember that you will encounter professors who have very different attitudes and methods of teaching. You may have one instructor who encourages questions and offers to work closely with you every step of the way as you learn the material. Then, you may encounter a professor who discourages excessive questions, refuses to "hold your hand," and believes that *you* must do all the work to succeed. As stated earlier, most instructors prefer the type of teaching that worked best for them as learners. Although not every teaching method will work for you, it is your responsibility to adapt to the different styles. Using what you know about your learning style, you should be able to adapt the instructor's style to yours.

When teachers aren't teaching. You will encounter many dedicated, qualified professors during your college career, but there may be an occasion when a professor is not doing her job to the best of her ability. If, for example, a professor is not covering the material or is never in class, consider reporting the problem to an administrator. Teachers who don't teach make it harder for you in the long run. The following are some signs that may indicate a problem that should be reported to a department chair or dean:

- Instructor misses many classes without notice or providing information about what to do until the next class.
- Instructor arrives late or dismisses the class early for most of the semester.
- Instructor does not know the material and has difficulty leading a discussion or answering questions.
- Instructor fails to return tests or papers in a timely manner or at all.
- Instructor does not use the required course materials, does not cover stated course objectives, or does not follow written grading criteria.
- Instructor sexually, verbally, or physically harasses or discriminates against students.
- Instructor is visibly impaired by drugs or alcohol.

A common concern among students who realize that an instructor is not doing her job is that the instructor will retaliate against them by lowering a grade or making communication in and out of class difficult. If you feel that reporting a problem during the semester may put your academic success in jeopardy, schedule an appointment with the professor's department chair or dean and voice your concerns honestly. The administrator may be able to provide reassurance that the complaint will remain anonymous and that final grades will be monitored for accuracy.

Advisors, Counselors, and Administrators

Some of the most important relationships you will forge during college are with people whose primary job is to make sure you succeed. Counselors and advisors will be key people in your academic career, so be sure to meet them and take advantage of their expertise when planning your schedule for future semesters.

Advisors. Your advisor may be the first person you encounter at college. An advisor will help you decide which courses you should take, how many hours you should take each semester, and how to plan remaining semesters. An advisor works for you—it is his job to see that you complete your degree with little difficulty. You may be lucky enough to have the same advisor throughout your college career. In that case, regular communication is important. If you have a different advisor each semester, try to find one person on whom you can rely to act as a regular advisor. That person may be a former professor or a counselor who advised you in the past. The goal is to find someone on campus who has an interest in your education beyond one semester. Each college has a different system for advising; determine how your college handles student advising and cultivate a relationship with someone who can help you plan and navigate your degree plan.

Counselors. You should get to know at least one counselor on your campus. Whether it is a career counselor or disability counselor, make it a point to

schedule an appointment with one while you are in college. Getting to know counselors is a great way to find out more about the school and its services. For example, a career counselor may inform you of a career fair or recruiting day. She can also help you prepare a resume and practice interviewing. Counselors who help students with personal issues are another valuable resource. Even if you do not need counseling, you may benefit from a relationship with one. This kind of counselor can help you manage stress and deal with difficult people. Look for opportunities that provide counseling services to students such as health fairs, job fairs, and transfer-university visits.

Some of the most important relationships you will forge during college will be with people whose primary job is to help you succeed, such as counselors and advisors.

Administrators. It may be more difficult to maintain a relationship with an administrator, but trying is worth the effort. Administrators, such as deans and library directors, can provide information and perspectives that you cannot get from other people on campus. One benefit of cultivating a good relationship with an administrator is that when you do have a problem, you already know with whom you will be speaking. One benefit of attending a community college is that administrators seem more connected and concerned with their diverse student body. You may be attending a college where the president is as eager to talk to students as an advisor is. If your college's administrators, such as the president or vice president, make an effort to talk to students about their concerns, try to share your thoughts and ask questions. You may be very surprised by the administrators' openness and willingness to take students' suggestions and make improvements. Don't let opportunities like that pass you by!

Creating Boundaries

Because you are surrounded by a diverse group of people of all ages, it may be difficult for you to create and maintain relationship boundaries. Whether an instructor or administrator is 20 years younger than you or the same age as you, it is customary to treat them with respect. Even if your professor's attitude is casual and friendly in class, it is in your best interest to be formal before and after class, during office hours, and in correspondence. If your instructors ask that you call them by their first name, then do so. However, as long as you are the student, refrain from inviting them to parties or special off-campus events or from spending several hours a week "hanging out" with them. In other words, create a boundary between you and your instructor, one that is friendly, yet respectful and professional.

Why should you create boundaries when you should be getting to know people on campus better or when you and your instructor share so much in common? Why should you refrain from fraternizing with professors even though you need them to get to know you if you are to ask for a referral or recommendation? Some colleges discourage personal relationships among instructors and students because of problems that can arise. Many companies prohibit a friendly relationship between supervisors and their subordinates; colleges see a close relationship between student and professor as problematic.

One possible problem is that intimate relationships can result in unfair evaluations or treatment. Because an instructor is considered a superior, the college views the instructor's role as one of authority and power. Sexual harassment policies and laws are based on the imbalance of power between a person in authority and the subordinates. Another possible problem is that other students may see the relationship as favoritism and feel as though they are being treated unfairly. There is also the possibility of a sexual relationship, which is strictly prohibited at some colleges. Read your student handbook for information about your college's policy regarding relationships between students and faculty.

If you get along well with your professors and genuinely enjoy their company, then respect the professor–student relationship while you are in class and continue the friendship after the semester over and if you have no intention of taking a class with the professor again. Some lasting friendships are made between professors and students, so consider cultivating them once the class is over. Make the decision that is best for you and the situation as to how friendly you should be with faculty.

Collaboration

EXERCISE 5.5

Working in a group, decide whether personal relationships between faculty and students should be encouraged and supported or prohibited. Be sure to provide support for your position.

Companion
Website

Handling Constructive Criticism

What is constructive criticism? An explanation of what it is *not* may be a good starting point because many people believe that all "criticism" is bad. Constructive criticism is *not* tearing down an individual through degrading and demeaning remarks. Constructive criticism is *not* a -

Critical Thinking PLUS*

You are aware that you are more right-brained than left-brained, which means you express feelings and emotions more. It also means that you look at the big picture rather than the details when completing a task. When you get your research paper back from your biology professor, who seems more analytical and detail-oriented than expressive, you become upset by all the comments about the lack of organization and undeveloped details. You thought you did a great job presenting the overall argument. Because you are an aural learner, you are not sure how to take your professor's written comments. What should you do to make the most of the feedback from your professor? If you decide to talk to the professor, how should you explain your concerns about the quality of your work?

Consider how understanding your personality style or learning preference can help you through challenging situations.

NOTES

*PERSONALITY + LEARNING STYLE = UNDERSTANDING SITUATIONS

personal attack. Constructive criticism is *not* excessively negative or petty comments about a person's work. Because of insecurities about their abilities, it is no wonder that many students fear constructive criticism. They often perceive any feedback that is not entirely positive as an indication of failure, or worse yet, they assume the person giving the constructive criticism does not like them. To better understand constructive criticism, think about its purpose in higher education: Because higher education expands your body of knowledge and worldview, the purpose of constructive criticism is to help you learn and improve so you can live an enriched, fulfilling life.

Some students, unfortunately, begin their college careers believing that constructive criticism should be avoided at all costs—either by refusing to receive it or by not giving it. You will find, however, it very difficult to have honest, open relationships with others if you do not know how to handle constructive criticism.

In order to improve your understanding of how to give and receive constructive criticism, think about what it is. Constructive criticism *is* a positive response to someone's work. Constructive criticism *is* feedback that is focused on the person's work, not the person. Constructive criticism *is* intended to help the other person improve and learn. Being able to handle constructive criticism is crucial to maintaining strong relationships.

Handling Conflict

All humans have conflict. It is a necessary and normal part of human behavior, so there is no doubt you will experience conflict at college. The conflict may be between you and another student, you and a professor, or you and a college employee. The most likely times for conflict are at the semester's beginning and end when stress and tension are high. Although you can't avoid conflict in your life, you can improve your reaction to it so you increase the chances that you will have a positive experience. Facing conflict and dealing with it instead of running from it allows you to learn more about yourself and others.

Messina and Messina (2003) describe conflict as any situation that causes you stress: Anger, lack of communication, threats, negativity, and risk of loss are all reasons people experience conflict within themselves or with others. Although you usually cannot control stressful situations, you can control how you react and what you choose to take away from the experience.

Messina and Messina (2003) suggest that you view conflict as a:

- Time of growth for the parties involved.
- Time in which problems can be solved creatively by looking together at a variety of alternatives.
- Chance to evaluate your performance objectively.
- Time for us to increase our knowledge of one another.
- Chance to reveal our unique ways of thinking, acting, and feeling.
- Chance to show understanding, respect, and acceptance of the unique ways in which others think, act, and feel. (www.coping.org/relations/conflict.htm#behaviors)*

The box that follows offers an example of a way you can take a common experience and change your attitude in preparation for handling the conflict.

Adjusting Your Attitude

CONFLICT SCENARIO

You started the semester off on the wrong foot by arriving late and unprepared for class several times, and you can tell the professor is not happy with your behavior. To make matters worse, you got a D on the first exam, and you are sure that she has decided you are a poor student. You would like to go talk to her to show her you are a good student—you were just distracted with personal issues—but you were told that she does not take excuses from students about their personal lives. The one time you did approach her, she did not seem interested in talking with you. In fact, you believe she was rude. What do you do?

CONFLICT SCENARIO SOLUTION

Your goal in this situation is to demonstrate that you are, in fact, a good student who had some personal problems and you are eager and willing to do the work that remains. Before you schedule a time to talk to your professor, make sure you are committed to doing better in class. If you believe you can devote more time and energy to the course, then ask your professor if you can meet with her. When you meet, explain that you are disappointed with your earlier work and that you don't usually have such a difficult time in a course. You don't have to explain the details of any problems you have; instead, say that you had outside distractions that are now resolved. End your conversation with the assurance that you will strive to do better work—and then keep your promise.

---

*Used with permission.

If you can view conflict, and stress in general, as a "time for growth" or an opportunity to improve yourself and others' view of you, you will be in a better position to overcome the challenges you face. Changing your attitude about conflict is as simple as changing the words you use to describe the stressful situation or person.

Some students turn their frustration into anger toward the professor, either by complaining to other students or by making a negative comment to her directly. Although the student may feel better after he verbally attacks someone or "lets off steam" by complaining, he is not really handling the conflict. Other students might retreat, ignore the conflict, and drop the course. It seems natural to have a fight-or-flight reaction to a conflict such as this, but neither response actually improves the situation.

In order to handle this conflict, you must recognize what is going on: First, you have internal conflict—you are worried that the professor has a low opinion of you because of your external behavior (coming in late and poor test performance). Second, you have perceived external conflict—the professor reacted negatively to you because of your behavior and performance. Once you realize what the conflicts are, you can make a plan to resolve them. It is important to handle this conflict appropriately because you may have to take another class with this professor or you may find yourself in need of a recommendation or advice. More importantly, handling this conflict with maturity and integrity shows others that you are a responsible and reliable student.

> **EXERCISE 5.7**
>
> *Reflection*
>
> How do you feel about receiving criticism? Is it something you avoid altogether or do you welcome it from certain persons? Explain your answer.
>
>
> Companion Website

Dealing with Difficult People

There may be times when conflict with others keeps occurring despite your best efforts to resolve the problem. There are just some people who are difficult to deal with no matter how hard you try. In Chapter 2, you learned about "toxic people" who make you feel bad about yourself and how to minimize your contact with them. In some cases, minimizing contact with a difficult person is impossible because he is a supervisor, coworker, dependent family member, or current professor. Dealing with difficult people takes practice and patience, so here are some tips to remember when you encounter them:

- Never take anything that anyone says to you personally. Difficult people are acting out their own insecurities and disappointments that have nothing to do with you.

- Consider that there may be a legitimate reason for their difficult behavior. They may be under a tremendous amount of stress because of personal, financial, or professional problems. The reason, though, for their difficult behavior is an *explanation*, not an excuse.

- Look for behavior patterns and avoid those people during the time when the behavior is likely to occur. Is it early morning or late afternoon when the difficult behavior is at its worst? Is it early in the week, late in the week, at certain times when work is due?

- Stay calm when you deal with a difficult person. Don't participate by being difficult too.

- Try to engage the person by asking about her life outside work. If she has family ask about them. A personal connection sometimes helps.

- If matters are unbearable or border on harassment, document the difficult behavior and talk to a supervisor.

- If at all possible, minimize contact with the person.

Integrity in Relationships

As you will see as you read the rest of this book, integrity is an important part of college life and the world at large. Integrity is defined in Chapter 1 as "a strict adherence to an ethical code of conduct," but the definition can be expanded to include relationships. Integrity in relationships requires being honest with other people and demanding honesty from them. Without integrity, relationships are superficial and meaningless. You might be better off by yourself than with people who do not demonstrate integrity in their relationships with you.

The underlying factor of integrity in a relationship is trust. If you can trust others, then you are able to learn, grow, expand, and improve yourself. If you do not have trust, then you may shut yourself off from others and experiences that are new to you. Trusting others takes time—it isn't developed overnight. Give people a reason to trust you and then deliver on your promises. Likewise, put your trust in others, giving them an opportunity to be trustworthy.

A specific part of trust in relationships is reliability or, expressed another way, doing what you say you will do. If your classmate asks you to take notes for him when he cannot be in class and you fail to do so, then you lack reliability, and your classmate can't trust you to help him. If you agree to take notes, knowing that you may not be able to, then you are not being honest—with him or with yourself.

Acting with integrity is not easy and doesn't always come naturally. Instead, it is a conscious decision to do what is right even when it makes things harder and more uncomfortable for you and others. Being reliable and trustworthy takes work because you may find yourself doing things (e.g., taking notes for a friend or taking a coworker home at the end of the day) that are inconvenient and time-consuming. Moreover, the rewards for acting with integrity are not always immediate; thus, to act with integrity, you must know that, despite how you feel now, the effects of your action are far-reaching and positive.

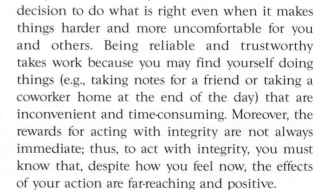

Collaboration

EXERCISE 5.8

As a group, describe three situations in which a friend can demonstrate honesty and integrity in the face of a difficult decision.

Companion Website

INTEGRITY MATTERS

Maintaining integrity in relationships requires being honest with others and with yourself. Building trust takes time and energy as well as conscious decisions to be honest. However, the rewards are great!

An Attitude of Gratitude

One of the most important and fulfilling ways to create and maintain strong relationships is to express gratitude for what people do for you. Giving thanks should not be a once-a-year event that accompanies eating turkey and watching football. Saying "thank you" to fellow students, professors, advisors, and other college employees helps you forge relationships that will last throughout your academic career and beyond. If a classmate lends her notes to you, be sure to thank her. If a professor goes out of his way to meet with you about your research paper, show your gratitude. If your college advisor sends you information about a scholarship she thinks you could win, tell her how much you appreciate her thoughtfulness.

If the favor or special consideration took a substantial amount of the giver's time and energy, be sure to write a formal thank-you note. Writing thank-you notes is a lost art that will be greatly appreciated by the recipient. Just a quick note that reflects how much the person's actions meant to you shows how thoughtful and considerate you are. People remember those who demonstrate their gratitude, which should be helpful when you need a favor.

Tips for Lasting Relationships

What a shame it would be to spend several semesters in college and not have one single friend to show for it. As discussed earlier, community college students do have a harder time cultivating friendships because of their busy schedules and because they do not typically spend four years with the same group of people. What can you do to strengthen the relationships you make in college?

- Get to know the other students in your classes.
- Exchange e-mail addresses or phone numbers with other students.
- Leave time in your schedule to talk with friends or meet with professors. If you must leave right after class to get to work, try to find some other time to meet with people.

Practice

EXERCISE 5.9

Choose a student in your class about whom you know little. Interview that student, and allow her to interview you. In addition to questions about her background, ask about strengths and weaknesses in college. Does she do well in a certain subject? Does she need help studying for a particular class?

Companion
Website

- Make an appointment with each instructor during the semester to ask questions or get feedback on your progress. Your ulterior motive is to cultivate a relationship.

- Learn to take constructive criticism with a positive attitude and remember its purpose is to help you improve.

- Approach conflict as an opportunity to learn more about yourself.

- Thank someone for a job well done or a favor. Return the favor when you have a chance.

- Always act with integrity. Relationships that last are ones built on trust and doing what is right.

Changes in Your Relationships with Family and Friends

Entering college is a new experience not only for you, but also for your family and friends, especially if they didn't go to college and are unaware of the changes you are going through. Communication is the key to weathering any changes in your relationships. They need to know how you feel about going to college.

While at college, you will experience changes in your outlook on life, your belief in yourself, and your attitude toward the future. When these changes occur, people around you will react differently. Some will be supportive and excited that you created personal goals and are achieving them. A few may, however, react negatively. These people may be jealous of your success or your new "lease on life" either because they did not have the same opportunities or because they squandered the opportunities they did have. Those who react negatively may be insecure about themselves and feel "dumb" around a person in college; these same people often fear that once the college student graduates, he will leave them for a "better" spouse or friend. Then there are parents of students who do not want to acknowledge that their children are adults who are and should be making decisions on their own; parents may also worry that their children will be exposed to a value system and beliefs that are very different from what they taught them. Regardless how the people around you react to the changes in you, know that you will survive.

Learning Styles Application

This chart lists the four learning styles and tips based on the chapter's main ideas. Locate your learning style and read the corresponding tips to maximize your success in college.

VISUAL

Visual learners like to see others in order to establish relationships with them. You may not like talking on the phone or e-mailing people in order to build relationships.

AURAL

For aural learners, talking and listening to others is the best way to start and maintain relationships. You enjoy talking both in person and on the phone. With today's technology, it is easy for you to stay in touch using a cell phone, voice mail, audio files, and webconferencing software.

READ/WRITE

Writing letters and e-mail is a great way for read/write learners to meet new people and create a relationship. You also like to share your personal writing and recommend books and articles to others as a way of establishing and strengthening relationships.

KINESTHETIC

For kinesthetic learners, participating in activities is a great way to learn more about others and work together. Whether it is creating something or playing a sport, you like to interact with others during physical activities.

Path of Discovery

Reflect on how the information about diversity and relationships made you think about how you treated others in the past. What mistakes did you make? What did you do well in terms of treating others with respect? What will you do in the future?

FROM COLLEGE TO UNIVERSITY

The relationships you foster now will open doors after transfer

The relationships you make in college will help you even after you transfer to a university. Your contacts with advisors, counselors, and professors should yield more contacts at your new school. Advisors and counselors can recommend certain programs and administrators. Professors can put in a good word with the people they know at your transfer school, which may mean extra consideration for admission into a program or for a scholarship.

These same people may also have inside knowledge of little known internships and aid, deadline extensions, and special transfer scholarships. Advisors, counselors, and professors can also provide advice about the particular challenges you may face once you complete the move. The closer the relationships, the smoother the transfer.

FROM COLLEGE TO CAREER

Making the most of diversity is key to success on the job

We sometimes think that once we reach our ultimate educational goal and start our dream career, we will be magically transported to a world in which everyone is an "instant" friend and everyone gets along. Unfortunately, we are brought back down from the clouds as early as the first day on the job.

You should continue to make positive connections with others and redefine established relationships. You will encounter diversity on a daily basis and have to rely on what you learned in college (and life in general) in order to consider others' feelings, beliefs, and attitudes. What you learned about other cultures, time periods, and philosophical and political ideas will make it easier to work with and appreciate the diversity of your coworkers.

Chapter in Review

1. Name and explain four types of diversity.

2. How will you use what you learned in this chapter to start and improve relationships with people on campus? Who will you seek out and why?

3. Using Exhibit 5.1, pick one of the diversity factors and its corresponding stereotypes. Create a list of other stereotypes that exist for the group. Then, explain why you think these stereotypes exist and what you can do to eliminate them.

4. Which of the teaching style types is your favorite? Which one is the hardest type to learn from? What can you do to make the most challenging teaching style more enjoyable?

5. How practical is the information in the chapter about dealing with difficult people? Can you think of situations in which the advice may not work? If so, create your own strategies for dealing with people in those situations.

Case Scenarios

Read the following case scenarios and determine what each person should do. Refer to the information in this chapter as you write a description and plan of action for each student.

1. Jonathan was raised in a very religious household. He believes that homosexuality is wrong, and he is struggling with an assignment that requires him to write about the issue from a sociological perspective. The professor wants the students to be objective, but Jonathan doesn't think he can be. What should Jonathan do?

2. Marie has been married for 14 years. She and her husband have twin girls who are 12. Since Marie started college, she has noticed that her husband seems less interested in her and what she is learning in her classes. He now belittles her desire to earn a degree. Although he initially encouraged her to enroll, he now seems to be against her continuing her education. Marie is discouraged by his reaction and is thinking about not enrolling next semester. What would you tell Marie to do?

3. One of Willis' professors missed three night classes in a row without telling the students beforehand and without providing a plan to make up the missed material. Willis really needs this class for his major in business, and he is worried that he won't be successful in subsequent classes. He is also worried that if he complains to the instructor, his grade will be lowered in retaliation. He may have to take a class from the professor again. What should he do?

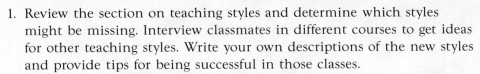

Research It Further

1. Review the section on teaching styles and determine which styles might be missing. Interview classmates in different courses to get ideas for other teaching styles. Write your own descriptions of the new styles and provide tips for being successful in those classes.

2. What does your college do to promote cultural appreciation on the campus? Collect examples of the college's promotion of multiculturalism and determine what, if anything, the college could do to enhance racial, ethnic, and cultural sensitivity and understanding.

3. What is your college's policy regarding relationships between students and faculty? In addition to reviewing your student handbook, interview students, faculty, and administrators about faculty–student relationships.

4. Research the topic of professor–student relationships. What are the benefits and drawbacks of intimate professor–student relationships? Use your findings to support your points.

References

American Association of Community Colleges. (2004). Retrieved July 13, 2005, from www.aacc.nche.edu.

Katz, N. (2005). "Sexual harassment statistics in the workplace and in education." Retrieved July 5, 2005, from http://womensissues.about.com/cs/sexdiscrimination/a/sexharassstats.htm.

Messina, J. J., & Messina, C. M. (2003). "Tools for relationships: Handling conflict." Retrieved July 27, 2005, from www.coping.org/relations/conflict.htm#behaviors.

U.S. Equal Employment Opportunity Commission. (2005). "Sexual Harassment." Retrieved September 17, 2005, from www.eeoc.gov/types/sexual_harassment.html.

Zemke, R., Raines, C., & Filipczak, B. (2000). *Generations at work: Managing the clash of veterans, boomers, xers, and nexters in your workplace.* New York: Amacom.

6 Listening and Taking Notes Effectively

Listening and taking notes effectively gives you an edge in college because you can take in more information and easily remember it. Laura can attest to the importance of developing an efficient note-taking system, especially for those students who have learning difficulties that prevent them from using just one style. This chapter discusses various note-taking strategies, including the method Laura developed. This chapter also helps you improve your listening skills. You will find answers to the following questions:

- How can I listen more effectively?

- What are the barriers to listening?

- What note-taking methods are available to me?

- How does my learning style strength affect my note-taking strategies?

- How can I still benefit from note taking if I have a note taker?

COMMUNITY · COLLEGE ·

Student Profile

NAME: **Laura Thomas**   AGE: **38**

MAJOR: **Social Work**

1. **What are your college goals? What is your ultimate career goal?**

   I want to get an associate's degree and have my dad see me graduate from college. I want to work in hospice care for the Veterans' Administration.

2. **What was your biggest obstacle when learning to take notes?**

   The hardest part about note taking is figuring out what to write down. I realized I don't have to write down everything the teacher says.

3. **What advice you would give to students who are learning how to listen and take notes effectively?**

   Sharpen your pencil, have plenty of paper, and stay organized with a binder that has dividers. Use hole-punched paper and keep your notes in the binder. Remove notes that you don't need after taking an exam and keep them in a safe place.

4. **What is your VARK?**

   Visual.

The Listening and Note-Taking Connection

Listening, memory, and note taking all have something in common: They are necessary in the process of learning. You will not make it through your classes successfully without doing all three. Retaining and recalling information, however, is only part of the process. This chapter helps you receive the information, which in turn helps you turn the information into a knowledge base that you can build on for the rest of your life.

Preparing to Listen

Active listening is a term you may hear in college classes; someone who listens actively is concentrating on what is being said and is taking steps to remember the information. To be an active listener, you must decide that listening is a worthwhile activity and that important information will be shared. The following suggestions are intended to help you listen actively and effectively.

The first step is to prepare to listen before you get to class—read the assigned pages or chapters ahead of time to identify the lecture or discussion topic and to become familiar with new words and concepts. Preparing to listen also includes reviewing your assigned readings before you get to the classroom. If you have a few minutes between classes or on the bus, pull out your book and skim the major headings, bold terms, and any text boxes.

To listen effectively while in class, avoid distractions. Sit up front away from talkative people, and put unnecessary textbooks, cell phones, pagers, and other distracting items away. Your best defense against interruptions is to clear your desk of everything except your textbook, a pen, and paper. If you need to get anything during class, such as a dictionary, minimize the disruption.

If you find yourself next to a chatty classmate or one who likes to write you notes, simply move. Even if you are politely listening or reading her messages, you are still disrupting the class. Talkative classmates make it difficult for you and others to listen, and they distract you from taking good notes.

Another good way to listen effectively is by maintaining a positive attitude about the class. If you think the class is a waste of time or is boring, you are less likely to pay attention. Even if your beliefs are true—and others bemoan the class as well—pretend the class is the only one left before you graduate and that if you don't pay attention and take good notes, then you will have to stay another semester.

Minimizing outside distractions is another way to keep a positive attitude. There will be times that you have to work late, stay up all night with a sick baby, or help a friend who just had a crisis. If not handled well, these stressful experiences can affect your class performance. As much as possible, leave your personal life at the door, and concentrate on the class you are sitting in. Even if the day's lecture is overshadowed by a personal problem, remember that you *can* handle both your academic duties and your personal life.

Finally, prepare for class psychologically by preparing physically. Eat something before class so you aren't interrupted by a growling stomach. Dress in layers in case the room temperature is uncomfortable. Nothing is more distracting than being too hot or too cold. Get plenty of sleep the night before class to help you pay attention and listen effectively. Although adequate sleep may be a luxury if you work a late shift, make an effort to get a good night's

Someone who listens actively is concentrating on what is being said and is taking steps to remember the information.

sleep as often as possible. You can't maintain your concentration and information retention, or even good health, without adequate rest.

Listening Critically

As stated previously, active listening requires focusing on the task at hand and concentrating on what is being conveyed, whether it be words or sounds. Another part of listening effectively is listening critically, or the act of processing and evaluating what you hear. Listening critically helps you make decisions about what is important and what is not, what is objective and what is biased, and what should be stored for later and what should be discarded.

Listening critically is a skill, one that must be practiced regularly. Your college professors should invite you to think critically and challenge assumptions (that is learning!). As you become comfortable with listening actively and critically, you will move from merely listening and taking notes to listening in order to evaluate and ask questions about the notes you took. Here are some questions to consider as you learn to listen critically:

- *Speaker.* Is the speaker a credible source? How do I know? What possible biases does he have? What is his experience with the topic?

- *Message.* What is the speaker's purpose? What are the details he uses to convey his message?

- *Details.* Is the speaker using facts or opinions? How do I know? Which type of details works best for what the speaker is trying to convey?
- *Self-knowledge.* What do I already know about the topic? How does what the speaker is saying conflict with or support my beliefs and opinions? Have I learned something new?
- *Larger picture.* How does what the speaker is saying fit into the larger picture? How can I relate the message to something I already know about life or the world? Are there any connections between what I heard and past experiences?

Answering some of these questions will get you started on the right path to listening critically. Even though you already listen critically and mentally ask questions about what you hear, you may still have to "tune in" when you hear something you don't agree with or don't understand.

Remember, *critical* does not mean *negative.* If you find that what you are hearing is contrary to what you know about the subject, you can still ask respectful questions. Most people do not mind being politely challenged or debated.

Collaboration

EXERCISE 6.1

Working with another classmate, take turns explaining why you are in college. Then, discuss how each of you listened critically. If there were any barriers to listening, describe what they were.

Companion Website

Potential Listening Barriers

Despite your efforts to prepare for class, you may find barriers to listening effectively, barriers that you cannot avoid no matter how prepared you are. For example, what should you do if your instructor talks too fast, uses technical jargon or an advanced vocabulary, is unorganized, digresses from lecture material (e.g., tells stories, allows too many irrelevant questions), or does not explain key concepts? Although you shouldn't coach your instructor in the art of speaking, you can ask her to slow down or define terms. Most professors do not mind repeating information or defining specialized terms and vocabulary because they want students to understand the material.

It may, however, be a little harder to ask the instructor to be more organized or to stay on topic. One option is to ask if she would provide an outline before each class. To bring the professor back to the original subject, ask a question about it or an upcoming exam or assignment that addresses the subject.

In addition to not getting enough sleep or sitting in an uncomfortable classroom, there are other barriers to

Reflection

EXERCISE 6.2

Think about a time when you heard someone speak and you did not agree with what was said. How did you listen? How did you react to what you were hearing?

Companion Website

listening effectively. If you have an unaccommodated learning disability or a hearing problem, you may not be able to listen productively. Discuss any learning or hearing difficulties with a counselor and ask for help. A more common hindrance to effective listening is the students' insecurities about their ability to do well in the course. It is not uncommon for a new student to feel, at first, intimidated by the course, the instructor, or other students. The reason for the discomfort may stem from a student feeling that she is not good enough or smart enough to be in college. A student also may feel that everyone, except him, knows what to do, what to say, and how to act. This fear is actually common and it usually subsides after the first week or two.

Remembering What You Heard

Once you have prepared to listen in class and have eliminated any barriers that inhibit your ability to take in information, turn your attention to remembering

what you hear in class. Taking notes, of course, is one way to retain information; however, there are other methods that will help you recall information at a later date.

One way to remember what you hear and learn in class is to ask questions. Asking questions may be difficult if you are shy or feel out of place in the classroom—some students refrain from asking questions because they don't want to look ignorant in front of their classmates.

Then there is the other end of the spectrum— the constant questioners. These students dominate the professor's time by asking questions that sideline the discussion or questions about material that was already covered. Don't be intimidated by a predominantly quiet classroom or by

Practice

EXERCISE 6.3

Choose a page from this textbook to read aloud to a classmate. Pair up with another student and take turns listening to each other's readings. See how much you can remember of the information your classmate read by restating the information.

Companion Website

those students who bother the professor with excessive questions. If you have a question, ask it. Some instructors believe there are no "stupid questions." If you don't feel comfortable asking questions during class, visit with your professor after class or during office hours. Some instructors ask students to write questions down and pass them up before class is over. Take advantage of such a practice; you will be able to ask questions without the fear of speaking up in front of classmates.

Participating in discussions and activities is an excellent way to remember key concepts. In fact, professors consider student participation a part of active learning. You are more likely to remember a concept if you can incorporate it into your own thinking. There is a reason that the most talkative students are usually the most successful—they make the material relevant to them, which makes remembering easier.

Another method of remembering, tape-recording lectures, is popular with students who have the time to listen to the tape. Listening to

Critical Thinking

EXERCISE 6.4

Describe the ultimate ineffective listening scenario. Write a scenario in which a student fails to use every kind of listening strategy. Present your scenario to the class.

Companion Website

INTEGRITY MATTERS

Listening with integrity means that you listen with an open mind and without judgment until the speaker is finished. Then, you can ask questions if there are points you don't understand. Listening with integrity also means that you avoid twisting the person's words to fit what you want to hear. Practicing active and critical listening will help you maintain integrity.

a tape recording works best if you have a long commute or if you go over your notes as you listen. Be sure to ask permission before you begin to tape and make sure you have fresh batteries.

How Information Is Presented

Learning to listen effectively is the first step to taking good notes, but you will also benefit from understanding how information can be presented during a lecture. As you attend more classes, you will notice that professors have a certain way they present material. Some follow the textbook in the same order. Others lecture only on new material not found in the textbook or other course materials. Then, others present a combination of the two. Reading assigned chapters and materials before attending class allows you to determine which lecture information is new and which is covered by the assigned reading materials.

As you will learn in Chapter 9, information can be organized in many different ways. Recognizing these various ways helps you keep your notes organized and provides strategies for revising and reviewing your notes when you begin studying.

Chronological. When notes are chronological, details are arranged by time (first this happened, then this happened, etc.).

EXAMPLE OF CHRONOLOGICAL LECTURE NOTES

1801: United Kingdom of Great Britain is created

1803: Louisiana Purchase is made by Thomas Jefferson

1815: Battle of Waterloo signals end of Napoleon's career

Cause/effect. In this style, details are arranged by presenting a cause and then its effects or an effect and its causes.

EXAMPLE OF CAUSE/EFFECT LECTURE NOTES

Cause: Civil War

Effects: slavery ended, industrialism began, the nation was brought back together, the federal government proved stronger than the states

Compare/contrast. In this style, details are arranged by similarities and differences.

EXAMPLE OF COMPARE/CONTRAST LECTURE NOTES

Similarities between Robert Frost and Walt Whitman: were males, used nature in their poetry, considered "poets of the people"

Differences between Frost and Whitman: Frost's poetry is more structured, while Whitman's is open and loose; Whitman's speakers are more positive and upbeat than Frost's; Whitman lived during the 19th century, while Frost's life spanned both the 19th and 20th centuries

Most important/least important. In general, details are arranged in order of importance. The most important detail can come first with minor supporting details following, or the least important details start a list that works up to a major detail.

EXAMPLE OF MOST IMPORTANT/LEAST IMPORTANT LECTURE NOTES

Self-awareness (purpose of education)

> Values
>
> Goals
>
> Mission
>
> Personality type
>
> Learning style

Note-Taking Strategies

There are numerous methods of taking notes, and your goal is to find the note-taking strategy that works best for you. Remember that you may have to adapt your note-taking style to each course, each teaching style, and each learning style strength. For example, outlining may work well in a history course in which the instructor writes key terms on the board and organizes her lecture around key ideas. If your professor prefers unstructured discussion, adapt your note-taking strategy to make the most of unorganized information.

Whatever you choose for a particular course, your learning style, or a specific situation, there are a few tips to remember when taking notes.

- *Listen for the main ideas.* Instructors will slow down and emphasize information, terms, and definitions. They may even use verbal signposts such as "The most important thing to remember is," "This may appear on an exam," or "Two crucial points about." If the instructor writes down or hands out an outline, you can be sure it contains the lecture's main points.

- *Leave plenty of "white space" (blank space on paper) when taking notes.* Don't try to fill your page with as much information as possible. You need the white space to add more notes later or to synthesize ideas once you have reviewed.

- *Review your notes as soon as possible after class.* Waiting two weeks to review your notes ensures that you won't remember everything you wrote or how it all fits together. Most experts suggest that you review your notes within two days of the class.

Develop a Shorthand

As you take more notes in each class, you will find yourself using some of the same words over and over again. These words are good candidates for abbreviating or denoting with symbols, creating your own shorthand. Shortened words such as *ex.* for *example, w/* for *with,* and *b/c* for *because* are abbreviations you may already use in notes and e-mail messages. Symbols you may already use include % for *percentage,* + for *add* or *and,* and # for *number.* If you develop a new abbreviation or symbol, make a note of what it means; for example, *TR* could mean *Theory of Relativity* in a science course and *Teddy Roosevelt* in a history course.

The following is a list of other commonly abbreviated words and symbols:

At	@
Between	betw, b/w
Decrease	decr
Department	dept
Does not equal	≠
Government	govt
Increase	incr
Equals	=
Example	eg, ex
Important	imp
Information	info
Regarding	re
Significant	sig

Developing a shorthand allows you more time to concentrate on what is being said. As you practice more, you become better at judging what information is worth writing and what is not, and your shorthand becomes more efficient. Just remember to read over your notes within a day or two so your abbreviations are fresh in your mind. It is a good idea to complete the words or concepts then so you won't struggle to remember what the shortened words mean later in the semester.

Outlining

An outline is a good note-taking method if the instructor is organized and presents information in a logical pattern. Some instructors encourage outlining by writing key words and concepts on the board or an overhead projecting device. If your instructor organizes lectures or class discussions, outlining your notes is easy. The key to effective outlines is to leave plenty of space between the items so you can add extra information. An outline for a lecture on effective listening might look like this:

I. Preparing to Listen Effectively

II. Listening Critically

III. Possible Listening Barriers

    A. External

        1. Hunger

        2. Climate discomfort

    B. Internal

        1. Feelings of self-worth

        2. Stress

IV. How Information Is Presented

    A. Chronological

    B. Cause/Effect

    C. Compare/Contrast

    D. Most Important/Least Important

Taking Notes in the Textbook

Writing in the margins of your textbook is another effective way to take notes, especially if the reading assignment is lengthy. If you don't mind writing in your textbook, you can summarize the main points you read. Writing brief summaries (two or three words) or questions in the margins helps you make sense of and remember what you read. Brief, marginal summaries also help you review material before class and after class when you start studying for an exam.

    Annotating in your textbook and writing down critical questions are two methods to further reinforce what you read and to prepare for note taking in class. Move beyond your summaries or retelling the material to drawing lines to connect major ideas and concepts and to asking questions such as "How do I know this to be true?" and "What else should be considered?" Annotating the textbook with your own notes not only reinforces main ideas, but also helps you synthesize the information in new ways to produce connections between concepts, making the material more memorable and more relevant.

    If you decide to write in your textbook, be sure it is not one you want to sell back to the bookstore. If you do not want to write in your book but still want the benefits of summarizing the material, write your summaries on a separate sheet of paper. Make sure to label each piece with the chapter title and page number of the book.

    Highlighting in your textbook is another method students use to take notes. A highlighter pen is used to mark important concepts for review, but don't highlight too much information. Over-highlighting the text has the opposite effect—instead of making it easier to understand key terms and information, too much highlighting makes everything seem of equal importance. If you do use a highlighter, use it sparingly. For example, don't highlight more than two sentences in a row. A better method is to use highlighting and written summaries together.

Practice

EXERCISE 6.5

Arrange your notes for this chapter using two different note-taking strategies.

Companion Website

Critical Thinking

EXERCISE 6.6

What are some drawbacks to using outlines when taking notes?

Companion Website

Annotating in your textbook and writing down critical questions are two ways to further reinforce what you have read.

Cornell System

Cornell University professor Dr. Walter Pauk developed a note-taking system that is popular with many students. The Cornell System, also known as the T System, is ideal for those who benefit from the visual impact of organized notes. The key to the Cornell System is dividing your notebook paper before you begin writing. To do so, draw a horizontal line across the paper two inches from the bottom. Then, draw a vertical line from the horizontal line to the top of the page about two inches from the left margin. The page should look like this:

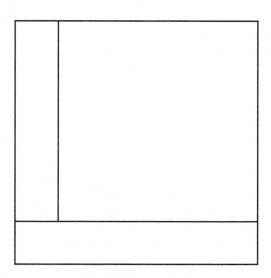

The largest area, the right column, is used for taking notes during class. The left column is used for noting questions if there is material you don't understand or if you think of possible exam questions as you write. The bottom section is reserved for summarizing your notes as you review them. The act of summarizing helps you understand and remember the information.

Note-Taking Strategies in the Disciplines

The following strategies for note-taking in the disciplines are just samples of what you may encounter in college. Although Chapter 8 discusses specific study strategies within disciplines, the following are note-taking strategies, grouped by discipline, that make reviewing and studying easier.

Art. In an art appreciation class, you have to identify eras (20th century), movements (Cubism), and artists (Picasso) as well their characteristics as seen in drawings, paintings, and sculpture. Quickly sketching the works in your notes and listing the characteristic details helps you record the information you receive through lectures. You may also notice that in the study of art there are times of intense change (usually coinciding with a world or cultural event) followed by artists who imitate or slightly modify the new style. As you review your notes, look for patterns within groups of artwork and for points of contrast.

Music. In a music appreciation class, the same suggestions for an art appreciation class work when taking notes. Instead of re-creating a painting or sculpture in your notes, write down descriptions of what you are hearing and what the sounds remind you of. Are the sounds fast or slow? Do you hear one instrument or many? Does it sound like a stampede or a trip down a lazy river? "Translating" music samples into written notes, as well as reviewing music clips on your own, strengthens your understanding of the material. As with your art notes, upon review, look for patterns across movements and eras and note contrasting ideas and elements.

Literature. Taking notes in a literature class requires that you complete the assigned readings before class and that you annotate and highlight your text. Because literature classes, even survey classes, focus more on discussion than lecture, be prepared to take notes on the analysis (how your classmates and instructor take the text apart and examine it) of the literature. As with music and art classes, being familiar with basic terminology before you get to class helps you take better notes. As you review your notes, look for ideas that pull the different readings together.

Languages. Foreign language classes center more on speaking and interacting than on listening to a lecture. Taking notes is not necessarily advantageous because you should focus all of your attention on listening actively, processing what is heard, and interacting based on what you hear. Daily preparation is essential to learning foreign languages; take notes as you encounter new material and ask questions in class to get clarification on anything you do not understand. Any notes you do take should be reviewed soon after class. As you review the notes, categorize material such as irregular verbs and include any tips for using or remembering the parts of language.

Science. Concepts and processes are key in science classes and your notes will reflect that. Prepare for class by reading the assigned material, making note of new vocabulary words, and studying diagrams and figures in the text and handouts. As with any class, ask questions if you have trouble following the steps of a process. As you review your notes, consider the different ways you can represent these concepts and processes visually and physically.

History. History class lectures are usually presented in chronological order, so using the tips for information that follows a time sequence will help you take notes in this class. However, you are also required to move beyond specific dates and events to considering overall themes, ideas, and movements.

In addition to chronological order, lectures may also use a cause/effect organization—you list and elaborate on the effects of a cause or the causes of an effect. For example, a history lecture topic is "The economic and social effects of the end of the Civil War." As you review your notes, look for major themes and recall actions that led to important events.

Math. Taking good notes in math classes requires that you prepare and attend each class meeting. As with foreign languages, studying for math should be an everyday occurrence because the skills you learn in each class build on the ones you learned in the class before. When reviewing your notes, recopy them to ensure that you understand, line by line, what you are copying. If you have any questions, write them in the margins of your notes to ask during the next class meeting.

Note-Taking Strategies with VARK

Visual Learners

Visual learners benefit from seeing the notes on the page, but they may also benefit from creating images of the material they wrote down. Take, for example, cause/effect information for the increase in electronic communication. An instructor may talk through or write down a few key ideas like this:

> In the late 1990s, electronic communication grows at home and in the workplace.
>   Effects: closer relationships with those who are far away, increased productivity, long distance costs decrease, decline in stamp sales, need for communication guidelines at work, problems with sharing too much information or sending junk, bombardment of spam and viruses.

A visual learner may take that same information and create a visual representation, as shown in Exhibit 6.1.

Aural Learners

Reading notes aloud, recording lectures, or recording yourself talking through material are all strategies for recording material. Although "taking notes" implies writing down words and then reading through them, there is no reason aural learners must suppress their learning style strength during the process. An aural learner can pair up with a read/write learner and talk through the material they heard in a recent class. The read/write learner can then record notes or annotate ones he already has and share them with the aural learner.

Collaboration

EXERCISE 6.7

Working in a group of three or more, discuss your VARK learning style strengths and weaknesses. Decide how you would take notes for an upcoming exam based on your learning styles and relevant note-taking strategies.

Companion Website

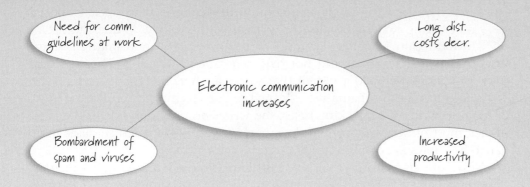

Need for comm. guidelines at work

Long dist. costs decr.

Electronic communication increases

Bombardment of spam and viruses

Increased productivity

Read/Write Learners

Read/write learners are at an advantage because their learning style strength is writing down notes and reading through them. However, not all instructors present information in a format that is easiest for read/write learners. As you read earlier, highly visual, aural, or kinesthetic disciplines are challenging for read/write learners to take effective notes. The key is in "translating" visual, aural, and kinesthetic material by describing with words what you experience. For example, in a music class, describe the sounds you hear or the rhythmic pattern; in an anatomy class, write descriptions or list the characteristics of organs to accompany pictures and body maps. Rereading your notes and annotating as you review reinforces what you learned regardless of whether you originally obtained the information visually, aurally, or kinesthetically.

Kinesthetic Learners

The act of taking notes by writing or typing them provides kinesthetic learners with a physical activity that makes remembering the written notes easier. Kinesthetic learners benefit from using more physical activity or objects when they review their notes shortly after taking them. For example, if you are using formulas to calculate volume in your math class, review your notes by creating your own volume problems in the kitchen. The act of pouring and measuring water and then calculating your measurements makes it easier to remember the process when completing homework problems or taking a test.

Likewise, a good way for a kinesthetic learner to study for an art class, or any class that uses visual images, is to re-create the artwork with paper and colored pencils. No need to strive for masterpiece quality when re-creating works of art; the physical activity of drawing the wavy lines in the background of Edvard Munch's *The Scream* will help you recall the piece on an exam.

Critical Thinking

EXERCISE 6.8

A friend is taking a visual arts class and is having trouble making sense of his notes because they pertain to specific artwork. The instructor did not hand out reproductions of the art, so the student tried to sketch the pieces during class, but that took too long. Do you have any suggestions for your friend on how to take more effective notes?

Companion Website

Finding Your Own Note-Taking Style

Laura Thomas, a student at a community college, developed a special note-taking system because of a learning disability. While taking an introduction to college course, she discovered the note-taking systems discussed in her textbook did not help her take good notes. Through trial and error, she developed a system that works for her.

Before class begins, Laura uses a pencil to date each page and leaves plenty of room to write. When taking notes, she writes on only one side of the page; in fact, most of her pages contain less than 50 words. Although she uses more paper, her notes are easier to read.

Next, she stars words that the instructor says are important. The most important part of her note-taking system is her use of arrows to make connections between ideas. By giving herself plenty of room, she can add any connections revealed later in the lecture. If her instructor reviews the material before an exam, Laura highlights what she already has and adds notes in the spaces. See Exhibit 6.2 for an example of Laura's notes.

One strategy Laura developed to help with her learning disability is that she doesn't worry about spelling. To make connections between ideas, she draws lines between words that relate to each other. She also makes charts for anything that is compared and contrasted. Finally, she keeps all of her notes in a binder that is divided for each class. Staying organized is an important part of her method. Although she uses only one binder during the semester, she keeps her notes organized by removing them after an exam. When she removes notes she no longer needs, she places them in labeled folders at home. She carries with her only the notes she needs at that time.

A Note on Note Takers

There may be a time when you have to rely on someone to take notes for you, or you may have a learning or physical disability that requires someone to take notes for you all semester. Student or professional note takers help unique learners and students with a disability receive the same education opportunities as others. Whether you depend on someone every once in a while or for the duration of your education, the following are some things you should consider:

- If possible, review the note taker's notes with the note taker or other classmates. Because the physical act of taking notes helps students remember information, you should find other ways to reinforce the material.

- Stay focused when you are in class. Find ways to help you remember the material such as creating visual maps or scenes in your mind.

EXHIBIT 6.2 *Laura's notes.*

Jewish Beliefs—Monotheism (1st)

Ancient — Jehovah

Jews divided — all humanity
Strictly-segregated

We (Jews) — They (Gentiles)

We (Jews)	They (Gentiles)
No outside conversion	non-Jewish
convenant with God	place on earth
↓	↓
chosen people	Tempters & obstacles
family-most important	
↓	Sacred text
society revolved around	Old Testament
Patriarchal male-dominant	
↓	Jehovah (Yahweh)
more rights	share-Christianity concepts (similar)
(+) marriage-lineage	(1) Fall of man from grace
(−) bachelor-frowned	(2) Day of judgment
male married by 24	(3) Immortality
prefer 20	(4) 1 God (worship)
Female-13 can marry	
↓	
more children	

- Prepare for class beforehand. Because you won't be taking notes, preparation is critical.

- Don't take your note taker for granted by missing class or not preparing. The note taker is not a surrogate student, she is only a supplement.

- If your note taker's notes are difficult to read, incomplete, or missing because he does not attend regularly, talk to the disability services counselor. She can arrange for a new note taker.

Critical Thinking PLUS*

Consider how understanding your personality style or learning preference can help you through challenging situations.

You are taking a chemistry class and your learning style strength is aural. The professor, however, relies on diagrams, drawings, and hands-on experiments to demonstrate concepts and processes. You are having trouble understanding the material, and it is only the third week of class. You spoke to your professor about your trouble, but because you are shy, you weren't completely honest about how frustrated and stressed you are. In fact, when you met with your professor, she suggested that you come by during office hours and go through the experiments again and again until the material sinks in. What should you do when you meet with her during office hours the next time?

*PERSONALITY + LEARNING STYLE = UNDERSTANDING SITUATIONS

Reviewing Your Notes

Notes are only as good as the extent to which you review them. If you never look at your notes after taking them, then they serve little purpose. Therefore, to make the most out of your notes, you must review them. As stated earlier, reviewing should be done within two days from the time you took them. With this said, it is easy to be lulled into a sense of "studying" by merely reading your notes again and again. When reviewing your notes, it is best to reorganize the material, make connections between concepts—even across disciplines—and ask questions about what you are learning.

If you use the Cornell System, then you have a built-in area for adding more information, summarizing, and asking questions. If you do not use a particular method, you can still benefit from filling in any blanks or holes in your notes with information you have since learned. As stated earlier, spell out any abbreviations that may cause confusion later. After filling in any gaps, you should include questions—either on the same page or a new page—to help you think about the material on a deeper level. For example, asking "Why is it important to know this?" helps you move beyond demonstrating your comprehension of the material to making it relevant and useful.

Freewriting about the material you learned is another way of remembering and understanding the information. This technique is often used as a way to generate ideas for writing, but it can also be used to take advantage of all the thoughts you have about the material. For optimum effectiveness, freewrite within a day or two of the class lecture. With or without your notes, write down (or type into a word processor) all the information you remember from the class.

The key to freewriting is continuation—do not stop writing even if you can't spell a certain word or get stuck on a particular idea. Give yourself 5 or 10 minutes to freewrite; then, go through your freewriting material and highlight or rewrite into complete sentences the information that pertains to the lecture. In essence, you learn the material in depth as you write about it.

Finally, reading your notes to a friend is a useful method for reviewing material. You can do this in person or on the phone. The benefits of reading your notes aloud and discussing them include filling in any gaps in the information and reinforcing what you learned. You can also critically question the material and take turns making connections between major concepts.

Tips for Successful Note Taking

- Prepare for class by reading *all* the assigned material before arriving. If you cannot read all of it, read as much as you can.

- Prepare to listen actively by removing distractions and bringing supplies.

- Listen actively; concentrate on what you are hearing, seeing, and experiencing.

- Listen critically by asking questions, either on paper or in class if your professor encourages class questions.

- Use a note-taking strategy that takes into account both your learning style strength and the subject matter.

- Go beyond reviewing your notes by rereading them; instead, focus on concepts and main ideas, make connections between the large ideas, and ask critical questions about processes and ideas.

- Continue the process regularly throughout the semester.

Learning Styles Application

This chart lists the four learning styles and tips based on the chapter's main ideas. Locate your learning style and read the corresponding tips to maximize your success in college.

VISUAL

Visual learners need a little extra help when preparing to listen because it is not their learning style preference. Visualizing concepts and creating visual representations of notes will help you reinforce what you heard. Also, pay attention to visual clues and nonverbal communication that signal major points, important contrasting ideas, and changes in thought.

AURAL

Listening is a strength for aural learners, but it doesn't mean you can ignore other ways to "hear" what is being said. Consider nonverbal communication as well as movement and text in order to get the full lecture.

READ/WRITE

Read/write learners work on their listening skills by practicing, writing what they hear, and reading their notes aloud to someone who can fill in any missing material. As a read/write learner, pair up with an aural learner to make sure your notes are complete.

KINESTHETIC

Kinesthetic learners benefit from lectures that include movement and activity. Hand gestures and body movements are important clues to the message being sent. You can translate a speaker's activity into your notes by recording when the speaker uses his hand, for example, to underscore an important idea.

Path of Discovery

Journal Entry

Have you ever experienced a time when you did not listen? What happened and what did you learn from the experience?

FROM COLLEGE TO UNIVERSITY

Improving your listening and note-taking skills when there are more distractions

When you transfer to a four-year university, the good habits you practiced at your community college will help you succeed. However, you may find that you have more distractions. There may be more people on campus and in your classes, more organizations and associations to join, more activities to participate in, and more stress when deciding on a major and getting ready to graduate.

In addition to distractions, you may also find that professors at four-year universities lecture less and rely more on student discussion and presentations. Your ability to organize the material into coherent parts is critical to making sense of the course. If you have trouble taking good notes, talk to others who have been at the university longer than you—they may have some tips. It is also a good idea to join a study group or at least find a "study buddy" to review your notes with. Although you may have done well studying by yourself at the community college, you may now realize that group interaction and work is not only encouraged but is also necessary for success.

FROM COLLEGE TO CAREER

Practicing critical listening skills gives you an edge at work

Most of the communication you do on the job involves listening: listening to clients' urgent needs, your employer's plans for the next six months, coworkers' explanations, and subordinates' questions. Being a good listener involves practicing the critical listening tips outlined in this chapter. Why do you need to listen critically on the job? Because you will be bombarded with information at all levels: above you from your boss, at the same level as you from your coworkers, and below you from those who work for you. Critical listening skills enable you to filter what you hear so you can act appropriately and avoid making errors in action and judgment. Consider, for example, a coworker who comes to you to complain about a company policy. By not listening actively and critically, you may disregard what the speaker is saying because you don't have time to do anything about it. However, if you take the time to analyze the speaker (Is she credible?), the message (Is its purpose to vent or change something?), what you know about the situation (Is the policy flawed and in need of change?), and the larger picture (How will this proposed change affect others?), then you are more likely to act appropriately and confidently.

On the job, as in life, you will not—and should not—respond to all messages you receive the same. Practicing critical listening skills makes it easier to determine which messages are critical and which can be acted upon later, making you a more efficient and effective employee.

Chapter in Review

1. List and describe the different note-taking strategies.

2. In what situations might taking notes distract you from learning? What other methods of remembering should you employ in those situations?

3. Describe the ultimate ineffective listening scenario. In a group or individually, write a scene in which a student fails to use any kind of effective listening strategy.

4. Using the information in this chapter, create note-taking guidelines for one of your classes. Keep in mind how the nature of the class determines how you take notes and how your learning style affects your strategy.

5. Which of the note-taking methods are the most effective for you? Which are the least effective? Explain your answers.

Case Scenarios

Read the following case scenarios and determine what each person should do. Refer to the information in this chapter as you write a description and plan of action for each student.

1. Theo borrowed Jon's notes for his algebra class and promised to return them before the next exam. However, Theo lost them, and with only two days left before the next test, he is not sure what to do. Jon is a good student and probably doesn't need them very much, but Theo wants to be able to borrow future notes from Jon. What should he do?

2. Karla has a learning difficulty, and she struggles with taking notes. The counselor assigned a note taker to takes notes for her in each class. Now that Karla is getting this help, she stopped preparing for class and listening closely. Sometimes she doesn't get the notes from her note taker until a week later. If you are Karla's friend or counselor, what advice would you give her about using a note taker?

Research It Further

1. Survey the students in one of your classes as to which note-taking strategies they use the most. Create a table from your results and present it to your classmates.

2. Using the keywords "note-taking strategies," search the Internet for websites that offer note-taking guidance. Choose two or three and review the information to determine which site offers the most practical and complete tips. Present your findings to the class.

3. Create your own note-taking or listening strategy and present it to the class, highlighting the benefits of your method over another method.

7 Reading Skills

an says, "You have to do the reading" in college, and he is absolutely right. Whether you love to read or you find the activity to be a challenge, reading is an integral part of your education in college. Can you imagine getting a degree and not reading a page? Technology changed the way we read and how we incorporate written information, but it did not change the importance of reading to being educated individuals. This chapter discusses different reading strategies for sharpening your reading skills, whether you are reading books, magazines, e-books, or Web articles. More specifically, you will find answers to the following questions:

- *What is the importance of reading effectively in college?*

- *How can I break down a long reading assignment so I can comprehend it and remember what I read?*

- *What is active reading, and what is the difference between skimming and scanning?*

- *What methods can I use to sharpen my reading skills?*

COMMUNITY • COLLEGE •

Student Profile

NAME: *Ian Dillon*   AGE: *20*

MAJOR: *Architecture*

1. What, if anything, surprised you about the reading expectations in college?

   The reading requirements are much more intense. The volume is larger, and the professors expect you to actually do it. You have to do the reading.

2. What reading strategies do you use when preparing for class?

   I highlight major ideas. Then, I skim my highlights before class.

3. What advice would you give other students about college reading?

   Get the major concepts from your reading because you are held accountable for them on tests.

4. What is your VARK?

   Read/Write and Kinesthetic.

College Reading Expectations

I f death and taxes are unavoidable parts of life, then reading is an inevitable part of college and lifelong learning; fortunately, reading is more enjoyable and more profitable than death and taxes. The bottom line is that you will not be a successful student if you do not read assigned and supplemental material regularly. Likewise, it will be difficult to practice lifelong learning after college without reading on a regular basis. As mentioned in previous chapters, reading class handouts, college publications, and your textbooks is essential to success in college. The reasons that reading is important to your college education and lifelong learning are many, but here are just a few incentives for making reading an integral part of your daily college work:

- Reading provides you with basic information you can use to create knowledge of a subject.
- Reading improves your understanding of others and the world around you by exposing you to new viewpoints, ideas, and cultures.
- Reading helps you understand yourself, which helps you make better life choices.

Having said that, it must be acknowledged that some students just do not enjoy reading because of bad experiences in school or learning difficulties. Thus, for some college students, reading is a challenge to academic fulfillment. Professors would be ecstatic if all of their students read well and enjoyed the assigned reading material. Realistically, students find some reading dull and difficult to comprehend, and they long to read something "exciting." The not-so-good news is that until you get into those classes that pertain to your major or career choice, you may very well feel that the assigned reading is uninteresting—the good news is that there are ways to improve your comprehension *and* enjoyment of the reading assignments.

In addition to the different subject matter you encounter in college reading, you will also find the reading load is heavier than in high school or for your job. If you are taking 4 three-credit-hour classes, you can expect to read over 100 pages a week if each professor assigns a textbook chapter. This number does not include full-length novels, supplementary articles, required periodical subscriptions, reserved library materials, online resources, and your own notes from class—all of which may be part of your weekly reading load. The truth about college reading is that there is plenty for you to read and you are accountable for reading, comprehending, and thinking critically about the material.

Reflection

EXERCISE 7.1

Which reading skills do you already have? Which ones do you need to work on?

Companion Website

What to Do with a Reading Assignment

When you first get a reading assignment, spend a little time preparing to read to help you maximize the time you have to complete it. No doubt, the first week of classes, you will be given handouts and syllabi and assigned chapters to read in your textbook. How do you manage it all without getting behind and becoming overwhelmed? First, all written material from your professors must be read. You will be held responsible for it at some point, so create a process for reading and remembering what you read.

Regardless of the assignment size, treat it seriously—make a conscious effort to read and remember important information. A positive attitude toward the reading assignment makes the other steps easier to complete. Before you begin reading, organize the assignments according to size, importance, and date due, starting with the most important documents. A shorter assignment can be completed first unless its due date is far off.

The reading load in college is heavier than in high school.

To increase your chances of reading effectively, establish a definite time and place to read. Just as you set a time to study or go to work, schedule time to read, preferably the same time each day. Finding a comfortable, quiet area to read is also important because it puts you in the mood to focus on what you are reading. Equally important to setting a definite time is establishing routine breaks. Get up, walk around the room, get a drink of water, and get the circulation going in your legs again. Taking breaks in which you physically move around helps your concentration and keeps you from falling asleep.

In addition to finding the right place, consider setting a purpose for reading to make the assignments easier to comprehend and complete. For example, if your reading purpose is to improve your understanding of networking, then when you sit down with your computer networking textbook, you are in the right frame of mind. Conversely, if your reading purpose is to be entertained when reading a chapter in economics, you may be disappointed and less receptive to remembering what you read.

As discussed in an earlier chapter, writing down your goals is the first step to realizing them. The same is true for reading. If your goals are to increase your reading speed, vocabulary, and understanding of the material, you should do more than give them passing consideration. Set specific, concrete goals for individual assignments or the whole semester. A reading goal example might be to increase the number of pages you can read in one sitting or to learn five new words a week and use them.

Finally, take care of yourself throughout the semester as you do the assigned work. You can't read effectively if you are tired, hungry, or sick. Don't force yourself to read if physical or psychological issues distract you. Too much sugar and caffeine and too little sleep make reading more difficult, as can certain medications and emotional distractions. If you cannot concentrate, return to the material when you feel better.

Another way to prepare to read effectively is to start a reading log to help focus your reading goals. A sample reading log appears at the end of this chapter (page 189) for you to photocopy and use.

Active Reading

Active reading, a term you may hear often in college along with active listening, means that you become fully engaged in reading by focusing your mind and body on the activity. Many first-time students read passively, rather than actively, and do not fully concentrate on the material. Just reading the words is not enough for college classes. Instead, you must be a part of the process by using some or all of the following reading strategies: skimming, scanning, breaking down material, building vocabulary, taking notes, checking comprehension, and reviewing and recalling what was read. The information that follows will help you become an active reader.

Skimming and Scanning

You may already be familiar with the terms skimming and scanning as they pertain to reading. *Skimming* is reading material quickly and superficially, paying particular attention to main ideas. This activity is used when you first get a reading assignment because it helps you get a feel for what the material is, how long it is, and how difficult it will be to read. To skim a text effectively, read the first and last paragraphs, the main headings of each section, and the first and last sentences of each paragraph. Of course, if time is a factor, delete some of the steps. Ideally, skimming is done before in-depth reading; however, sometimes skimming may be the only chance you have to read the material. If this is the case, pay attention to the major headings of each section and the first and last paragraphs of the material. Don't be surprised, though, if you miss major ideas sandwiched in the middle.

Although it now has a meaning similar to skimming, scanning is a reading method that traditionally meant "examining a text closely." Nonetheless, some reading experts define *scanning* as looking quickly for a specific item or topic as you would scan a phone book for someone's name or a dictionary for a particular word. Scanning also includes examining the table of contents and index to narrow your focus and prepare you to find what you are looking for. Similar to skimming, scanning requires that your eyes move quickly over a page. However, the difference is that you know what you want to find and will slow down once you find it. Scanning is particularly useful when reviewing sources to use for a paper. You can determine rather quickly if the source pertains to your topic or not. After scanning, you then skim or read the text actively.

Breaking the Material Down

As stated earlier, part of scanning a text is examining its parts. Certain pages hold valuable information for deciphering its purpose. Students who want to "hurry up" and read the meat of the assignment often overlook some of the most important parts: The title, author, table of contents, chapter titles, introduction, section headings, headnotes, bibliography, and index are wonderful and revealing components of a piece of writing.

Title. The title of an article or book gives you a clue as to what it is about. For instance, the title to this book is *The Community College Experience* because the information in it reflects the unique needs of community college students, not students at other types of institutions of higher education. When reading any material, take time to think about the title's significance and go back to it to look for additional meaning once you complete the whole text.

Author. Who the author is can be just as important as what she has to say. Authors' reputations can lend credibility to their words or instantly make readers suspicious. If you recognize the author's name, then you should have a good idea what the text is about. The more you read, the more you encounter writings by certain people, and you will expect certain viewpoints from them.

Table of contents. Most books have a table of contents that shows how the book is organized. A table of contents lists the chapters as well as many subsections. The table of contents also contains the beginning page number for each chapter or section. Familiarize yourself with the table of contents to make it easier to find information when you need it.

Introduction. Sometimes overlooked, the introduction can provide all the information you need to determine whether a particular book is what you want. When researching a topic, you can decide whether or not a book is a good source for you by reading the introduction. Introductions typically tell the reader what the book is about, what unique features it contains, and what viewpoint is supported.

Chapter titles. Chapter titles are a good indication of what you can expect to read. They also help you locate information quickly. Can you imagine trying to find information from this text about taking notes without any chapter titles? You would have to scan each chapter until you found it.

Section headings. Section headings work the same way as chapter titles— they indicate how the material is organized and give you a sneak peek of what is to come.

Headnotes. Headnotes appear at section beginnings or before essays and explain or briefly summarize what you are about to read. Headnotes can provide biographical information about the author or indicate the essay's main points.

Bibliography. A bibliography, or list of references or works cited, usually appears at the end of an article or a book, right before the index. Literally, a bibliography is a list of books the author has read or used to prepare his text. This section of a book or article is often overlooked, but it actually contains a wealth of information for the reader. If you want to learn more about a topic the author mentions briefly, look at the bibliography to see what other books are listed about the subject. Also, if you are doing research and need instant access to a list of more sources, an author's bibliography can supply you with that information.

Index. One of the last elements of a book is its index, which is an alphabetical list of major ideas and concepts that are keyed to the pages on which they appear. If you need to find information on note taking, for instance, use the index to pinpoint the exact page where it appears. Indexes (or indices) are especially helpful when evaluating research sources for whether or not they contain material about your subject. For example, if you locate a book on African American playwrights and need some information on Lorraine Hansberry, look for her name in the index to see if she is mentioned in the book. If she is not listed, then you know the book is not a good resource for you.

Practice

EXERCISE 7.2

Read the introduction to this book if you have not already done so, and write down what you think the central theme is.

Companion
Website

You may think that breaking the material down is time consuming and unnecessary, especially if you do not have much time to spend reading anyway. Yes, at first it takes more time, but the more you do it, the less time it takes because you know what to look for. Also, your reading speed and comprehension will improve, which means you can complete your assignments quicker.

Building Your Vocabulary

Increasing your vocabulary is another benefit to reading regularly. Some students get sidelined when they read because they encounter unfamiliar words. Few students take the time to look up words they don't know and subsequently miss out on learning new ideas or understanding the author's intent. Although it is well worth your time to look up words when you read, there are some methods you can use to decrease the time you spend flipping through a dictionary.

The first method is to look for context clues in the sentence. Many times you can figure out what the word means by how it is used in a sentence or by the words that surround it. Consider the following sentence:

Students often use context clues to *decipher* the meaning of unfamiliar words.

If you didn't know that *decipher* means to figure out, you can still understand the sentence by considering that students are using something (context clues) in order to do something to (decipher) unfamiliar words. You might deduce, then, that students are making the unfamiliar words more familiar by using context clues. Now, try this sentence:

> It was not until we traveled to Beijing that we realized how *ubiquitous* American fast food is. On every street corner, we saw a McDonald's or a KFC.

If you are not familiar with modern-day Beijing, you may not know that American restaurants are plentiful. Thus, to understand the meaning of *ubiquitous*, the second sentence provides the context clues. With the phrase "On every street corner," you should realize that *ubiquitous* means *everywhere*.

Although context clues allow you to make sense of most unfamiliar words, there will be times you cannot rely on the other words to help you. For example, can you tell what the words *amenable* and *obsequious* mean in the following sentence?

> Charles was *amenable* to going out to eat with Sheila's *obsequious* mother.

In this case, if you don't know what the words mean, the sentence offers little assistance. Does Charles want to go out to eat or doesn't he? Is Sheila's mother someone who is enjoyable to be around or isn't she? To answer these questions, you may need to look the words up. Here is what you find if look them up in *Webster's New World Dictionary*:

> a·me·na·ble (əme′nəbəl) *adj.* [[<Ofr , L *minare*, to drive (animals)]] 1 responsible or answerable 2 able to be controlled; submissive—a·me′na·bil′i·ty *n.*–a·me′na·bly *adv.*

Now, look up *obsequious* for yourself and see if you can decipher the sentence.

Another way to figure out what words mean is to know some common Latin and Greek root words, prefixes, and suffixes (see Exhibit 7.1 for examples). For example, if your professor calls astrology a *pseudoscience*, and you know that the Greek root *pseudo* means false, then you can understand that your professor is claiming that astrology is not a true science. In order to learn the common roots of everyday words, study words' origins. Taking a college reading class or using a dictionary regularly will help you learn to recognize the roots in other words.

TIPS FOR BUILDING VOCABULARY

- Purchase or borrow discipline-specific dictionaries that contain a large amount of terminology (e.g., medical or scientific dictionaries, foreign language dictionaries, and glossaries for literary terms).
- Before asking your professor or classmate what a word means, look it up.
- Don't be afraid to look up words, even the same word multiple times. You will eventually recall the meanings.
- Use new words in conversation to "try them out." Using them regularly helps you remember what they mean.

EXHIBIT 7.1   *Common Latin and Greek root words.*

ROOT	MEANING	EXAMPLE WORD	DEFINITION
Ante	Before	*Antebellum*	Before the war, specifically referring to the American Civil War
Anti	Against	*Antibiotic*	Against life, specifically against microorganisms
Auto	Self	*Autobiography*	Writing about the self
Biblio/Bibl	Book	*Bibliography*	A list of books
Cede	Go, leave	*Secede*	Leave an organization or alliance
Chrono	Time	*Chronological*	Events ordered by time in which they occurred
Cogn	Know	*Recognize, cognizant*	To know from before; fully informed
Graph	Write	*Autograph*	Person's own signature
Inter	Within, between	*Intermission*	The period between performances
Phil	Love	*Philanthropy*	Love of humankind
Photo	Light	*Photography*	Producing images using light in the process
Pseudo	False	*Pseudonym*	False name

● Write a new word on a 3x5 index card along with a sentence using the word. Look up the definition when you have time and add it to the card. Take the cards with you and review your new words while waiting in line or stuck in traffic.

● Buy and browse a thesaurus, a book that contains synonyms for words. A thesaurus is handy when you are searching for a word that is similar to another.

● If you have an e-mail account, subscribe to a word-a-day service that sends you a new vocabulary word each day, or buy a word-a-day calendar.

● Subscribe to magazines that challenge your reading skills: *The Atlantic Monthly*, *The New Yorker*, and *Harper's* are examples of print magazines that contain interesting and challenging material.

Practice

EXERCISE 7.3

Rewrite the sentence on page 179 using synonyms for the words *amenable* and *obsequious*.

Companion
Website

Taking Notes While You Read

If it is not too distracting, take notes as you read, either in the textbook or a notebook. Writing down any key ideas, terms to look up later, and questions you have as you read is an excellent way to stay focused and improve comprehension—taking notes helps you remember what you read.

Questions to consider and answer as you read include the following:

- What is the reading's main idea?
- How would I summarize the main idea of each paragraph in two or three words?

ACTIVITY *Calculate Your Reading Speed*

Knowing how quickly you read is helpful when planning reading time and marking your progress. The goal is to increase your speed *and* your comprehension. To calculate your reading speed, time yourself while you read the following article from *The Chronicle of Higher Education.**

COMMUNITY-COLLEGE STUDENTS' REASONS FOR DROPPING OUT ARE FAMILIAR ONES, STUDY FINDS

David Glenn

Community-college students drop out at much higher rates than do students in four-year colleges, but for similar reasons, according to an ambitious new study that was described here on Tuesday at the annual meeting of the American Sociological Association.

The study's central finding—that the dynamics of dropping out of community colleges and four-year colleges are essentially the same—might not sound like heart-stopping news. But the study's author said that her work should dispel any suspicions that community-college students are so different from their four-year counterparts—in age, ability, and life circumstances—that the traditional explanations for dropping out don't apply to them.

Indeed, community colleges probably should follow some of the same dropout-combating advice that has been given to four-year colleges during the past decade, said the author, Regina Deil-Amen, an assistant professor of education at Pennsylvania State University at University Park. In particular, Ms. Deil-Amen said, community colleges should pay attention to their students' levels of academic integration (how frequently they interact outside of class with teachers, librarians, and other staff members) and social integration (their participation in campus clubs and friendship networks).

The terms "academic integration" and "social integration" derive from the work of Vincent Tinto, a professor of education at Syracuse University who during the 1970s developed a widely-used model of how students decide to drop out. Students who face identical intellectual and financial obstacles can vary widely in their propensity to drop out, Mr. Tinto observed—and the difference often has to do with how well students believe that they fit at a particular college.

Many recent studies have empirically supported Mr. Tinto's basic insights, Ms. Deil-Amen said, but few of them have looked specifically at the community-college context. In her project, Ms. Deil-Amen drew on a large-scale federal research project known as the Beginning Postsecondary Longitudinal Study, which followed students who first enrolled in college in 1995. From that study, Ms. Deil-Amen took data concerning 3,300 students who entered four-year institutions and 3,600 students who entered community colleges.

Ms. Deil-Amen's analysis found that, among community-college students, "participation in clubs or arts activities, study groups, and frequent interaction with faculty and advisers outside of class were all significantly negatively associated with dropout." This appeared to be true even for students who attended part-time, who had low grades, who had children, and who worked many hours outside of college.

Participating in study groups turned out to be one of the most powerful variables in Ms. Deil-Amen's analysis. All else being equal, joining study groups appeared to reduce a community-college student's odds of dropping out by approximately 28 percent.

Among four-year students, study groups had no statistically significant effect. That was one of the few strong differences Ms. Deil-Amen found between the two groups.

Along with her quantitative analysis, Ms. Deil-Amen conducted detailed interviews with community-college students and dropouts in the Chicago area. In her paper—titled "Do Traditional Models of College Dropout Apply to Non-Traditional Students at Non-Traditional Colleges?"—Ms. Deil-Amen quotes one of those students on the value of study groups and social networks: "When you doubt yourself, your intelligence, everything . . . you feel as though you can't make it, you're not going to make it, it's a horrible feeling. . . . When you find a student who says, 'Yes, I know what you're talking about. Yes, I have that same problem'—even if she's never solved it and you're still experiencing add it, you're not alone anymore."

This article is 580 words long. To calculate your reading speed, divide the number of minutes it took to read the passage into 580. For example, if it took you 2.5 minutes to complete the passage, then you read at a rate of 175 (580/2.5) words per minute.

Number of words	580	580/ ___ (number of minutes) = ___ WPM
Number of minutes	___	

Average readers read between 200 and 250 words per minute, but that does not reflect their comprehension of the material. Techniques for improving speed are worth learning and practicing. Your college may offer a speed reading class, or you may be able to read about methods for improving speed through books or websites.

Practice

EXERCISE 7.4

Without referring to the article, answer the following questions:

- What is the article's main idea?

- What do the terms *academic integration* and *social integration* mean?

- According to the article, what is the one overwhelmingly consistent factor in the retention of community college students?

Companion Website

Checking Your Comprehension

The most important aspect of reading is comprehending and remembering what you read. If your textbook has questions after each chapter to help you reinforce what you learn, get in the habit of answering them when you finish a reading assignment. Even mentally answering the questions helps you understand the material. If your textbook does not have questions, create your own or write a short chapter summary. To reinforce what you learn, trade summaries with a classmate.

A high reading speed means very little if you do not remember anything you read. Your goal is to improve your reading speed to help you keep up with the reading demands of college and to improve your retention and comprehension of the material.

Reading in the Disciplines

he following are strategies for reading in the disciplines you may encounter in college.

Math. Take your time to read the written information and explanations as well as the visual representations of problems and steps to solving them. Reading assigned chapters *before* you get to class helps you check your reading comprehension.

Literature. You may find you have more reading in literature classes—novels, short stories, plays, and poetry. Start early on these long reading assignments, and take notes along the way. Depending on the literature's complexity, you may have to read it a few times, especially poetry. Sounding out individual words, or subvocalization (see the Reading Difficulties section in this chapter), is often considered a reading difficulty, but it may be necessary to slow down and read short pieces of literature aloud. Also, pay attention to details when reading fiction and poetry.

Languages. The goal of reading in a foreign language is to improve your comprehension. Use a dictionary the first time you encounter new vocabulary and work on improving your speed.

Sciences. Reading in the sciences takes time and focus as you encounter new concepts and processes. Look for visual representations of the content in your textbook.

Social Sciences. Large amounts of assigned material are part of any social science class. Start reading early and look for key ideas. People and their theories or their actions (in history) are key components of the reading. Learning the who, what, when, and where of the material makes it easier to remember.

INTEGRITY MATTERS

One definition of integrity is doing what you say you will do even in the face of adversity. Acting with integrity in college includes making a commitment to complete reading assignments in all your classes even if you face challenges. Reading in college is not optional; rather, it is crucial to success. When you make the commitment to enroll in college, you must also follow through and tackle the reading that is part of the experience.

Improving Your Reading Attention Span

Each semester gets more demanding in terms of reading because you are advancing in your degree program and are encountering new, more challenging content. Therefore, the more practice you have reading effectively, the easier it is to complete larger reading assignments. If you find that your reading attention span is not long, then work on lengthening it.

First, determine how many pages you can comfortably read without getting distracted or tired. Record the number in your reading log, a notebook, or a calendar. Each time you read an assignment, note how many pages it is. See if you can "beat" the number from the previous reading session. The more you read and the more you challenge yourself with reading, the better you will get. Just be patient.

Thinking Critically When Reading

In addition to all you learned about preparing to read and improving your reading skills, you must also consider reading critically. As stated earlier, critical thinking is required in college classes. Your instructors not only want to impart basic information to you through the lectures, class discussions, and assigned readings, but they also want you to think critically about the information in order to add to your understanding of yourself and the world around you. It is not enough to know that Lincoln's Emancipation Proclamation was delivered on September 22, 1862; instead, you should think critically about

Taking notes while reading will help you remember, understand, and think critically about the text.

why the speech was given, the effect the speech had on its audience, and the far-reaching implications of its message long after it was given.

How can you begin to think more critically about your reading? First, make sure that you understand what you are reading. Improving your vocabulary and reading comprehension is essential in understanding the material. Second, get comfortable taking notes whenever you read. Writing in the margins or a designated notebook is the foundation for remembering what you read so you can think critically about it.

The next logical step is to question what you read. Reading critically means that you question everything from the author's background and expertise to the information she presents and how she organizes it. You may think that published authors are always right—or they wouldn't be published—so you may find questioning an authority on a subject uncomfortable at first. "Who am I to say this person is wrong?" may be a question that runs through your head as you begin to read and think critically. The answer is that you are the perfect person to question the author because you are his audience, the person for whom he is writing. If you have questions about his ideas, then others may as well.

The following are some standard questions you should ask of every reading:

- Who is the author? What is her background? What makes her knowledgeable on this subject? Does she have any bias toward the subject?

- Who is the audience for this material? Are the length, vocabulary, and organization of the information appropriate for the audience?

- Are there any factual errors? Does the author misrepresent information or oversimplify it?

- Does the author say anything that seems confusing?

- Do the author's examples support her overall point? If not, which ones do not? Why don't they support it?

- Does the author omit anything from the information?

- What else do you want to know about the subject?

- What questions do you have about the information that the author did not answer?

- Overall, how do you rate the reading?

When you first start thinking critically about your assigned readings, answer as many of these questions as you can. You don't have to answer all of them each time you read, but the more you read with a critical eye, the more questions you will have.

The OK5R Reading Strategy

Many different reading strategies have been developed to help students read critically and effectively. What most methods share in common is a multiple-step process that involves spending time reading, writing, and thinking about the text.

EXERCISE 7.5   *Critical Thinking*

SQ3R, which stands for survey, question, read, recite, and review, is another popular reading strategy. Compare these five steps with those of the OK5R method and determine which method might be easier for you to use.

Companion
Website

Devised by Dr. Walter Pauk (1984), the OK5R method divides the process into seven steps—notice that actually reading the text is in the middle.*

- *(O) Overview:* Chapter by chapter, look at the titles, headings within the chapters, and the subheadings. This sampling gives you an idea of the book's overall emphasis. According to Pauk, there is no need to read whole paragraphs; instead, "taste" the text.

    - *(K) Key Ideas:* To find the key ideas, read the beginnings and endings of each chapter. You should have a good grasp of the key ideas from your overview.

    - *(R1) Read:* Now, read your text more closely, stopping frequently to ask yourself how each paragraph, with its details, supports the book's main idea.

    - *(R2) Record:* For each paragraph or page, write a one- or two-word summary of the key ideas. Mark any sentences or words that do not make sense, and note any questions you have.

- *(R3) Recite:* To improve your ability to remember the material, stop to recite, or say aloud, what you learned. Do not look at the book or your notes when reciting. When you are finished, check your notes and the book to see how well you remembered what you read.

- *(R4) Review:* Look back over your notes and see if you can fit all the "jigsaw" pieces, as Pauk refers to them, of ideas together into one picture. Review your notes soon after you read and make a point to review them later.

- *(R5) Reflect:* Take some time after you read to think about how the ideas fit into your life. The more you understand how your life is affected by the main ideas, the more likely you will remember the reading and create knowledge from it.

Putting the Pleasure Back into Reading

One of the most difficult reading obstacles every college student faces, no matter how well he reads, is generating interest in the material. A common student complaint is that the reading is boring. True, some college material is dry and dull, but you can change how the reading affects you by changing your attitude about the reading itself. Sometimes, you just need to trick yourself into enjoying what you read, and one way to do that is to tell yourself that you will learn something new and useful.

*From W. Pauk, *How to Study in College*, Third Edition. Copyright © 1984 by Houghton Mifflin Company, p. 192. Used with permission.

Reflection

EXERCISE 7.6

What do you enjoy about reading? What kinds of writing do you like to read and why?

Companion Website

Another way to put pleasure back into reading is to seek out pleasurable reading yourself. If you have favorite authors or types of writing, go to a bookstore or library and get a copy of a book or magazine that may spark your interest. Make an effort to find reading material that is interesting, stimulating, and even fun. Reading or browsing through a magazine or newspaper each week helps your reading skills. A habit of reading also makes it easier to stick to the schedule you set for reading class material. If you have a good book waiting, it serves as a reward for completing those less exciting reading assignments. Once you develop good reading habits, you will find yourself reading—and enjoying it—even after classes are over. You will soon discover you have a curiosity to learn new things and reading will satisfy your thirst for knowledge.

Collaboration

EXERCISE 7.7

Working in a group, create criteria for good college reading material. What do you think is essential to hold the interest of a college reader?

Companion Website

Reading Difficulties

For some students, no matter how much they want to read well, the activity is difficult. Having to deal with reading difficulties makes a short reading assignment seem like climbing Mount Everest and makes it hard to stay motivated. This section describes some common reading difficulties students experience. It is not intended as a comprehensive list, nor is it intended as a diagnosis of problems you may experience. If you think you may have a reading difficulty or a learning disability, see your college counselor for a proper diagnosis. Your college's counseling services can also provide you with resources to help alleviate any problems you have because of a learning difficulty.

Some reading difficulties are more bad habits than disorders. Subvocalization, or pronouncing each word in your mind as you read, is one type of bad habit that some readers experience. Reading the same words or sentences over and over again, or regression, is another. Improving your reading speed, or the rate at which your eyes move across the page, often eliminates the reading habits that slow you down. Moving a finger, pen, or pencil across the page as you read slows down your reading speed. Unless you are stopping to take notes along the way, eliminate the use of an instrument to keep your eyes moving. Finally, poor concentration negatively affects how quickly you read. In some cases, poor concentration is part of a larger issue that may be diagnosed by a health professional. If poor concentration is just a bad habit, work toward improving it by eliminating distractions and following the suggestions outlined in this chapter.

Reflection

EXERCISE 7.8

What, if any, reading difficulties have you had? What did you do to overcome them?

Companion Website

Critical Thinking PLUS*

Consider how understanding your personality style or learning preference can help you through challenging situations.

You have right-brain and aural learning style preferences and a large reading load this semester. In your economics class, you will read over 800 pages during the semester. You also have four novels to read in your American literature class, and a biology textbook and lab manual for your biology class. You don't consider yourself a strong reader because it often takes you a long time to complete even short assignments. You love to listen to mystery novels on tape, but when it comes to reading through textbooks that contain unfamiliar terminology and abstract concepts, you are discouraged. What can you do to successfully complete the reading assignments and improve your reading skills?

NOTES

*PERSONALITY + LEARNING STYLE = UNDERSTANDING SITUATIONS

Dyslexia is a neurological disorder that makes it difficult for people to comprehend and recognize written words; they may also have trouble writing and spelling. According to the International Dyslexia Association, (2004), 15–20 percent of all students are dyslexics and most dyslexics have average or above-average intelligence. The good news about dyslexia is that many · students learn to cope with the disorder and succeed in college and careers.

Attention deficit disorder (ADD) and attention deficit hyperactivity disorder (ADHD) are behavioral disorders in which a person has difficulty paying attention. Reading becomes just another obstacle that someone with ADD or ADHD must overcome. To work through any difficulties that ADD/ADHD may cause, contact your counseling center. As with dyslexia, ADD/ADHD can be managed so that your reading skills get sharper.

Some reading difficulties are actually the result of vision problems. A regular eye exam can determine if your difficulties are caused by the need for corrective glasses or contacts. If you think your eyes are the reason you have trouble reading words, get your eyes checked by a doctor. You may want to stop first at your college's health clinic, if one is available, for a screening. Also, take advantage of any health fairs offered on your campus where you can get a free screening that may pinpoint the problem.

Reading Log

Title of text or chapter _____

Number of pages _____

Author _____

Class _____

Instructor _____

Date reading should be completed _____

Estimated time to complete _____

Reading goals _____

Actual time to complete _____

Reading goals achieved   YES   NO

Skimmed   YES   NO   PARTIALLY

What is the reading about?

What did I learn from the reading?

What questions do I still have about the reading?

What difficulties, if any, did I have while reading?

New Vocabulary Words

_____   _____   _____

_____   _____   _____

_____   _____   _____

_____   _____   _____

Learning Styles Application

This chart lists the four learning styles and tips based on the chapter's main ideas. Locate your learning style and read the corresponding tips to maximize your success in college.

VISUAL

Students with visual learning preferences often find reading a stimulating activity because it involves visual processes. You may also appreciate diagrams and drawings that represent key concepts.

AURAL

Those with aural learning preferences may benefit from reading some material aloud, especially material that requires you to slow down and pay attention to detail. One word of caution: subvocalization can slow reading speed, which may inhibit you from reading large amounts of material in a short amount of time.

READ/WRITE

Students with read/write learning preferences often enjoy taking in information in a written format. You may find it easier to remember what you read by taking notes as you read.

KINESTHETIC

Students who prefer to learn kinesthetically may need to work through processes and problems in order to grasp the material. You will retain what you read if you incorporate some movement during the reading process.

Path of Discovery

Journal Entry

How do you plan to improve your reading skills in college?

What do you hope reading well will do for you?

FROM COLLEGE TO UNIVERSITY

How the reading load and expectations will change

You may have noticed that with each chapter's discussion of college to university, the demands become greater—the reading expectations are no exception. The reading load will increase significantly—you may find you have hundreds of pages to read and comprehend each week. You may also find you are expected to do more than just recall the information. You have to think critically about the reading by asking questions of the author and of yourself. Professors in upper-level classes require you to discuss the readings in class, and the discussion will move beyond the reading's content to the formulation of new ideas and opinions about the topic. The more you can contribute, the more you will learn from the reading and the class.

FROM COLLEGE TO CAREER

How reading skills help you succeed

There are very few, if any, careers that do not require some level of reading—jobs in computer programming and networking require constant reading to stay on top of new developments and trends in the field, as do industrial careers that require you stay abreast of the latest regulations and laws. No matter how hard you try, there is just no escaping a career that requires reading.

The good news is that after completing your certificate or degree, you will be a better reader and will understand the importance of reading regularly. A better vocabulary, an improved reading comprehension, and a faster reading speed will help you do your job better. An employee who reads well is an asset to a company because she is usually more attuned to the latest trends and ideas. An employee who reads effectively also knows what is happening in the company and can handle challenges more efficiently.

Chapter in Review

1. Which reading skills are essential to success in college?
2. What, if any, reading difficulties have you had? What did you do to overcome them?
3. What do you enjoy about reading? What kinds of writing do you like to read and why?
4. How do you evaluate a text?

Case Scenarios

Read the following case scenarios and determine what each person should do. Refer to the information in this chapter as you write a description and plan of action for each student.

1. Daicki hates to read, and he will do anything to keep from reading in college. He does, though, like to read home improvement magazines. He is working on his associate of arts degree. What can he do to read, read well, and enjoy reading?

2. Meghan thinks she may have a reading difficulty, but she has never been diagnosed. Instead, she works extra hard to keep up with and understand her reading assignments. However, as her classes get more difficult, she worries that she won't be able to keep up. What can she do to stay on top of her reading assignments?

3. Wilson can't remember anything he reads for class, even though he reads for hours the night before. He also has difficulty remembering what words mean. Although he is building his vocabulary slowly, he still finds himself looking the same word up several times before he can remember. What should he do?

Research It Further

1. Interview three people about their reading habits and preferences. Find out what kinds of reading they do for their job and what kinds of reading strategies they use to complete the reading. Also, ask if they read for pleasure and what types of reading they enjoy most. Write down your findings and present them to your class.
2. The National Adult Literacy Survey (Kirsch, et al., 2004) found that over 40 percent of Americans are functionally illiterate, which means they can function in society but cannot perform complicated reading tasks. Most of these Americans are at a disadvantage socially and economically.

Do your own research as to what challenges people who cannot read or cannot read well face.

3. Create a survey that asks members of the campus community what can be done to encourage students to read more. For example, are they willing to participate in a book club or host a local author on campus?

References

Glenn, D. (2005)."Community-college students' reasons for dropping out are familiar ones, study finds." *The Chronicle of Higher Education*, August 17, 2005. Retrieved August 22, 2005, from http://chronicle.com/temp/email.php?id=fowli7bl7ngbg247gi98ku57kxkareq2.

International Dyslexia Association. (2004). "Dyslexia basics." Retrieved May 18, 2004, from www.interdys.org.

Kirsch, I.S. (2004). "Executive summary of adult literacy in America: A first look at the results of the national adult literacy survey." National Center for Education Statistics. Retrieved March 13, 2004, from http://nces.ed.gov//naal/resources/execsumm.asp#econ.

Pauk, W. (1984). *How to study in college* (3rd ed.). Boston: Houghton Mifflin.

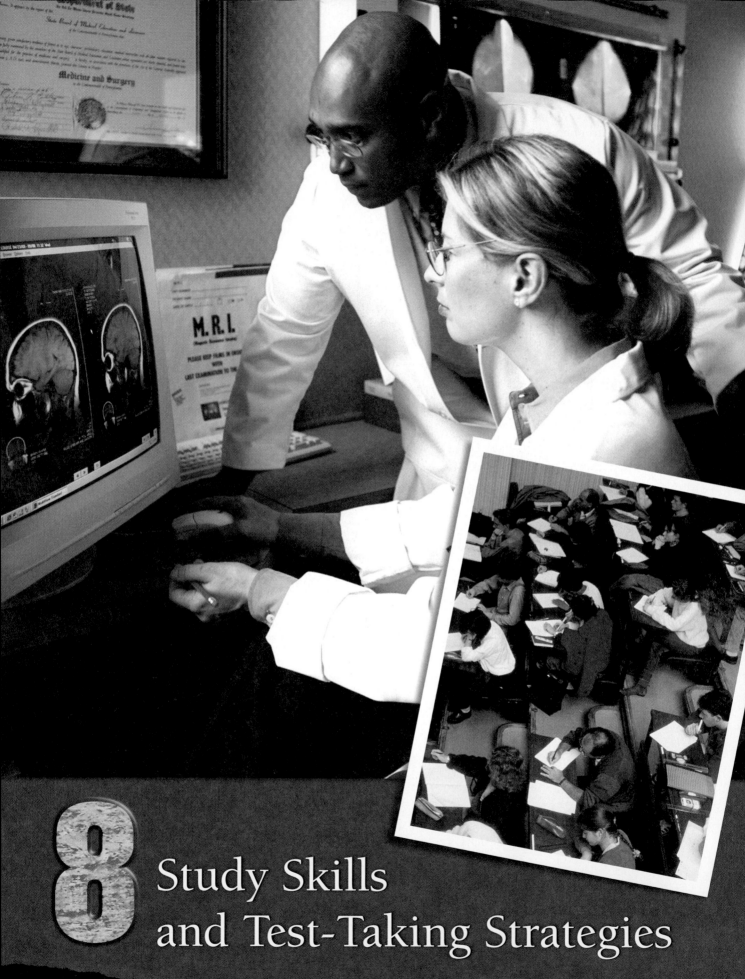

8 Study Skills and Test-Taking Strategies

tudying and school share more than the letter "s." For some students, the words invoke both fear and anxiety when spoken in the same sentence. Although going to college and studying do go hand in hand, studying doesn't have to be a dreaded activity. In fact, you may learn to look forward to studying, especially as you take classes that interest you and apply to your career. This chapter's purpose is to help you improve your study skills, which will in turn help improve your test-taking strategies. No matter what you have heard, successful students study frequently and effectively. If you have never been "good" at studying, you can improve by following the steps that work best for you.

This chapter provides you with study strategies and tips for making the test-taking process easier. Specifically, this chapter addresses the following questions:

- How much time and effort should I spend studying?
- How do I make studying in groups worth my time?
- What tips are there for improving the outcome of studying?
- What kinds of test questions will I encounter and how can I best answer them?
- What are the best strategies for taking tests?

COMMUNITY · COLLEGE ·

Student Profile

NAME: *Jacob*　　　　　　　　AGE: *23*

MAJOR: *Undecided*

1. What study skills do you use?

   I take good notes, read the chapters, and participate in study groups.

2. What are your most effective test-taking strategies?

   Read everything—notes, chapters, answers in the back of the book.

3. What advice would you give a fellow student who is having trouble taking tests?

   Study hard and do not try to learn everything the night before.

4. What is your VARK?

   Multimodal.

How Much Time Should You Spend Studying?

How much time should you devote to studying? For first-time students, this question is hard to answer because they have not experienced the rigors of college classes before. Many first-time students seriously underestimate the amount of time needed to study for a class. As discussed in an earlier chapter, a common formula used to teach students how to predict the amount of study time is to spend three hours studying for each hour you are in class each week. For example, for a class that carries three credit hours and meets three times a week for one hour, you should study 9 hours a week. Now, if you add 40 hours of work on the job to 12 hours of schoolwork and class, you get 52 hours that you are working, either for your job or your classes.

Exhibit 8.1, a sample weekly calendar of someone who works a typical 40-hour week and spends 10 hours in class each week, will help you better understand how much of your time should be spent studying.

Given the schedule shown in Exhibit 8.1, will this student be able to reach the 48 hours of study needed for her college classes? In order to reach 48 hours, this student would need to study at least 5 hours each day during the week and 11 hours on Saturday and Sunday. In other words, every waking moment that she is not at work, in class, or taking care of herself and her other responsibilities, she should be preparing for class, completing homework, writing papers, and studying for exams. If she could not devote that much time to her college classes, she would need to take fewer classes, ask for help with home responsibilities, or cut back on her hours at work.

Many students opt to cut back on studying because other activities, such as running errands, exercising, and socializing, are necessary parts of their lives. Although you may be able to reduce your study time for a few classes, that won't be possible for most classes. Taking college classes is a tremendous time commitment and you have to work in your other responsibilities (except maintaining your health) as best you can. To be successful in college, you have to make a conscious effort to put studying near the top of your priority list most of the time.

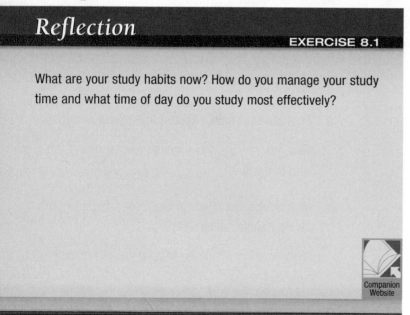

Reflection

EXERCISE 8.1

What are your study habits now? How do you manage your study time and what time of day do you study most effectively?

Companion
Website

When and Where Should You Study?

The best time to begin studying is when the semester starts and you have notes to review. Even though you are not in class every day, you have to study every day. Studying the night or day before an exam may be too

EXHIBIT 8.1   *Sample weekly calendar.*

MONDAY	TUESDAY	WEDNESDAY	THURSDAY	FRIDAY	SATURDAY	SUNDAY
6:30–7:30 Get ready	6:30–7:30 Get ready	6:30–7:30 Get ready	6:30–7:30 Get ready	6:30–7:30 Get ready	7:00–10:00 Clean house, shop	7:00–10:00 Study
7:30–7:45 Travel	7:30–7:45 Travel	7:30–7:45 Travel	7:30–7:45 Travel	7:30–7:45 Travel	10:00–11:30 Soccer	10:00–11:00 Church
8:00–12:30 Work	8:00–12:30 Work	8:00–12:30 Work	8:00–12:30 Work	8:00–12:30 Work	11:30–12:15 Lunch w/ team	11:15–12:30 Lunch w/ parents
12:30–1:15 Lunch, errands	12:30–1:15 Doctor's appointment	12:30–1:15 Lunch w/ friend	12:30–1:15 Lunch, walk 1 mile	12:30–1:15 Lunch, study	12:15–2:00 Errands	12:45–3:45 Study
1:15–4:45 Work	1:15–4:45 Work	1:15–4:45 Work	1:15–4:45 Work	1:15–4:45 Work	2:00–6:00 Library, do research	3:45–5:45 Yard work
4:45–5:00 Travel	4:45–5:00 Travel	4:45–5:00 Travel	4:45–5:00 Travel	4:45–5:00 Travel	6:00–7:00 Dinner	6:00–7:00 Dinner
5:00–5:45 Dinner, study	5:00–5:45 Dinner, study	5:00–5:45 Dinner, study	5:00–5:45 Dinner, study	5:00–7:00 Dinner w/ friends	7:00–9:00 Study	7:00–8:00 Walk 3 miles
6:00–9:00 Classes	6:00–9:00 Classes	6:00–9:00 Classes	6:00–9:00 Classes	7:00–9:30 Movie	9:00–10:00 Answer e-mail, watch TV	8:00–10:00 Laundry, get ready for next week
10:00 Bed	10:00 Bed	10:00 Bed	10:00 Bed	10:00 Bed	10:00 Bed	10:00 Bed

late to review and remember all the material covered over the past several weeks. As stated in Chapter 6, start reviewing your notes within 24 hours of taking them. If possible, you should start studying for future exams right now, today.

If you are a typical community college student, then your time is limited. You may not have the luxury of large blocks of time, so be creative about studying. Because it is more effective to study for short periods of time, you can study in between classes, during breaks at work, and on the way to work and school (provided you are not driving). One way to ensure that you study during the day is to bring notes or a book with you whenever you anticipate waiting for long periods of time. You may decide to get up earlier or stay up later to get some studying in before starting or ending your day.

If you have the luxury of choosing when you study, pay attention to the *time of day* you are most alert and receptive to learning. As you recall from

Chapter 3, the best time for you to study is dependent on your energy levels and your regular daily activities. Some people know that they are "night owls," while others claim to be "morning people." If you know when you are at your best, study your hardest subjects or most difficult concepts at that time. If you have a predictable schedule all semester, plan to study at the same time each day.

The environment in which you study is just as important as the time of day and the length of time you spend. Again, consider the kind of environment that works well for you. Some people need complete silence with no visual distractions, while others need a little background noise to stay focused. Create a place that is comfortable, has good lighting, and has space for your supplies and books. It is easier to make time to study when you have a place to do it. If you have nowhere at home that is quiet and roomy, then search for a place on campus or in a local library that offers study space. Some people find that studying away from home is better because they are not distracted by the television, phone, or family members.

If you have small children, make a concerted effort to find a quiet spot. If necessary, hire a babysitter or find a classmate who can trade child care with you when you want to study. Many college students who are also parents only have time to study when their children are asleep. Therefore, their best studying takes place late at night or early in the morning at home. Whatever works best for you is what you should do. Just remember that small children may make it difficult to find quiet time.

How to Study Effectively

Setting Study Goals

After you determine when, where, and how much you need to study, it's then time to set study and test-taking goals. Just as you learned in Chapter 2, write down the goals you want to achieve when studying or taking a test—to make it happen, you must write it down. The same is true for something as short term as studying for and taking a test. Your goals might be as simple as the following:

- I will use my time wisely so I am able to study all my notes.
- I will ask the instructor questions about any notes I do not understand.
- I will remain calm before, during, and after the exam by practicing breathing techniques and relaxing.

Of course, your goals could also be studying with a group or making a high grade. If you have never established goals for studying or taking tests, start small. Once you achieve your study and test-taking goals, create newer, more challenging ones for each test:

- I will improve my writing skills by practicing the essay questions in a timed environment.
- I will improve my overall retention of the material after the test.

Creating a Study Log

After establishing your study goals, create a study log to help you track your tests and preparation steps. Exhibit 8.2 is an example of a study log.

Understanding Course Objectives

Another step in studying effectively is to understand the course objectives. You will find the course objectives in the syllabus or other material handed out in class. If a course objective is to identify the processes of cell replication, you can be sure that you will be tested on that topic in some manner. Studying the material referenced in the course objectives helps you focus your time and energy on the right course content.

Using Time Wisely

The type of learner you are influences how much time you spend and how many sessions you schedule. You might start with studying for 45 minutes three times a day over a week to see how well you retain and remember the material. Adjust your schedule as needed. Just remember to be conscious of how effective your study sessions are. If they are not helping you meet your study goals, then change your schedule.

No matter how much time you spend studying, it won't be effective if you are unable to concentrate. Many times you will be distracted by external and internal commotion. Externally, you may have a noisy or messy house, or you may have others who need or want your time and attention. Illness, stress, self-doubt, and fear are examples of internal distractions. Both internal and external distractions make it difficult to study effectively, so you must either eliminate them or tune them out. If not, the time you spend studying will not be productive.

EXHIBIT 8.2   *Sample study log.*

Class	Chemistry
Date	Tuesday, October 27
Material	Chapters 4–7, extra lecture material
Practice/Previous Tests	In library on reserve; answer key for practice test
Question Types	Multiple-choice, problem-solving
Study Methods	Review notes, work through extra problems, go through practice test, study with group
Time Needed	6 hours
Approved Materials for Test	Paper, pencil, calculator
Number of Points	150, 15% of overall grade

For some students, planning ahead to study effectively is not an option. Because of poor time management or procrastination, these students often try to study in one long session of cramming. Cramming and marathon sessions should be avoided just before an exam because they usually produce more anxiety than learning. If you do find yourself in a situation in which you must cram, try to maximize the effectiveness of the long hours. Organize your time into short periods (no more than one hour) and take many breaks. When you return from your break, review the material you were studying before you begin new material. Try a combination of writing down what you know, drawing pictures to represent the material, reciting key concepts aloud, creating songs with the material, or building a model of a key idea. The more intelligences you use to understand the material, the better your chance of remembering it all for the test.

VARK Study Strategies

The VARK study strategies, shown in Exhibits 8.3 through 8.6, come from Neil Fleming's website www.vark-learn.com and are used with permission. Study each one and decide which learning style is closest to your own.

Study Tips, Tricks, and Skills

When it is time to sit down to study, you may think that all you have to look forward to is hours of reading, highlighting, and memorizing material—but studying does not have to be so boring. Knowing some clever tips, tricks, and skills to liven up your study sessions will help.

Mnemonic Devices

Mnemonic devices, strategies for remembering, are simple ways to recall what you learn. You may remember using mnemonic devices to help you recall steps in a process or a group of items. Although not recommended for deep concepts, mnemonic devices such as acronyms, rhymes, and acrostic sentences are good for remembering keywords or the order of steps in a process. Mnemonic devices can work in a pinch, but they are no substitute for learning the material well. Use them to start the studying process, but work toward a thorough understanding of the course content.

Visualization Strategies

Sometimes visualization strategies are lumped in with simple mnemonic devices, but they can be more complex and take more effort to create. Roman rooms are one method for storing information and recalling it when needed. This technique is useful when trying to remember a string of seemingly unrelated items or complex material that needs to be pulled together.

EXHIBIT 8.3 *Visual learning strategies.*

If you have a strong preference for **Visual (V)** learning, you should use some or all of the following:

INTAKE
To take in the information

maps
charts
graphs
symbols
diagrams
overviews
underlining
flow charts
highlighters
different colors
colorful brochures
designs, patterns, posters
textbooks with diagrams, models, maps
word pictures (e.g., "marching up the slopes")
different spatial arrangements on the page (like this list)
colorful language (e.g., "*crashing out of space,*" "*circling like vultures*")
watch and listen to teachers who use gestures and picturesque language
white space (makes the blank areas around text more significant)

SWOT (Study Without Tears)
To make a learnable package

Convert your notes into a learnable package by reducing them. Make three pages into one page using your diagrams.

Turn tables into graphs.
Draw pictures to show ideas.
Use logos, designs, WordArt®, symbols.
Read the words and convert them into diagrams.
Make complex processes and lists into flowcharts.
Redraw your newly designed pages from memory.
Replace the words with symbols, pictures, or initials.
Look at your pages. Remember their shape and format and color.
Use all the techniques above to make each study page look different.
Reconstruct the images in different ways—try different spatial arrangements on the page.

OUTPUT
To perform well in the examination

Practice turning your visuals back into words.
You still have to practice writing exam answers.
Recall the "pictures" made by your study pages.
Draw things. Use diagrams to answer the questions.
Recall the interesting and different formats of the pages you made.

You like to see the whole picture so you need some overall diagram to make sense of complex material. You like to see where you are up to. You are often swayed by the look of an object. You are interested in color, layout, and design. You are probably going to draw something.

EXHIBIT 8.4 *Aural learning strategies.*

A

If you have a strong preference for learning by **Aural (A)** and **Oral** methods (hearing and speaking), you should use some or all of the following:

INTAKE
To take in the information

use email and cellphones

explain new ideas to others

explain what happened to others

discuss topics with other students

discuss topics with your teachers

use a tape recorder so you can listen again and again

text a summary of the main points of the class to a friend

attend as many classes and teaching sessions as you can

leave spaces in your class notes for later recall and "filling"

attend discussion groups and other opportunities to share ideas with others

describe the overheads, pictures, and other visuals to somebody who was not there

remember the interesting examples, stories, and jokes that people use to explain things

SWOT (Study Without Tears)
To make a learnable package

Convert your notes into a learnable package by reducing them (three pages down to one page) into memorable ways for you to hear.

Read your summarized notes aloud.

Explain your notes to another "aural" person.

Ask others to "hear" your understanding of a topic.

Talk about your learning to others or to yourself.

Put your summarized notes onto tapes and listen to them.

Your notes may be poor because you prefer to listen rather than take notes. You will need to expand your notes by talking with others and collecting notes from the textbook.

OUTPUT
To perform well in the examination

Practice speaking your answers.

Listen to your voices and write them down.

Tune into your teachers talking about the topics.

Spend time in quiet places recalling the big ideas.

If the system allows it, choose an oral examination for your learning.

You may still have to practice writing answers to old exam questions.

Imagine you are talking with the teacher as you write your answers.

You would prefer to have this entire page explained to you. The written words are not as valuable as those you hear. You will probably go and tell somebody about this book and this chapter. You want to discuss some issues in it.

EXHIBIT 8.5 *Read/Write learning strategies.*

R

If you have a strong preference for learning by **Reading (R)** and **Writing,** you should use some or all of the following:

INTAKE
To take in the information

- lists
- notes
- essays
- reports
- contracts
- textbooks
- glossaries
- definitions
- quotations
- dictionaries
- PowerPoint©
- printed handouts
- wordy mind maps
- readings—library
- laboratory manuals
- websites and webpages
- meanings in headings
- taking class notes (verbatim)
- computer and other mechanical manuals
- listening to teachers who use words well and who have lots of information in sentences and notes

SWOT (Study Without Tears)
To make a learnable package

Convert your class notes into a learnable package by reducing them, three pages down to one page.

- Write out the words again and again.
- Read your notes (silently) again and again.
- Do the "extra" reading requested by the teacher.
- Rewrite the ideas and principles into other words.
- Organize any diagrams, graphs into statements (e.g., "The trend is . . .").
- Use a word processor to arrange your ideas and to "play" with words.
- Turn reactions, actions, diagrams, charts, and flow diagrams into words.
- Imagine your lists arranged in multiple-choice questions and distinguish each from each.

OUTPUT
To perform well in the examination

- Write exam answers.
- Re-order your lists into priority order.
- Practice with multiple-choice questions.
- Refer to publications—citing references.
- Use your word processor to prepare answers.
- Write your notes into lists (a, b, c, d; 1, 2, 3, 4).
- Write paragraphs; their beginnings and endings.
- Arrange your words into hierarchies and bullet points.
- Search the Internet for new ideas and confirmation of old ones.

> You like this page because the emphasis is on words and lists. You believe the meanings are within the words, so talk is OK, but this book is better. You are heading for the library for more books to read or you are going to write somebody about this.

EXHIBIT 8.6 *Kinesthetic learning strategies.*

K

If you have a strong preference for **Kinesthetic (K)** learning, you should use some or all of the following:

INTAKE
To take in the information:

field trips

case studies

trial and error

applied opportunities

examples of principles

do things to understand them

exhibits, samples, photographs

laboratories and practical sessions

teachers who give real-life examples

hands-on approaches (e.g., computing)

recipes, solutions to problems, previous exam papers

use all your senses—sight, touch, taste, smell, hearing

videos and pictures, especially those showing real things

National Geographic and the History Channel on television

collections of rock types, plants, shells, grasses, bones

listen for the examples—they hold the key to understanding the abstract bits

SWOT (Study Without Tears)
To make a learnable package

Convert your class notes into a learnable package by reducing them—three pages goes down to one page.

Remember the "real" things that happened.

Talk about your notes with another "K" person.

Search for the reality and the applications in any ideas.

Go back to the laboratory or your lab manual or your practical notes.

Use case studies and applications to help with principles and abstract concepts.

Find pictures and photographs that illustrate an abstract idea, theory, or principle.

Your class notes may be poor because the topics were not "concrete" or "relevant."

Recall the experiments, field trips from which you learned the applications and turned them into principles.

OUTPUT
To perform well in the examination

Role-play the exam situation in your own study room.

Put plenty of examples into your notes and your answers.

Write practice answers, paragraphs. You cannot avoid writing.

You want to experience the exam so that you can understand it.

Recall previous examinations, especially those on which you did well.

You like the ideas above because they emphasize examples and real, concrete things. You enjoy learning by doing things and trying things out for yourself. Practicing and experimenting is your way of trying things. You are probably going to try some of the ideas mentioned above to see if they really work.

Common Mnemonic Devices and Examples

Acrostic sentences. By taking the first letters of the items in a series, you can form sentences to help you remember the items and their order. For example, in music, students remember the order of the keys with the sentences "Every Good Boy Does Fine" and "All Cars Eat Gas." When remembering the planets and their order, the following sentence is useful: "My Very Elegant Mother Just Sat Upon Nine Porcupines." To recall the order of the biological groupings used in taxonomy, just remember "Kids Prefer Cheese Over Fried Green Spinach."

Acronyms. If the first letters of the items in a series spell a word, you have an *acronym*—a simple memory device. Here are a few examples of acronyms we use every day: AIDS (Acquired Immune Deficiency Syndrome), SADD (Students Against Drunk Driving), REM (Rapid Eye Movement), and SCUBA (Self-Contained Underwater Breathing Apparatus).

Rhymes. Rhymes are a little more difficult to develop than acronyms and acrostics, but you may have an easier time remembering them. Who cannot remember "Thirty days hath September . . ." and "In 1492, Columbus sailed the ocean blue"?

To create a Roman room, visualize a familiar place, such as a room in your house. If this room is connected to other rooms, then you have more "places" to put ideas. When you visualize your room, pay particular attention to details already in the room such as furniture, peeling paint, or favorite pictures. The more vivid the visualization, the easier it is to remember the items you place there.

Once you have your room memorized, add items you want to remember. For example, if you want to remember the process for writing an essay, your visualization might be something like the following:

Practice

EXERCISE 8.3

Companion Website

Create a Roman room for the reading strategy OK5R, which appears in Chapter 7. Once you visualize your room, draw a picture of it, placing the five reading strategies in the room.

> Before I even walk into my house, I see the **topic** pasted on the front door. When I open the door, I see people in my living room who will be my **audience.** I hand them the topic, which I have taken from the door, and they tell me my **purpose.** I then go to the fireplace where I light logs that have the word "ideas" on them. The flames and the smoke carry my **specific details** in them and the ashes fall to the floor. I sweep up the ashes, which are my specific details, and carry them to the dining room where I lay them out. Using paper and glue, I attach the pieces of ash to make a visible representation of the paper. The glue helps connect the pieces of ash as **transitions** connect ideas within and between sentences. When I am finished, I show my work to the audience in the living room and they tell me if they understand what I did.

Of course, depending on the complexity of the material you are studying, your room can be much more detailed; the more unusual the details, the easier it is to remember them, which should trigger the connection you made.

"Cheat" Sheets and Index Cards

Creating "cheat" sheets was once considered an activity only for those who intended to cheat; however, many educators acknowledge the benefit of creating such sheets. You may have a professor who says you can bring a 3-by-5 index card to an exam with anything you want written on it. Students who didn't study much beforehand usually jump at the chance to cram as much information as possible in that tiny white space. The result is the students retain more information than they would had they not created the cheat sheet. Many times, the cheat sheets are not needed because the student has, in effect, studied adequately.

Even if you can't bring a cheat sheet—and only do so if given permission—you can still reap the benefits of this technique by closing your books and notes and writing down as much as you can remember about the subject. For example, if you have a test on genetics, take a blank card and write everything you know about DNA on the front and back. Organization is not important unless you will be using it for an exam; what is important, however, is to see how much you have learned already. Once you fill the card, go back through your notes and books to see what you missed.

Previous Exams and Practice Tests

If allowed by the instructor, study copies of old tests. Your instructor will put them on reserve in the library, post them online, or hand them out in class. Previous exams are an excellent source of questions you will be asked. If someone offers you his old tests from the previous semester, ask your instructor first if you can study from them before taking them.

Equally beneficial to understanding how your professor will test you is to take advantage of any practice exams offered. Some instructors provide opportunities for students to take a practice exam during office hours or online.

Having a Good Time

There is no reason that studying cannot include having fun. There are books, magazines, and websites that offer games and fun quizzes to help you study. You don't have to look for games produced by others—you can create your own. Create flashcards to quiz yourself or others if you are in a study group. Or tape record questions and answers; play the question, stop the tape and answer it aloud. Then, play the answer to see how well you did. If you can push yourself to enjoy studying, you will do it more often.

Studying in Groups

One of the most underused and underrated ways to study for a class is to form a study group. A *study group* is two or more people taking the same course who get together to study the course material. The benefits of studying in groups, rather than alone, are many. First, you benefit from others' notes—both to fill in gaps in your own and to cover a class you missed. Sharing notes exposes you to the others' perspective on the subject, and you may find your classmates can explain major concepts better than the professor. Another advantage is a built-in support system. These people may become good friends during the process of studying.

Key to a successful study group is limiting the group to four or five participants. More than five participants makes it harder to remain on track. It is also best to study with people who are not close friends to minimize distractions and off-topic conversations. When choosing group members, find out what each expects from the group. You want members who will contribute and take on specific responsibilities to benefit the whole group.

Once the participants are selected, exchange contact information (cell phone numbers and e-mail addresses) and choose a leader. The leader can change from meeting to meeting, but one person should be responsible for contacting everyone to announce the time and place for the first session. The leader is responsible for keeping everyone on task and assigning roles to the members.

When the group meets, be sure that each person contributes to the study session and "teaches" the assigned part. Take breaks periodically to keep people focused. To make studying comfortable, meet in a quiet location that allows food and drink; this reduces the need for breaks for those who are hungry and thirsty. Consider taking turns bringing snacks or chipping in for pizza. Better yet, go out for a meal *after* studying—everyone then has a goal to look forward to.

Forming study groups at a community college may be hard because many students lead full lives and have little time to schedule extra activities. Their free time may not be consistent because of work or their daily family responsibilities. To make your study group work, be creative with scheduling and organizing time. For example, join a chat room or use e-mail to make assignments or quiz each other about exam material.

Another study group type consists of two people—you and a person who took the class previously. Try to find a partner who is taking a class that you

One key to a successful study group is to limit the group to four or five participants.

have finished. The information exchange helps each person learn the new material. This kind of study group is harder to form because it requires that both participants be taking a similar class schedule or degree program. However, the potential benefits make it worth trying.

GENERAL TIPS FOR STUDY GROUPS

- Start with a small group—three to five people.
- Choose a leader for each meeting.
- Keep a master list of contact information.
- Schedule a time and place that is convenient, comfortable, and conducive to studying.
- Be creative about meeting. Try doing some of the work (e.g., creating sample test questions) online using chat rooms or e-mail.
- Assign each person part of the material to "teach" the group.
- Do your homework before meeting by preparing to "teach" your material.
- Review notes with each other.
- Quiz each other over the material before leaving the meeting.
- Be respectful of others' commitments.
- Take frequent breaks.
- Stay on task.
- Meet often for shorter periods rather than in "marathon" sessions.

Studying Alone

If you can't or don't want to belong to a study group, there are still advantages to studying alone: You don't have to worry about someone slacking off or taking control of the group, scheduling conflicts, and misinformation. Because you are in control of the studying, you will receive all of the glory of doing well on exams.

Test Question Types

Learning how to take tests is just as important as learning the material. Knowing how to answer each possible type of test question makes taking an exam just that much easier; at least, your anxiety will be reduced because you know what to expect.

There are two categories of question types: objective and subjective. *Objective questions* ask you to recall facts and concepts and usually take the multiple-choice, true/false, fill-in-the-blank, and short-answer forms. *Subjective questions* ask for your opinion about the material or ask you to apply the material in a new way. Essay and problem-solving (critical thinking) questions are subjective because there are many ways to answer them correctly. Some students believe that there are no "wrong" answers to subjective questions, and that may be true, but there *are* better ways to answer them. The next sections discuss typical test questions and how to answer them.

Critical Thinking PLUS*

A self-described left-brain and read/write learner, you have three different exams on one day and only two days to study. Your algebra test will be the easiest, you think, while your history test will be the hardest. However, you really need to raise your grade in the computer concepts class. If you have two periods of 12 hours to study, how do you best divide your time? What study strategies might work best for you?

Consider how understanding your personality style or learning preference can help you through challenging situations.

*PERSONALITY + LEARNING STYLE = UNDERSTANDING SITUATIONS

Multiple-Choice Questions

Multiple-choice questions test information recall or they assess your ability to apply information or analyze situations. Despite a reputation for being easier, expect more difficult and time-consuming multiple-choice questions on college exams and don't be alarmed if the answers are not obvious.

To answer multiple-choice questions, first, read the question or statement carefully. Then, mark any special words in the question or statement such as *not*, *always*, and *only*. Before looking at the choices, try to answer the question. For example, consider the following question:

1. **What should you NOT do to alleviate anxiety when taking a test?** [Notice the word NOT and think in terms of what is not an acceptable answer.]

   a. **Arrive early for the exam.** [This is something you SHOULD do, so it is not the correct answer.]

   b. **Skip over the directions.** [This is something you should NOT do, so it may be the right answer. Lightly mark this one, but keep reading the rest of the choices.]

   c. **Pay attention to the time limit.** [This is something you SHOULD do, so it is not the correct answer.]

   d. **Read all of the questions before answering.** [Again, this is something you SHOULD do, so it is not the correct answer.]

After reading through all of the choices, it is apparent that B is the only correct answer.

Consider another multiple-choice question:

2. **When answering an essay question on a test, be sure to**
   a. **Answer each part of the question thoroughly.** [This is something you should do. Keep reading the rest of the choices.]
   b. **Organize your essay before writing it by sketching out a quick outline.** [This is something you should do. Keep reading the rest of the choices.]
   c. **Read the directions carefully.** [Again, this is something you should do. Keep reading the rest of the choices.]
   d. **All of the above.** [This seems the best choice because all of the other choices are correct.]

After reading all of the choices, D is the correct answer because A through C are correct statements.

Read each choice carefully and eliminate any that are obviously wrong. If you have to guess, eliminate any answer that has a misspelled word (usually a sign that the instructor hurriedly added false answers) or any answer that is shorter than the others. Also, pay attention to any "All of the above" and "None of the above" choices. If you determine that at least two of the choices are correct, then "All of the above" is probably the correct answer. Likewise, if at least two of the choices are not correct, then "None of the above" is probably the correct answer.

Examples of multiple-choice questions. Circle the correct choice for each question.

1. The reading strategy OK5R includes the following steps:
   a. Overview, key ideas, read, record, review, remember, and recite.
   b. Overview, key ideas, read, record, recite, review, and reflect.
   c. Overview, key concerns, read, record, review, remember, and reflect.
   d. None of the above.

2. SQ3R stands for survey, question, read, recite, and:
   a. Record
   b. Reflect
   c. Review
   d. Remember

3. The step in the OK5R process where you look back over your notes to see if you can fit all the jigsaw pieces together is called:
   a. Review
   b. Reflect
   c. Recite
   d. Remember

4. Which of the following activities describes the "Reflect" step of the OK5R reading strategy?
   a. For each paragraph or page, write a one- or two-word summary of the key ideas.
   b. Take some time after reading to think about how the ideas fit into your life.

    c. Look over your notes soon after reading.

    d. Go through the assignment and look at chapter titles, headings and subheadings.

5. Which of the following statements is the MOST accurate assessment of the SQ3R and OK5R reading strategies?

    a. Both strategies have the same number of steps.

    b. OK5R includes taking time to think about how the reading material fits into your life, while SQ3R does not.

    c. SQ3R includes questioning the text, while OK5R does not.

    d. SQ3R includes a step for getting a broad idea of what the reading will be about, while OK5R does not.

Matching Questions

A matching section presents you with two columns: a list of words or phrases that are to be matched with a list of descriptors. Matching sections usually require a basic recall of information, but read the directions *carefully*: There may be more than one match for an item or there may be extra descriptors.

    To answer matching questions, read through both lists completely. Then, answer the easiest ones first, progressing to the more difficult. Be sure you write the correct letter in the appropriate blank—check your work after you finish.

Examples of Matching Questions. Match the interests and strengths descriptions with the appropriate multiple intelligence. The multiple intelligences may be used more than once; some may not be used at all.

_____ 1. Enjoy outdoor activities	A. Verbal/linguistic
_____ 2. Know how and why they act	B. Logical/mathematical
_____ 3. Good at design, architecture	C. Visual/spatial
_____ 4. Choose careers in science, computer technology, engineering	D. Bodily/kinesthetic
_____ 5. Use voice or instruments to express themselves	E. Musical/rhythmic
_____ 6. Enjoy reading and writing	F. Interpersonal
_____ 7. Can read others' feelings well	G. Intrapersonal
_____ 8. Fascinated with pictures	H. Naturalistic

True/False Questions

True/false questions can be tough even though there are only two possible answers. Guess or randomly answer true/false questions only as a last resort. Read the statements carefully, noting keywords that could point to the correct answer—*frequently*, *sometimes*, and *a few*. These words usually indicate a true statement. Words such as *never*, *only*, and *always* usually indicate a false statement. If you have trouble answering a true/false question, don't confuse yourself worrying about how the statement is worded—go with your gut instinct. If you are not entirely sure what the statement is expressing, write down a justification for your answer on the test. Some professors give partial credit if the wrong answer is clearly justified.

Examples of true/false questions. Determine if the statements are true or false. Circle the appropriate choice.

1. Howard Gardner's theory of multiple intelligences includes the category Nutritional/Health.
   a. True
   b. False

2. OK5R is a test-taking strategy.
   a. True
   b. False

3. Priorities are beliefs shaped by experience and are not the same for everyone.
   a. True
   b. False

4. A mission statement is important because it declares your beliefs and your goals.
   a. True
   b. False

5. A priority is something that keeps you from achieving your goals.
   a. True
   b. False

Fill-in-the-Blank/Short-Answer Questions

Fill-in-the-blank and short-answer questions require you to recall definitions of key terms or items in a series. To complete these questions, read the sentence or question carefully. Often, points are lost if you don't provide an exact answer or you misspell the correct term.

Examples of fill-in-the-blank/short-answer questions.

1. The T System for taking notes is also known as the _____.

2. Abbreviating words and phrases is called _____.

3. An instructor who is difficult to understand is an example of a listening _____.

4. _____ listening includes making a decision to concentrate on what is being said.

5. _____ is a method of note taking that involves numbering items and organizing them.

Problem-Solving Questions

Problem-solving, or critical thinking, questions usually require students to demonstrate or apply the concepts or ideas they learned. To answer problem-solving questions, read the question carefully, marking any multiple steps or parts in the directions. Next, determine what information you need to solve the problem. Then, break the problem into parts and write down the process or operation you need to perform. Work through the problem, and once you arrive at an answer, check the question again to make sure your answer is adequate.

The following is an example of a problem-solving question:

Beatrice has a scholarship that requires her to maintain a 3.2 GPA while in college. During her first semester, she took four 3–credit hour courses and made two As and two Bs. Now, she is taking 1 four-hour course and 4 three-hour courses. Can she make an A in her four-hour course and Bs in her three-hour courses and still keep her scholarship?

To answer this question correctly, you have to know how to calculate a GPA. Breaking the steps down further, you have to know the definitions of grade points and quality points, and how a GPA is calculated for more than one semester. Finally, you have to know how to multiply, add, and divide. These sound like commonsense steps, but writing down every necessary operation enables you to answer the question correctly and helps you check your work.

Practice

EXERCISE 8.5

Answer the question about Beatrice's GPA. Will she be able to keep her scholarship? Show the steps you used to answer the question.

Companion Website

Examples of problem-solving questions.

1. Lenise's history class grade is determined by her scores on four exams. So far, she has a 65 and a 74. What are the lowest grades she can get to earn a C in the course? Is it possible for her to earn a B?

2. In Carlos' biology class, the final grade is comprised of the following: homework (20 percent), mid-term exam (30 percent), and final exam (50 percent). If Carlos gets an 85 on his final, a 71 on his mid-term, and a 68 for his homework, what is his final average?

3. Lester needs a 3.63 GPA to be inducted into the Phi Theta Kappa honor society. This semester, he earned two Cs, an A, and two Bs. Will he be inducted? Show your work.

Essay Questions

Instructors use essay questions to measure the students' ability to analyze, synthesize, and evaluate the concepts they learned; this question type gauges more than the students' recall of facts or terms. You will encounter more essay questions in college because they allow students to demonstrate a deeper understanding of the material.

Although you won't have a great amount of time to complete an essay (typically, 15–20 minutes), your professor still expects your answer to be thorough and clear. Always read the directions carefully. If the question has more than one part, be sure to mark each part in the body of the essay. If the

directions specify a length, be sure to meet it. Before you begin writing, create a brief outline of what you want to cover. Make a short list of transitions and details you can refer to if you get stuck during the exam.

Finally, because your professor will be reading and grading many essays, a clearly organized essay stands out and makes it easy for her to tell whether you discussed the key points. Give yourself plenty of time to write the essay and use any remaining time to proofread and edit your work.

Practice

EXERCISE 8.6

Create two sample test questions for each type described. Base your questions on material in this chapter.

Companion Website

Examples of essay questions.

1. Do you think colleges should strive, at whatever cost, to ensure that their campuses are diverse?

2. Should colleges prohibit personal and/or intimate relationships between professors and students? Support your position and refer to the college's policy regarding student–professor relationships in your essay.

3. How have your relationships at home and work changed since entering college?

Test Types

Just as important as the types of questions is the type of test you can expect in different classes; for example, a math test looks quite different from a music test. The strategies for studying for them and taking them are different. The next sections discuss only a few of the various tests you may encounter in college, but you can apply the same tips to exams in other disciplines.

Math and Science Tests

For math and science tests, it is best to first work through the problems you know. Then, tackle the problems you do not know as well. If you finish the test early, consider reworking the questions again on another sheet of paper and comparing the answers. If you discover two different answers for the same problem, determine which answer contains the error. Always show your work and complete as many parts of a multiple-part problem as possible. You may receive partial credit for doing the process correctly even if you do not arrive at the right answer.

When answering science test questions that involve processes or major concepts, draw a picture to create a visual of the process to help you answer questions about the steps. Regardless of the question types, you will be required to recall terms and definitions.

Fine Arts and Literature Tests

When taking exams for fine arts and literature classes, it is as important to explain the significance of a selected work as it is to identify key passages, authors, terms, and eras. Work through the easier questions first and save plenty of time for the written portions. Think about the major themes and the historical importance of the works and look for those themes to be part of the test questions. Although recalling facts about eras, dates, and creators is tested, there should be more emphasis on synthesizing the material.

Open-Book and Take-Home Tests

On occasion, you may be given an open-book or take-home test. Although they sound easy, professors who give open-book tests make sure you work hard to answer the questions. They may be harder than in-class, closed-book exams. Even if you know ahead of time that the test will be open-book, you still have to study for it so you don't waste time looking through your book and notes for the answers. Take-home exams are also often more difficult and time-consuming than a regular test. Your instructor expects more when he allows you to take the test home. Because the expectations are higher, give yourself plenty of time to formulate your answers and check your work. Even though the exam is unsupervised and you may be expected to use a variety of resources, you must still maintain integrity. Unless you receive permission from your instructor, do not accept or give help.

Online Tests

As discussed in Chapter 4, whether you take an online class or not, you may be required to take a quiz or test through an online learning system or through a website, such as a publisher's site that supports your textbook. Online tests are usually timed, which means you must be aware of how much time is left after you answer each question. Instructors often place a time limit on online exams to discourage students from reviewing notes, using the text, or surfing the Internet for answers. If your professor provides a practice test, consider taking it so you get a feel for how much time it takes and what types of questions are included. Additional considerations include reviewing the questions, if possible, to ensure you have not chosen the wrong answer for a multiple-choice question; saving your answers before submitting your exam; and not sharing exam information with other students who have not taken it yet.

EXERCISE 8.7   *Collaboration*

Working in a group, brainstorm a list of tips to help students study and effectively take tests. Divide your tips into visual, aural, read/write, and kinesthetic categories.

Companion Website

General Test-Taking Strategies

Preparing for the Exam

Before you can begin to think about a test and how you should study, you must make sure you are taking care of yourself. Eating and sleeping are fundamental to doing well on tests. If you are not healthy, you cannot perform at your highest level. Just as athletes prepare in advance by eating carbohydrates and resting, you should focus on getting regular sleep

and eating well days before the exam. At the least, get a good night's rest the night before and avoid refined sugar (e.g., candy, cakes, and cookies) and caffeine. For more specific information on staying healthy, see Chapter 12.

Maintaining a good attitude as you prepare for the exam is an effective strategy. Monitor and eliminate any negative self-talk about your ability to do well. Instead, visualize yourself taking the test successfully and earning a good grade.

Reflection

EXERCISE 8.8

What common health mistakes do students sometimes make before tests?

Companion
Website

Taking the Exam

If you properly prepare for the exam, both physically and mentally, you should be ready to take it. Before leaving for class, be sure you have the appropriate supplies: Do you need a watch, paper, pen, pencil, a calculator, or a dictionary and thesaurus? Are there any approved test-taking aids you should bring as well? Can you use your textbook or a cheat sheet with formulas on it? Once you arrive in class, sit away from distractions where you feel comfortable. If you are not wearing a watch, sit somewhere you can see a clock. When taking tests that use a Scantron or bubble form in which you mark your answers by filling in circles, be sure to bring at least two sharpened pencils.

When you first get the exam, read through all of the questions, noting which will take longer to answer. Taking the time to read all of the questions is actually a time-saver because you then know what to expect and can pace yourself. Turn the paper over and check the back—it may be a two-sided test.

Read the directions for each section carefully and mark any special instructions. For example, in a matching section, there may be more than one match for an item; in an essay section, there may be a choice of topics. Also, be aware of how many points each section is worth. If one section is worth half of the points for the entire exam, spend half of your time on that part.

Pacing yourself during the exam is very important. Before beginning the test, determine how much time you should spend on each section based on the question types, your comfort level with the questions, and the amount of points it is worth. As a general rule, spend less than a minute on each multiple-choice and true/false question and 15 minutes or more on each essay question. For the other types, spend somewhere between one and five minutes. If you get off track and spend too much time on one section, don't panic—just work quickly and carefully on the rest of the exam.

Work the easiest questions first and mark those questions you don't know or find confusing. Don't come back to them until you finish all of the questions you can easily answer. If you are unsure of an answer, mark the question and review it before turning in your exam. If the question or problem has multiple parts, work through as many of the parts as possible. Do not leave questions unanswered. Partial answers may receive partial credit.

Finally, leave yourself 5 to 10 minutes to check your work. If you finish an exam early, always go back through to ensure that all questions are answered and all parts are completed. If there is an essay, read through your response, checking for grammatical, spelling, and punctuation errors. Initial and number each page of your essay, if appropriate. Turn in your exam with any paper you used to work problems or draft an essay.

Maintaining Integrity

You may have read about the new ways students try in order to cheat on exams or plagiarize. Advances in technology make cheating easier and make it seem widespread. Although there is no clear evidence that more students are cheating now than they did 30 years ago, there does seem to be more confusion about what constitutes cheating. For example, some professors require group presentations and project collaboration; however, very few offer guidelines on who should do what and how to doc-

ument the part each student does. In addition, collaboration on homework assignments, which was encouraged in high school, may now be prohibited in college. When in doubt about how you should complete homework or group projects, ask your instructor for specific guidelines.

Before beginning the test, determine approximately how much time you will need to spend on each section.

The integrity rules are a little clearer when taking a test. Unless otherwise stated, do not use notes, books, or classmates as references for the exam. Most instructors ask you to clear your desk of any material except paper and a pen or may ask that you move away from the nearest person. All of these requirements ensure there are no questions about the originality of your work. Other instructors are more trusting and may leave the classroom or give the class a take-home test. An instructor who allows such freedom is sending you a message about integrity: He trusts his students to act maturely, responsibly, and honestly. Violating that trust can have grave consequences because not only did the cheating student create problems for herself, but she also damaged the trust relationship for the entire class.

Act with integrity when taking an exam, whether supervised or not—do your own work and keep your work surface clear of books, papers, folders,

INTEGRITY MATTERS

According to Dr. Donald McCabe at the Center for Academic Integrity, 75 percent of college students admit to some cheating. Almost 25 percent admitted to serious cheating, while nearly 50 percent admitted to cheating in one or more instances.

Source: "CAI Research." Retrieved August 2, 2005, from www.academicintegrity.org/cai_research.asp.

cell phones, pagers, and even drink bottles. If possible, distance yourself from other students so they are less likely to cheat off you. If you are ever in doubt, however, about your actions or the exam requirements, ask your professor.

Beating Test Anxiety

All of the information in this chapter is difficult to put into practice if you have an overwhelming anxiety about taking tests. It is not unusual to experience nervousness, anxiety, and fear before or during an exam, but extreme anxiety accompanied by excessive sweating, nausea, or crying is not normal. If you experience such reactions, see a college counselor or other professional. However, if you occasionally experience mild anxiety, there are some techniques to help minimize it. Remember that some degree of nervousness is normal.

To cope with mild anxiety, use basic relaxation techniques such as deep breathing and visualizations to take the edge off. Take the time to breathe deeply whenever you feel overwhelmed. Also, visualize yourself relaxing or succeeding on a test to help you get beyond self-defeating doubt and stress.

Critical Thinking   EXERCISE 8.9

Do you procrastinate when studying? Brainstorm a list of reasons why you procrastinate, then brainstorm a list of goals you can achieve by studying.

Companion
Website

Learning Styles Application

This chart lists the four learning styles and tips based on the chapter's main ideas. Locate your learning style and read the corresponding tips to maximize your success in college.

VISUAL

As a visual learner, work through test-taking anxiety by visualizing yourself going through the exam questions and answering them successfully. You may want to use images of success to decrease test anxiety.

AURAL

Learners who learn best by hearing may be able to talk through test anxiety with a close friend or family member. Listening to soothing music is another way you can ease the stress of anticipating a difficult exam.

READ/WRITE

Read/write learners who are experiencing test anxiety can alleviate symptoms by journaling or reading something for fun rather than for studying. You may also create a studying blog that will help you channel your frustrations.

KINESTHETIC

Getting out and moving is a good way for kinesthetic learners to relieve tension from test anxiety. Deep breathing exercises and stretching will relax you as well.

Path of Discovery

Journal Entry

How do you study best for tests? How did you develop these study habits? What do you want to change, if anything, about how you prepare for an exam?

FROM COLLEGE TO UNIVERSITY

How studying and testing may differ after transfer

One of the biggest differences that community college students notice when they transfer to a four-year university is the amount of material they must read and study. The number of exams and papers seems to get fewer, but their importance to the overall course is greater. Some classes may require only one exam or paper, which means you will not know how well you did until the class is over. Your reading load will increase and the subject matter will get more technical. You may also find yourself reading a variety of material: textbooks, journal articles, lab manuals, dissertations, novels, surveys, charts, graphs, and statistics.

When you take upper-level courses, you are expected to move beyond summarizing, or retelling, the material presented in class to formulating your own opinions and ideas about the material or applying the material to new situations. Your critical thinking skills are essential to making it through these courses. Your professors expect you to have strong study skills and solid test-taking strategies.

This is not to say that university professors are cold and uncaring about your learning; instead, they are more concerned with pushing your abilities in terms of thinking and learning. If you have a solid foundation of skills and strategies, then you will be successful—just monitor your progress and make adjustments as necessary. For instance, if you have not studied with a group before, at the university, you may find that study groups are essential to cover the massive amounts of material. Your goal should be finding what works best for you and what continues to help you succeed.

FROM COLLEGE TO CAREER

Preparation counts

Just as you prepare for exams and presentations in college, you will use the same skills at work. Time management, attention to detail, and careful preparation are necessary to be successful in your career. Depending on your career choice, you may have to pass proficiency tests or certification exams at least once or even once a year. Although failing an exam in college does not mean the end of your academic career, failing a licensing exam or a certification test could very well be the end of your job. Thus, the stakes—and the stress—are much higher.

The pressure to pass is greater, but because you attended college, and passed many tests, your test-taking skills will get you through exams at work. In addition to reviewing the test-taking strategies outlined in this chapter, take advantage of any test preparation seminars your employer offers. Also, now is the time to demonstrate your ability to study with others. There is no better study group than your coworkers because they all have the same interest as you: They want to pass the exam in order to keep their jobs or advance to a higher position.

Chapter in Review

1. List the different study strategies for visual, aural, read/write, and kinesthetic learners.
2. How would a kinesthetic learner best study for an exam in music and an exam in biology?
3. What are the drawbacks to using mnemonic devices to remember key concepts?
4. Compare and contrast studying in a group with studying alone. What are the benefits of both? What are the drawbacks to both?
5. What is the purpose of tests? Can they truly measure a student's understanding of course material?

Case Scenarios

Read the following case scenarios and determine what each person should do. Refer to the information in this chapter as you write a description and plan of action for each student.

1. Sylvia's accounting professor announced to the class that he allows students to study from old tests. In fact, he keeps a folder of previous exams in the library for students to access. One of Sylvia's classmates asks her if she wants to study for the test, and she agrees. When they meet, her classmate pulls out a copy of a test with the current semester's date on it. Sylvia questions her classmate, who says that the professor gave her a rough draft of a test that he decided not to use. When Sylvia gets to class, she recognizes every question because it is the same test her classmate had. What should Sylvia do?

2. Ryan does not think he knows how to study well. He glided through high school without opening a book. Now, he is in college and taking five classes: Intermediate Algebra, Reading Improvement, Introduction to Sociology, Speech Communication, and Concepts of Health and Wellness. He is struggling with his health and math classes. What can you tell him about studying for those subjects to help him get back on track?

3. Betty gets sweaty palms and wants to throw up each time she takes a test. She failed classes before because she couldn't calm herself enough to take a major test. This semester, though, Betty wants to do better because she cannot keep dropping or failing her classes. What advice can you give Betty to help ease her fears? What can she do so she can be successful?

Research It Further

1. Investigate methods of cheating that occur with "high-stakes" testing such as licensure and college-entrance exams. Write a report about these methods and the effects they had on how organizations test.

2. What are the most popular ways that students study at your college? Create a questionnaire that asks students how, when, and where they study. Once you tally the results, determine whether the students need a one-page reminder of how to study effectively. If you think they do, create one based on the shortcomings of their study methods.

3. Using the material in this chapter, create two or three games that can help students remember and understand course material.

9 Writing and Speaking Effectively

Regardless of your major or final career destination, you will be asked to write and speak in college and at work. As Jill explains, writing well is an important skill, and just as important is learning to speak effectively.

Although a discussion of all aspects of speaking and writing is beyond the scope of this chapter, it does give you an overview of both writing and speaking well. It will also serve as a good reference after completing your composition and speech classes to refresh your memory of what effective writing and speaking are.

Specifically, this chapter answers the following questions:

- Why is writing well a necessary skill for success?

- What kinds of writing will I have to do in college?

- What will professors expect from my writing?

- What steps do I follow to give a good speech?

- How do I improve my speaking skills?

COMMUNITY · COLLEGE ·

Student Profile

NAME: **Jill Lampe**   AGE: **19**

MAJOR: **Public Relations**

1. What writing have you done so far in college?

   I have taken Composition I and Composition II as well as a creative writing class. I have written essays, research papers, stories, and poems.

2. What do you think students should know about writing in college?

   They shouldn't hold back what they feel. They also have to prepare—you can't procrastinate when writing a paper. Procrastination wears you out and the paper won't be very good.

3. How have you improved your writing?

   I learned how to follow the MLA format. I learned how to tie all my ideas together, organize the papers so the ideas flow together.

4. What is your VARK?
   Aural.

Writing in College

Writing well is important to your success. Although your composition class is the place to learn how to write, this chapter gives you an overview of the basics. Writing research papers is discussed in Chapter 11.

In a society that craves "quick and easy," there is nothing quick and easy about writing effectively. Whether you are just learning grammar and spelling basics or you are comfortable with preparing 20-page research papers, writing is hard work. Students often ask, "What can I do to be a better writer?" Writers and professors always have the same response: Read and write every day. To become a better writer, you must be a good reader and you must practice writing regularly just as a concert pianist or a star athlete practices frequently. Regular reading and writing help you recognize the grammatical construction of sentences, build your vocabulary, and improve your spelling. You don't have to read a book and write a paper each day to keep your skills in good shape. No matter what you read and write, nor how often, you will improve your skills just as any amount of exercise a day is better than none.

Another tip for writing well in college is to buy a good dictionary and thesaurus—and carry them everywhere. Although the spell checking function and www.websters.com are fine sources for writing papers on the computer, they don't beat the convenience and portability of paperback reference books. Be sure, though, that both books are appropriate for college students. Some reference books do not have words commonly used in college texts, so the *American Heritage Dictionary* and *Roget's Thesaurus* are excellent choices for college students. Surprisingly, some dictionaries with the word "college" in the title often are not comprehensive enough for college classes. Be sure to use the dictionary any time you encounter an unfamiliar word. The best ways to learn new words are to write them down, look them up, practice saying them aloud, and use them in your writing.

Reflection

EXERCISE 9.1

Do you write regularly? If so, for what purposes? How is writing an integral part of living?

Companion
Website

Top Eight Writing Skills for College

The demands of college writing are more than they were in high school. Although the standards may be higher, they are achievable. At the very least, your writing during the first two years of college should be clear and to the point, yet adhering to the assignment. The following eight skills are required for effective college writing.

1. Fulfillment of the assignment. To receive full credit for writing assignments, read the directions carefully to ensure you fulfill all requirements. Omitting one element—such as a reference page—could lower your grade significantly.

All good writing must have a clear point, a main idea.

2. Main idea or point. All good writing must have a point or a main idea. Make sure your main idea is clear throughout the assignment. One question to ask yourself as you read the sentences and paragraphs is "How does this relate to my topic?"

3. Clear organization. Even if your ideas are insightful and enlightening, without clearly organized details, those ideas will not be communicated effectively. It is a good idea to start with an outline before you begin writing.

4. Focused paragraphs. Paragraphs that handle one minor idea at a time are considered focused. Each minor idea must support your overall point for the writing assignment. Paragraphs that cover too many different things are unfocused.

5. Concrete, specific details. Concrete details are the specific examples used to support your main idea. For example, if you are writing a review of a restaurant, provide concrete, specific details to re-create the experience. Writing merely "The main course was delicious" does not allow your readers to visualize or experience the meal—the detail is not specific or concrete. Instead, revise the sentence to: "The main course of chicken parmesan in the tangy tomato sauce that generously covered a bed of pasta was irresistible. Although the breading was crunchy, it was not overwhelming, and the melted mozzarella cheese created a perfect complement to the juicy chicken." Besides appealing to the readers' senses, providing specific details shows your professor you thought about the assignment and took the time to respond thoughtfully.

6. Neat presentation. Although the paper's presentation is not as important as clearly expressing the main idea, make sure it is neatly printed on quality paper. Your professor may have more specific guidelines to follow. If your paper looks messy or does not follow the format requirements, the first impression is that you hurried through the assignment.

7. Grammatical sentences. Good grammar is essential to effective writing. Some instructors demand near perfect grammar, while others allow for a few errors in an otherwise well-written paper. If you know that you make the same grammatical mistakes in each writing assignment, get help from the professor, the writing or tutoring center, or the resources in your library. There are many websites, as well, that offer grammar help. Do not rely, however, on the grammar checking function in your word processor. Most of the time, the grammar suggestions are incorrect.

8. Correct spelling. With the advent of the spell checking function in word-processing programs, most students do not correct spelling errors by using a dictionary. Although spell checkers are more accurate than grammar checkers, they cannot correct every misspelled word. For example, if you use "there" when you mean "their," your computer software considers the word spelled correctly. Correct spelling does not necessarily indicate a good paper, but it does show your readers that you pay attention to details. There are students who have difficulty spelling because of a learning disability such as dyslexia. These students have to take more time to check spelling, but they shouldn't let spelling overwhelm them. Instead, they should talk to their instructor about their spelling difficulties.

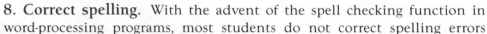

Reflection

EXERCISE 9.2

How do you feel about your writing skills? What would you like to improve? How will you make those improvements?

Companion
Website

Different Types of Writing Assignments

Many students underestimate the importance of reading and understanding the writing assignment before they begin writing. Carefully reading and noting what you are asked to do saves you time—and points—in the long run. One of the benefits of writing well is that you can easily move from one assignment type to another. The key to fulfilling an assignment is to know what the professor wants you to do. The following is a discussion of the common writing assignment types.

Summarize. A summary is a brief retelling of a subject. A summary covers the main points of an event or text, but does not contain your opinion on the subject.

EXAMPLE

Summarize Freud's contributions to psychology.

Evaluate, review, assess, state your opinion, critique.

An evaluation assignment asks for your opinion. You should consider the subject's strengths and weaknesses, and provide specific examples to support your ideas.

EXAMPLES

Evaluate a website's use of graphics.

Assess the effectiveness of the information you received from the financial aid office.

Synthesize.

A synthesis assignment sounds more complicated than it is. If you have ever written a research paper using two or more sources, then you wrote a synthesis. When your professor asks you to synthesize two articles' approaches to understanding the impact of immigration, read those two sources, form an opinion about them, and use information from the two sources to support your opinions.

EXAMPLE

Read two articles on the importance of higher education and write a synthesis paper contrasting the points made in each article.

Describe, define, discuss, explain.

Any time you are asked to describe or explain a subject, you must know the topic well. Discussion questions are usually intended to assess how well you know a topic. The more specific details you provide, the more likely you have described or defined the subject adequately.

EXAMPLES

Explain the major events that led up to the Civil War.

Define the terms "values," "goals," and "mission statement."

Analyze.

To analyze a subject is to break it apart and look at its components carefully. Once you have investigated the parts, you must put the subject back together again. When you analyze a poem, you might break it apart into "rhyme scheme," "language," "images," and "speaker." To examine each of these parts is to analyze the poem. Once you have completed your examination, bring the parts back together again with commentary on how the parts all work together. For those more mechanically minded, analysis can be used to figure out why your computer won't connect to the Internet—you analyze different components of the computer to discover the problem. "Putting it all back together" is your final diagnosis of the computer's problem.

EXAMPLE

Analyze the character of Willy Loman in Death of a Salesman.

Compare and contrast.

The purpose of a compare/contrast essay is to examine two subjects more carefully. When you are asked to compare and contrast two subjects, first make a list of the similarities and then list the differences. After discussing the similarities and differences, make a point about them. For example, if you are asked to compare and contrast apples and oranges, first describe their size, color, texture, and taste. Then you have to make a significant point about those details. Is one more nutritious than the other? Is one more popular than the other? Expressing the significance of the similarities and differences satisfies the purpose of your compare and contrast.

EXAMPLES

Compare and contrast two types of welding techniques.

Compare and contrast two kinds of bacteria.

Persuade, argue. Persuading an audience and arguing a point demand that you take a stand about a topic. Whether or not you are passionate about the assigned topic, you must argue passionately about it. An argument is most effective when specific, accurate details are presented. Effective persuasion requires that you treat your readers with respect and present your argument fairly. Exaggeration and misrepresentation are not characteristics of a successful argument.

EXAMPLES

In an essay, persuade the college administration that students should have a study day before finals.

Write an essay in which you argue that the American legal system should be reformed.

Reflect. When you are asked to reflect on a topic, you are being asked for your thoughts about it. Reflections are usually used in an informal setting and are a way for the professor to get to know more about you. If you are asked to reflect on your progress during the semester or how you felt about writing a research paper, be sure to provide plenty of details that explain your ideas. Some students hurriedly answer reflections because they do not understand their importance or they think the professor is not really interested in their answers. Saying "I have done well" or "I can't wait to get the paper written" is not what your instructor is looking for. Elaborate on your answer to such a question; the more details you provide, the more thoughtful and helpful your response is.

EXAMPLES

What have you learned about the writing process so far this semester?

How did you feel about your performance on the last exam?

Audience, Purpose, and Length

Audience, purpose, and length are other key factors to understanding writing assignments. For many assignments, you will be assigned a *length* such as a two-page paper or a 1,500-word essay. Professors assign a length to help you gauge the development necessary to fulfill the assignment adequately. For instance, if your instructor assigned you a one-page review of a website, don't turn in a 10-page paper. Conversely, if you have a 2,500-word research paper to write, don't turn in a 750-word paper. Obviously, a paper that is shorter than the required length does not contain enough information and reflection to fulfill the assignment. If you are worried that you cannot meet an assignment's length requirement, talk to your instructor as soon as possible. She can help you narrow or expand your topic so you have enough material to work with.

The *audience* for your assignment is both the immediate readers and the potential readers of your paper. When creating a writing assignment, many professors assume that the audience is your classmates or people interested in your subject—many students, however, assume that the only audience is the professor. If an audience is not specified for your assignment, imagine you are writing for college students who are studying the same subject—such as your classmates. How you present your ideas and the words you use should be appropriate for other college students.

There may be, however, times when you are assigned a particular audience as part of the requirements for a writing project. The reason professors assign a particular audience is to help you focus your ideas, language, and argument. Consider, for example, an assignment that may be part of a health class:

WRITING ASSIGNMENT

> *In a three-page paper, discuss the latest information about sexually transmitted diseases.*

This is a straightforward assignment that can be completed by anyone who has access to the current information. However, how might the assignment change if your audience is 12-year-old public school students? What information would you add or eliminate? What kind of language would you use? Would you include diagrams and definitions or cartoons? How much detail would you provide? These are all new considerations because your audience has certain limitations. Unfamiliar vocabulary, technical terms, detailed information, and photographs may be inappropriate for these students. Simple terms, diagrams, and personal stories about kids their own age may be a better way to convey the more complicated information.

Now, consider the same topic with a different audience: 70- to 80-year-old men and women who live in a nursing home. Again, you have the same questions: What information would you add or eliminate? What kind of language would you use? Would you have to include diagrams and definitions or cartoons? How much detail would you provide? Obviously, this audience has different needs than the young students. Because your audience is much older and experienced, you have to think about how to approach a topic that they have definite ideas about. Some may be resistant to hearing about the topic because they believe it is not appropriate to discuss it in an open setting; others may feel they know enough to make their own decisions about their bodies. Still others will not see the relevance for them. These challenges are unique to your audience and, as you have seen, changing *who* you are writing for changes *how* you approach the presentation of information.

A final consideration for your assignment is your *purpose*. Your purpose for writing is usually closely connected to your assignment, but there

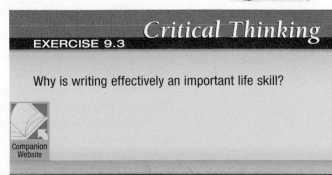

Critical Thinking

EXERCISE 9.3

Why is writing effectively an important life skill?

Companion Website

are other purposes for writing. For example, in addition to evaluating a website, another purpose could be to make your audience laugh. When you compare two popular diet plans, your purpose could be to persuade readers that one plan is a healthier choice. The purposes for writing are endless, but it is important to ask yourself why you are writing and what you want to accomplish. The answers to those questions are your purpose for writing, and knowing that purpose will help you complete your assignment effectively.

Prewriting Techniques

Once you have read and understood the writing assignment, it is time to use one or more prewriting techniques to get your ideas down on paper. You may have your own way of writing, but it is worth investigating some of these proven methods for generating ideas. Most student writing suffers from a lack of appropriate, specific details, in part because they skip this first step in favor of saving time. In reality, using a prewriting technique before you begin to write saves you time in the long run because you have plenty of ideas to work with.

There are three common prewriting techniques you can use to generate details for your paper. *Freewriting* is an easy way to get ideas down on paper. The only rules to freewriting are to start with an idea and stop only after you have filled a page or after a certain amount of time has passed. When freewriting, allow your mind to wander off the subject; you must, however, write down everything that comes to mind. Later, when you start organizing your details, you can eliminate anything that does not pertain to your subject. If you are a good typist, you can freewrite by typing. Don't worry about spelling, grammar, or punctuation when you freewrite—the purpose is to free your mind of that little voice that censors everything you think.

FREEWRITING ON THE TOPIC "FINANCIAL AID"

Financial aid is a great way to help students go to college, but it is so hard to fill out all those forms and get all the information that I need. I can't think of anything harder to do than fill out a financial aid form correctly. when I applied I forgot to put my social security number and I can't believe I did that. They called me to tell me that my application had been delayed because of the oversight. I could have died because I needed to buy my books and get an apartment. I don't think they understood that I didn't have time to waste; I had bills to pay and I needed my financial aid to get into my classes and start school. Now that I got everything straightened out I am glad I went through the process. I know how to do it and know what to watch for and overall it hasn't been that bad but I was really stressed those first few weeks. Maybe the school needs to have workshops for new students that show them how to fill out forms and that stress the importance of filling them out correctly. That would be a good idea.

Note that the student didn't worry too much about punctuation or even where she was going in the freewrite. Instead, she listed all of her thoughts about financial aid—she recently experienced what it was like to be stressed because her financial aid was delayed.

Clustering is another method of prewriting that works well for those who are strong visual learners. Clusters, or think links, are visual representations of ideas and their relationship to each other. The key to clustering is to start in the middle of your paper—leave yourself plenty of room—by writing down

EXHIBIT 9.1   *Clustering for the topic "Sexually Transmitted Diseases."*

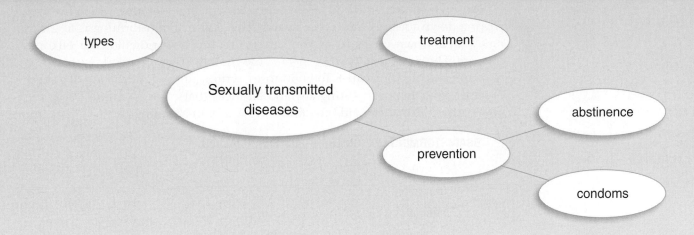

your topic and circling it. Draw a line from your subject and write down a related topic. For instance, "types," "prevention," and "treatment" are all parts of the topic "sexually transmitted diseases" (see Exhibit 9.1). Then, there are subtopics that branch off "prevention"—"abstinence" and "condoms." The words and phrases that surround a topic or subtopic must be connected to it, both logically and literally by drawing a line.

Practice

EXERCISE 9.4

Fill in the cluster bubbles below.

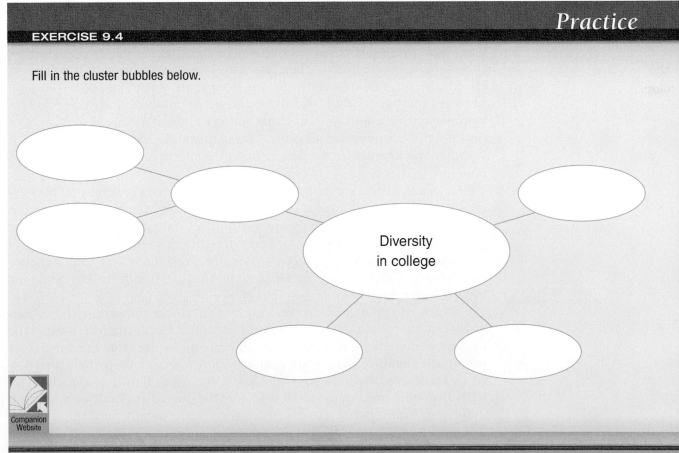

Companion
Website

Another effective method of generating ideas is *brainstorming*, which involves writing down ideas as they come to you. The goal in brainstorming is to get as many ideas down on paper as you can, no matter how ridiculous or off-topic they are. The more details you generate, the more you have to work with as you begin organizing your paper. To brainstorm, write your topic at the top of a sheet of paper, and then start listing any and all ideas that come to mind. Using the same subject, "financial aid," the following is a brainstorming list.

BRAINSTORMING LIST ON THE TOPIC "FINANCIAL AID"

Forms

Information

Financial Aid Officer

Trouble getting the information filled out properly

Fear that I won't get enough money to pay my college bills

Worried that I won't be able to pay it back

Feel good about how helpful the people at school are

Need to know more about when I start paying it back

Need to find out what I need to do to renew it each year

Wish there was a handbook for students that is easy to read and reassuring

As you can see, the first details are just a few words, but further down the list, the details get more specific and yield more ideas to work with.

Organizing Details

Once you have a list of details you want to use, give some thought to how they should be organized. There are a variety of ways to organize a paper effectively. You can arrange the details from most to least important or least to most important. Details can also be arranged chronologically, especially if you are writing about an event that follows a specific time line. Moreover, details can be arranged from general ideas to specific details or vice versa. It is important to organize the details logically, and this depends on your purpose and audience.

For example, you are writing a paper on the greatest challenges to diversity on your campus, and your details include the lack of cultural appreciation activities, a recent racially motivated incident, few minorities in administrative roles, and the lack of African American literature classes. The current order of the details provides no logical connections between them, and your audience will have a difficult time understanding the magnitude of the problem. Instead, order them according to importance.

Which of the details do you think is the most important indication of the challenges to diversity on your campus? Certainly, the most striking is the racially motivated incident. You might use it as the first, most important detail to grab your readers' attention and keep them interested in and sympathetic to your thesis. On the other hand, you might start with the least important detail and use the incident detail as your last, most important point. How you arrange your details, as long as each detail builds on the others and supports your thesis, depends on your purpose for writing.

Writing Paragraphs

A *paragraph*, a group of sentences considered one complete unit, is the building block of an essay. Paragraphs begin with an indentation, known as a tab, on the left-hand side of the page. Well-developed paragraphs, the mark of a thoughtful writer, can be any length; however, if a paragraph is too short, the reader may think something is missing. If they are too long, your reader may get lost in what you are trying to say. The keys to writing a good paragraph—and you will write many in your college career—are to stay focused on one topic at a time and to let your reader know what that main idea is by using a *topic sentence*. A topic sentence can appear at the beginning of the paragraph, in the middle, or at the end. As long as your reader knows what the whole paragraph is about, then the topic sentence has done its job.

After you determine what the paragraph will focus on, start putting the details in place. Just as you consider the overall arrangement of the details in your paper, give some thought to arranging the details *within* the paragraphs. The same detail organization for an entire paper works for paragraphs as well: general to specific, specific to general, order of importance, or chronological. You can use a different method for each paragraph as long as all of the paragraphs support your thesis. Here is an example of a chronologically ordered paragraph on the racially motivated incident that demonstrates your campus has challenges to diversity:

> One of the most important reasons I believe our campus needs to overcome its diversity problems is the recent racially motivated incident that occurred after the football game [topic sentence]. The incident started when a group of black and white students from our school started yelling insults at the predominantly white team members [first detail in chronological order]. Then, the taunting turned into throwing bottles at the white team members [second detail in chronological order]. While some of the team took cover, others fought back with rocks [third detail in chronological order]. The incident ended with three people in the emergency room, being treated for cuts, scrapes, and a broken bone [last detail in chronological order]. If our campus did more to promote cultural sensitivity and racial diversity, then outrageous behavior such as this would be a part of history rather than the present [conclusive statement that restates the point of the paragraph].

Transitions

To make your sentences flow smoothly and your paragraphs relate clearly to one another, use transitions. *Transitions* are words or phrases that signal to the reader that you are moving from one thought to the next. Imagine describing over the phone how to get from the college to your house. If you didn't use transitions, your listener may be confused as to how to get there. Words such as *first, next, then,* and *after* are transitional words that help your reader see how each sentence relates to another.

When you move from paragraph to paragraph in your paper, you definitely need a strong transitional phrase or sentence to indicate that a new idea or point is forthcoming. Phrases such as "In addition to . . . " and "Even though . . . " and "Contrary to the point above . . . " are strong enough to slow the reader so he pays attention to your next major point. The following paragraph contains bolded transitions so you can see how each word or phrase is used:

> **The first step** to effective listening is to prepare to listen before you get to class. You should read the assigned pages or chapters before class so you know what the lecture or discussion topic will be. **If you read the chapters ahead of time,** you will be familiar with new words and concepts. Preparing to listen **also** includes reviewing your assigned readings before you get to the classroom. **If you have a few minutes between classes or on the bus,** pull out your book and skim the major headings, bolded terms, and textboxes.

The bolded words and phrases indicate the beginning of an idea and how each idea connects to the others. The words "The first step," tell you something important: This idea is the first in a series of steps that will follow. The transition "also" tells you that another point is being made in addition to the one at the beginning of the paragraph. Finally, the phrases that begin with the word "If" in two different sentences tie the ideas from the previous sentences to the ones in the next sentence. They serve as a bridge to connect the ideas together.

In addition to connecting ideas, transitions also improve the paper's readability. If you read your work out loud and it sounds "choppy" or repetitive in rhythm, you may have to add transitions. Adding transitions effectively takes practice. The list below gives examples of transitions of various types. If you need help, see your instructor or someone in the writing center at your college. With a little work, the flow of your writing will improve.

COMMON TRANSITIONAL WORDS AND PHRASES

- *Transitions of addition:* also, and, in addition, moreover, furthermore, again, first, second, last, finally, next, another point.
- *Transitions of compare and contrast:* likewise, on the other hand, in contrast, in comparison, however, nonetheless, nevertheless, but, on the contrary.
- *Transitions of conclusion:* in conclusion, as a final note, in sum, therefore, thus, in summary, on the whole.
- *Transitions of example:* for example, for instance, to illustrate, in this case.
- *Transitions of time:* first, second, next, after, before, then, finally, a few hours later, immediately.

Essays

The word *essay* has its origins in French and means "an attempt" or "a trial." For college students, writing essays is an attempt, or a trial, in some sense, to complete the assignment without going crazy! In the context of college, an essay is a composition on a particular subject that offers the author's view. If, for example, you are asked to write an essay on the death penalty or obesity in children, then present your view on the subject. Essays do not usually contain research; instead, they are based on your observations, details, and opinions. They are, in essence, an attempt by you to convey your view on a subject.

When assigned an essay for a class, you should include some basic components. Without all of them, your essay is just a piece of writing—just as a few bones do not make up an entire skeleton. At a minimum, the essay should contain the following five parts:

Title. All essays must be titled, preferably something original and a reflection of the essay's topic.

Introduction. This is a paragraph that introduces the topic and explains to the audience why you are writing the essay. It can also function as an attention-grabber that lures the reader into the essay.

Thesis. The thesis is a sentence or two that tells the reader what you will be discussing, or proving, in the essay. For example, your thesis could be: "The worst summer I ever had was in 2000." Your reader, then, will expect you to prove to her why the summer of 2000 was the worst.

Body paragraphs. Without body paragraphs (three or more, depending on the assignment), you don't have an essay. A general rule, for a short essay, is to have three body paragraphs, each making its own point. Continuing the earlier example of the summer of 2000, one paragraph might discuss breaking up with your girlfriend. The second paragraph deals with losing your job, and the third paragraph might talk about breaking your leg in a water-skiing accident.

Conclusion. The final paragraph of your essay should convey your concluding ideas about the subject. You might conclude your essay on the worst summer of your life with reflections on what you learned from all of the disasters. The reader should understand how all of the points come together to support your thesis.

Portfolios

A *writing portfolio* is a collection of your writing throughout the semester. Portfolios are popular with composition instructors because they allow students to work on their writing all semester. Instead of getting a grade on the first draft, students can revise their papers until they meet the minimum standards for the course. The benefit of the portfolio method is that students can focus on the process of writing instead of a final product. Some students, however, find it difficult to do because they are not used to the way portfolios are evaluated. Some students want to get a grade, no matter what it is, and move on to a new project; the thought of rewriting and rewriting until the paper is "perfect" is not appealing to them at all. On the other hand, some students like the idea that they can improve their grade on a paper by reworking it.

The best way to handle a writing portfolio is to review its requirements, including due dates and policies on completing final drafts. If you have questions about the expectations, especially if you have not done a portfolio before, ask your professor and schedule periodic meetings to ensure you complete the components successfully. Take advantage of the opportunity to submit multiple drafts and receive feedback on them. Although revising essays for a portfolio is time-consuming, you receive extensive feedback and help with improving your writing.

INTEGRITY MATTERS

HOW TO AVOID PLAGIARISM

- Do not buy or download a paper from the Web and turn it in as your own.
- Do not cut and paste any amount of material from a website without telling the reader who the original author is and without placing the material within quotation marks.
- Do not borrow a paper from someone else to turn in as your own.
- Do not ask someone else to write a paper for you.

Avoiding Plagiarism

No word strikes fear and confusion in students more than plagiarism. Simply defined, *plagiarism* is the use of another's words or ideas without proper acknowledgment. If the information or the expression of the information came from another source, not your own brain, you must let the reader know what that source is. Plagiarism is discussed further in Chapter 11.

Critical Thinking
EXERCISE 9.5

A friend is taking a course you took last semester and asks to borrow the paper you wrote for the research requirement. You worked hard on the paper and made a good grade, but you fear that your friend wants to copy part or all of the assignment. What can you do to help your friend without compromising your integrity?

Companion Website

How College Professors Evaluate Student Writing

College professors vary in the methods they use to evaluate student writing. Some look for and reward keywords and concepts, while others mark and take off for grammatical, mechanical, and organizational problems even if the key concepts are easily identified. You will soon learn, if you have not already, that each instructor has his own criteria for grading written assignments, and the sooner you learn what the criteria are, the better your writing will be. Remember, instructors expect you to write at a college level. Your instructors' job is to make you a better thinker and writer, no matter the subject, and they will correct errors and make suggestions for improvement. Sometimes, students are shocked when they receive extensive feedback on their writing from instructors in disciplines other than composition. Your job, therefore, is to consider feedback from all of your instructors and make the improvements they suggest.

Knowing When to Get Help

There may be times when a writing assignment is confusing or overwhelming. If at any time you don't understand what you are supposed to do, contact your instructor as soon as you can. Professors know you

have other responsibilities and classes and are often willing to work with you if you plan ahead and ask for help early.

If your college has a writing center, make an appointment with a tutor as soon as you realize you need some help. Because writing center tutors are employed by the college, their job is to help you with the kinds of assignments instructors give. Writing center tutors may also be able to explain what you should do to complete the assignment.

Other students in the class and friends who are not in the class can be other sources for getting help, but be careful. Your classmates may not know much more about the expectations than you. Moreover, your instructor may prohibit any kind of collaboration—even if it is only to better understand the assignment. Getting help from people who are not in the class or not taking college courses should be your last resort because they don't know your instructor's expectations. The most they may be able to help you with is the grammar and mechanics.

Collaboration

EXERCISE 9.6

Working in a group, write down three career paths. Then, brainstorm a list of writing activities that you might do in each job. Also, consider what skills will be most important in those writing activities—accuracy, clarity, grammatical correctness, brevity. Present your information to your classmates.

Companion Website

When You Have Received Too Much Help

How do you know when you have received too much help on a writing assignment? If someone else writes whole sentences, paragraphs, and pages for you or supplies you with many main ideas and examples that you use in your paper, then you have probably received too much assistance on your writing assignment. Some professors disapprove of editing and proofreading services as well. When in doubt, check with your professor and explain what kind of help you are getting.

Common Writing Mistakes Students Make

- Not following directions, including format requirements (e.g., cover page, works cited page, copies of sources).
- Not asking questions about how to complete the assignment.
- Not managing their time properly (e.g., trying to write a paper the night before).
- Not believing that writing rough drafts is a good use of time.
- Not writing the paper themselves (e.g., allowing someone else to help too much).
- Not writing formally for college (e.g., using slang or informal language to discuss academic issues).

Speaking in College

Speaking effectively is a skill that will benefit you not only in your career, but also in life. For example, you may have to speak on behalf of the parents at your children's school as president of the Parents and Teachers Association, or you may be asked to make weekly announcements at your church. In your college classes, you usually get a specific assignment (a five-minute persuasive speech on a current event) or a specific topic (cloning). However, not all speaking experiences begin with detailed directions. You may be asked to introduce someone or to "talk for 10 minutes about whatever you think will interest the audience." Regardless of how you are assigned a speech, the process is the same: You have to plan, prepare, deliver, and assess.

Planning

Choosing a topic is the first step in preparing to speak. Sometimes you will be given a topic, but in some of your classes—or for some occasions—you will be allowed to choose your own. Speech topics can come from your personal experience, current events, or from in-depth research. If you are not sure which topic you want to explore, use brainstorming or another method of generating ideas to determine which topic interests you the most.

Deciding on your purpose is the next step. You may have to inform, persuade, or entertain your audience. If informing them on your topic, use

Not all speaking is formal speaking—your assignments or job may involve many types of presentations.

Types of Speeches

- **Impromptu.** A speech delivered on the spur of the moment with no time for preparation. Impromptu speeches sometimes occur at award ceremonies when a person is asked to "say a few words."

- **Extemporaneous.** A speech where the speaker is given a topic, allowed time for research, and then delivers the speech from notes. Extemporaneous speeches are often assigned to help students develop time management, research, and organization skills.

- **Memorized/Manuscript.** Both the memorized and manuscript speeches are written in advance. The memorized speech is delivered without notes. The manuscript speech is read either using pages at a podium or a TelePrompTer. Memorized and manuscript speeches are often used by politicians or those delivering a speech that is broadcast on television.

certain details and language to present the information in an unbiased manner. If persuading your audience, use examples and language to change their attitudes or beliefs. Entertaining your audience requires you to use information, details, and language to amuse. Your speech may have more than one purpose—and sometimes all three—but one will be emphasized the most.

Just as writers must decide who their audience is before they begin writing, speakers must also consider who they will be addressing. Audience analysis is the process by which speakers determine who will be the receivers of the message.

Here are examples of audience analysis questions:

How many people will be in the audience?

You may need to modify your delivery style if you have 200 as opposed to 20 people. Fewer people often means more opportunities for interaction, while more people means fewer opportunities.

What are the characteristics of the audience (e.g., gender, ages, race, culture, educational background, learning style)?

Depending on the audience's makeup, your language, tone, and use of examples will change. You will speak very differently to a group of Japanese businesswomen than to a group of retired military men—even if it is the same topic and thesis.

What are their attitudes toward your topic? What do they know about the topic?

Your audience may be very knowledgeable about your subject, but they are looking for new ways to think about it, or they may have preconceived notions about the issue and be more difficult to persuade.

Are there any other aspects of the audience's makeup that you should consider?

Did the group just experience something exciting and energizing, or did they just suffer a tremendous physical or emotional blow? What you know about their recent collective experience colors how you speak, what words and examples you choose, and how you carry yourself.

Here are examples of occasion analysis questions:

When are you speaking? Will you be speaking first thing in the morning, before or after lunch, or in the early evening?

Typically, an audience's energy level in the morning is a little higher than right after lunch. It may be easier to speak about important, serious issues early in the day, while taking a lighter, more humorous approach in the early afternoon. You may not always get to change your presentation to match the audience's energy level, but keep in mind how you might alter your delivery depending on what the time of day is.

How long do you have to speak?

An important part of planning is knowing how much time you have to speak and then preparing a speech that is appropriate in length and scope. Unlike writing a paper, how much time it takes to deliver the speech can mean the difference between success and misery. Remember, your audience expects you to manage your time; if you don't, even a brilliant message may get lost in the process.

What is the space like?

Is it outside or inside? What is its size and shape? Are there architectural elements, such as columns, that might prevent people from hearing or seeing? These are questions to ask so you can determine what body movements you can make and how you should use your voice.

What kind of equipment will be present? Will you be videotaped? Will you have access to audiovisual equipment?

Again, the kind of equipment available, whether it is a computer with a data projection device or an overhead projector, determines how you make your points during the presentation. If you are being videotaped, your movement may be limited and you have to be conscious of speaking loud so the microphone can pick up your voice.

What else will you need? Visual aids, handouts, or time for questions or discussion?

All of these miscellaneous questions help you decide how to prepare and what to bring.

Preparation

Once you determine your topic, purpose, and audience, it is time to generate ideas, research if necessary, organize the details, create an outline, draft

You have right-brain and visual learning preferences and were asked to speak in front of the college's Board of Trustees (most of whom have left-brain and read/write learning preferences) about creating a fine arts program at your institution. You feel strongly that theatre, music, and art classes will enhance the learning environment at the college, but you know that two of the board members are against adding any liberal arts classes because they feel these classes take away from the college's emphasis on technical and industrial career preparation. With this information in mind, how do you plan your persuasive speech?

Consider how understanding your personality style or learning preference can help you through challenging situations.

*PERSONALITY + LEARNING STYLE = UNDERSTANDING SITUATIONS

the speech (citing sources if necessary), provide transitions between main ideas, revise, and practice. This may sound like plenty of work, but if you break the steps down and focus on one at a time, then the process is easier to complete.

To generate ideas, try freewriting or brainstorming. If you need to do research to gather details, follow your instructor's directions on citing sources and write down the material's source. You may organize your speech chronologically (this happened first, this second), from most important to least important, or general idea to specific idea. Choosing the right organization for your speech depends on your topic, purpose, and audience.

Organizing your details and writing an outline are usually completed at the same time. An outline, though, can be a formal written assignment that you must turn in before or after you make your speech. For example, the following is an outline on public speaking anxiety:

I. Causes of public speaking anxiety
    A. Fear of the unknown
    B. Fear of negative feedback

II. Effects of public speaking anxiety
    A. Physical effects
    B. Psychological effects

III. Methods of reducing public speaking anxiety
    A. Mental exercises
    B. Physical exercises

(Remember that when you break a main point or subpoint down, it must have at least two parts to it.) Once you have an outline ready, start drafting the speech. A benefit to writing out the speech, even if you do not have to turn in a final draft, is that it helps you determine how to elaborate on each point. You may even want to note stories or elaborate points to ensure you include all necessary details. As you draft your speech or create a more developed outline, remember to credit any source you used to prepare your speech. In addition to citing sources in the outline or speech manuscript, verbally cite the source before providing the audience with the information. Cite the information on any visual aids such as handouts and slides as well.

As you draft and shape your speech, consider the different elements that make a speech fit together and flow well. An introduction, or opening, sets the stage for the topic and provides the audience with your thesis. Give some thought to what you will use as an attention getter. Your audience is listening to instead of reading your introduction, so you may pose a question, relate a story, or even sing a verse or recite a poem.

As you move to the body of your speech, pay attention to the use of transitions. Unlike readers, listeners cannot go back to your earlier statements and review; thus, your audience needs clear signals that you are moving from one idea to another; for example, "**Even though I experienced anxiety for five years,** I learned to cope by using visualization techniques." The bolded part of the sentence reminds the listener the speaker has moved from telling us about her suffering to a method she used to manage her fear. You may also reference visual aids, such as slides or handouts, to indicate a change in point or idea.

Saying "That's all folks!" or "That is the end of my speech" are not effective ways to conclude a presentation. There are many more effective ways to provide closure and underscore your main point. Leave the audience with a question, quote, or visual element such as a cartoon, or tell a funny story to make your point and leave an impression.

Practice

EXERCISE 9.8

Using the topic "first day of the semester," make a list of details that you could use in an extemporaneous speech. Then, put the details in an order that you think would be most effective for new students.

Companion
Website

Delivery

Vocal. What if you crafted a fantastic speech and no one ever heard it because they couldn't understand what you were saying? Sound impossible? It has, unfortunately, happened before: a great speech is lost because the speaker didn't project his voice or mumbled through the words. For vocal delivery, then, the most important aspect is getting the words out successfully. Consider the following suggestions when practicing and delivering a speech:

- Pay attention to the tone and pitch, or vocal quality, of your voice. Is it soft or harsh? Do you sound angry or giddy? Audience members prefer voices that are easy to listen to.

- Speak slowly and deliberately, making sure that you are properly pronouncing words (check the dictionary) and using correct grammar (consult a writing handbook). Open your mouth and move your lips to ensure you are enunciating. Speaker credibility is lost when words are not used properly or are poorly pronounced.

- Use variety when speaking. Vary volume, pitch, and speed to create interest. Pause between points for effect. Do you remember the monotone teacher in the movie *Ferris Bueller's Day Off*? He didn't vary his volume, pitch, or speed, and his students were either asleep or not paying attention.

Speak slowly and deliberately, enunciating clearly, to gain credibility as a speaker.

Physical. Appropriate nonverbal communication while speaking can mean the difference between an effective and an ineffective speech. Paying attention to and practicing your body movements will help you develop good physical habits when speaking. Here are just a few to consider:

- Dress appropriately. If you look professional, you appear more credible. Unless you are making a point by dressing down or in a chicken outfit, dress up. A neat and clean appearance also suggests attention to detail and importance.

- Smile at the audience. It demonstrates a positive attitude and puts the audience at ease.

- Plant your feet firmly on the floor and stand up straight. Slouching or slumping lessens your effectiveness.

- Act naturally. The more you practice, the more comfortable you will be with your body movements and the less likely to use unnatural, mechanical hand gestures and head movements.

- Move from the waist up only. Shuffling and pacing are distracting.

- Step out in front of the podium when speaking to groups of 30 or fewer. With larger audiences, using a podium works well and focuses the audience's attention to you. In smaller settings, moving from behind the pectern creates intimacy and connection.

- Use hand gestures appropriately. Keep your arms and hands close to your body. Avoid pointing your finger to emphasize an idea; instead, use a closed fist with thumb slightly up. Open hands work well, but avoid banging on the lectern or table.

- Remember to maintain eye contact with your audience.

Assessment

After you deliver your speech, you have one more step left: assessment. Assessing both the audience and yourself helps you determine what you did well and what you need to work on the next time. Although it may sound challenging to evaluate yourself and those who listened to you, there are some techniques you can use to determine how successful you were.

The questions below are just a few to start you thinking about self-evaluation and improvement. As you become more experienced speaking in public, you will become better at gauging your effectiveness and the audience's reaction. You will also be more open to asking for feedback from your audience.

Self-Assessment

PREPARATION ASSESSMENT

- Did I prepare adequately for the speech?
- Did I anticipate what I should do to deliver an effective presentation?

DELIVERY ASSESSMENT:

- Did I use nonverbal communication effectively? Did I smile, move my body, and keep eye contact?
- Did I clearly state my topic and thesis? Did I provide adequate transitions and use repetition to keep my message focused?
- Did I provide a clear conclusion that effectively ended my speech?
- Did I enunciate and project my voice so I could be heard?
- Was I generally successful?

Audience Assessment

NONVERBAL AND BEHAVIORAL ASSESSMENT:

- Did they seem interested?
- Did they react appropriately to what I said or showed them?
- Did they leave quickly after the speech?

VERBAL AND WRITTEN ASSESSMENT:

- Did some of the audience members stay after my presentation to give me verbal feedback?
- If I provided a survey, what did the results show?

Tips for Effective Speaking

s with learning to write effectively, there are tips for successful speeches. Just a few of them appear below.

Repetition. "Tell them what you are going to tell them, tell them, and then tell them what you told them" is often-heard advice about speaking in public. It merely means that you should repeat your main idea at least three times during your presentation: in your introduction as your thesis, in the body of your speech, and in your conclusion as a summary of your main idea. The repetition of words, phrases, and images is also very effective. One example is Martin Luther King Jr.'s "I Have a Dream" speech, in which he repeats the word "dream" to make the point that the dream has not died for him and for African Americans.

Eye contact. Avoid reading your speech or looking anywhere except at your audience. People want to connect with you, and looking at them improves that connection. Maintaining eye contact also demonstrates confidence and improves credibility.

Time. A speaker who uses her time wisely is considered effective. When you speak, be conscious of the time remaining and what you have left to cover. Practice repeatedly to make sure you are delivering your speech in the allotted time.

Humor. Starting the speech off with a joke or a short funny story that relates to your topic is a great way to put an audience at ease and make them lean forward to hear what you have to say next. It also demonstrates that you are a confident speaker.

Dealing with Anxiety

Preparation and practice will make you less anxious when you give your speech, but there may be times when you feel nervous no matter what you do. Be assured, though, that we all get nervous at some time. Try some of these tips to relax:

- *Breathe deeply.* Slow, deep breathing calms your nerves and gets oxygen to much-needed parts. You will think more clearly and respond appropriately.

- *Get into the mind-set.* Focus your thoughts on the task at hand and relax. Imagine yourself walking through the door, walking to the podium, and delivering your speech. Then, imagine yourself concluding, waiting for applause, and exiting the room. Mentally rehearsing the actions you will perform eases your uncertainty and helps you relax.

- *Practice, practice, and practice your speech.* The more you know the speech and what you are going to say, the more likely you can recover from a stumble along the way.

- *Think positively.* Imagine that the audience is enjoying what they are hearing from you. Visualize smiling faces and nodding heads.

- *Consider that what you have to say is important and may change someone's life for the better.* If you think you have an opportunity to make a difference in the world, then your message becomes more important than your nervousness.

- *Recruit loyal friends and family to attend if possible.* Ask them to sit within view so they can provide nonverbal support. Experienced speakers look to others who can provide some sort of positive feedback.

- *Keep water within reach to moisten your mouth if it gets dry.* A little pause to take a drink may be the moment you need to gather your thoughts and move to the next point.

- *Remember that everyone, even experienced speakers, gets nervous in front of others, especially their peers.* If you feel the same sometimes, it is perfectly natural. Remember, you will feel more nervous than you look.

Reflection

EXERCISE 9.9

Do you fear speaking in public? If so, what is it about public speaking (preparation, audience, etc.) that worries you the most about speaking in front of a group?

Companion
Website

Troubleshooting

As you get more comfortable with speaking in public, you will feel more confident in handling everything when it all goes right. But what happens if something goes wrong? First, be assured that well-prepared speakers rarely run into problems, but there may be a time that you are confronted with something that throws you off and turns a good speech into a bad one.

If you do experience a problem, remember that most audience members are generally sympathetic toward you. Many realize how much work it takes to prepare and deliver an effective speech. They also may help you because they want you to succeed. At the very least, they will feel more at ease if you handle the situation professionally and with a sense of humor. Acting angry, speaking negatively, breaking down in tears, and walking out are not options for effective speakers. You will win your audience over more readily if you take unexpected obstacles in stride and continue as best you can with what you have.

In some cases, there are specific actions you can take to minimize the damage from a bad situation. What do you do when:

- *You arrive or start late?* If you arrive late, apologize and explain why you were delayed if appropriate. Make a joke if you can think of something quickly. Then, get going with your speech and be sure to end on time. If there is important information you must leave out, provide contact information for those who may be interested in hearing or reading the omitted points.

- *Your audience is bored or hostile?* Again, humor may defuse a sticky situation in which your audience is not receptive to what you have to say. Another tip is to talk about nonverbal feedback you are receiving; then, highlight why what you have to say is important and why you are enthusiastic about it. Acknowledging their lack of receptivity may be all it takes to change their attitudes. If not, providing time for questions and comments usually defuses tense situations. At least remain calm, especially if someone in the audience is argumentative, and treat the audience with respect.

- *You forget a piece of equipment or visual aid, or something does not work properly?* If you have time, replace the item. You may have to start your presentation and wait until someone can bring a replacement. Any audience that has dealt with technology will usually be sympathetic to someone who has a few technical difficulties. You might modify your presentation and keep going.

- *You trip, spill, tear, or break something?* Accidents happen. Unless it is too obvious, be discreet about the accident and keep on going. Allow people to laugh if it is rather ridiculous, and join in with them. Otherwise, don't mention it and stay focused.

Reflection

EXERCISE 9.10

Have you ever witnessed a speaker who had a challenge like the ones listed? If so, what did the person do, if anything, to recover? What was your impression of the speaker before and after the mishap?

Companion
Website

- *You draw a blank or lose your place?* First, breathe. Second, if you are using an outline or a written text, glance down to find your place. If you don't remember what you need to say about a particular point, move to the next point. You may be able to go back to the previous point if you remember it later. If you are not using any aids, ask for questions from the audience. A pause in your speech can add drama and may not seem as terrible to the audience as it seems to you.

Learning Styles Application

This chart lists the four learning styles and tips based on the chapter's main ideas. Locate your learning style and read the corresponding tips to maximize your success in college.

VISUAL

Those who learn best with visual stimulation find learning to write easier when they can "see" how an essay is supposed to look. It may be helpful for you to draw the organization for your papers. You enjoy using visual aids when making a presentation because they add interest and are helpful when making strong points.

AURAL

Aural learners may benefit from reading their essays aloud to determine if the paragraphs flow smoothly and fit together. You also enjoy speaking and usually are adept at using your voice to highlight major points and mark transitions in your presentations.

READ/WRITE

Those who learn best by reading and writing are more comfortable writing ideas down on paper and organizing them into a cohesive whole. You enjoy brainstorming and outlining your speeches, but you may have a little difficulty writing speeches for the ear rather than the eye.

KINESTHETIC

Kinesthetic learners enjoy the physical aspects of writing—moving the pen on the page or typing at the keyboard. To help organize your writing, you can try cutting up your essays or outlines and rearranging them until each point flows logically. You also enjoy using your body to make points more clearly when you speak.

Path of Discovery

Journal Entry

How have the writing and speaking expectations changed for you since high school? What do you expect the writing and speaking expectations to be like on the job?

FROM COLLEGE TO UNIVERSITY

How writing assignments and expectations may change

When you take upper-level courses at a university, you will write more and the expectations will be higher. Your professors will definitely assume that any writing challenges you had during your first two years of college have been overcome. Your professors are more concerned with the strength and originality of your argument and with the depth and breadth of your research than with grammar, punctuation, and spelling. Likewise, they expect that lower-level issues such as grammar and mechanics are mastered.

You will be writing more to discover what you think about a particular topic. You will also find writing and research more enjoyable as you settle into a major course of study. Most students who transfer learn that they enjoy writing about subjects that will help them in their careers. This kind of satisfaction takes time, and although you may not enjoy every writing assignment in community college, realize that with each writing assignment, you become a better writer and thinker, which will help make your transition to a four-year university that much easier.

FROM COLLEGE TO CAREER

Why strong speaking skills set you apart at work

Don't think of your speech communication class as the last time you will speak in front of peers and superiors. No matter what career path you take, you will have to use those communication skills to work in groups, relate to your boss, and instruct or present information to your coworkers. You may have to make a presentation to a client, summarize the company's goals and projects for new employees, or present to management a new idea for efficiency. Just as good writing skills are essential to on-the-job success, solid public speaking skills will set you apart from your coworkers as someone who can communicate even the most complicated or mundane aspects of the company. That kind of ability will garner respect and admiration from those who work with you.

Chapter in Review

1. What are the different elements of writing effectively?
2. What should you consider after being assigned a speech?
3. How are speaking and writing different?
4. How do you evaluate a speech or piece of writing? Create your own criteria for what you think makes a speech or text successful.

Case Scenarios

Read the following case scenarios and determine what each person should do. Refer to the information in this chapter as you write a description and plan of action for each student.

1. Renée is barely passing her literature class. She did not do well on the tests or the writing assignments, so she asked someone to help her write her final literary analysis paper. A friend of her mother's, Joan, offered to help her. When Joan meets with Renée, she offers to write down all of Renée's ideas, organize them, and reword her sentences. The result is that Renée's paper earns an A, something that she has not achieved all semester. What do you think of the help Renée received? Is there some other way that she can improve her writing without that kind of help?

2. Paul is having a hard time understanding the research assignment his government professor handed out to the class. He had two months to work on the paper, but he hasn't done anything yet, and now he has only two weeks. Where should he start and what should he do?

3. Jennifer's professor writes very few comments on her papers, so she is not sure how he arrives at her grades. She wants to improve her writing, but she doesn't know where to start. What should she do?

4. Pietra is afraid of public speaking and postponed taking her speech class until her last semester in college. The professor lectured about overcoming speaking anxiety, and she read the material in her textbook, but she doesn't think she can pass the class. What can she do to overcome her intense fear and pass the class?

Research It Further

1. Search the Internet and create a "hot list" of sites that are beneficial to college students. You can focus on a particular aspect of writing such as grammar, or create a list of several topics that concern college writers.

2. Interview two people whose careers are in fields other than writing and ask them how important writing is to their jobs.

3. Interview two people whose careers are in fields other than professional speaking and ask them how speaking effectively is important to their jobs.

4. Create a survey of students' attitudes toward and concerns about public speaking. Poll your class and other students and compile your results. Present your findings to your class.

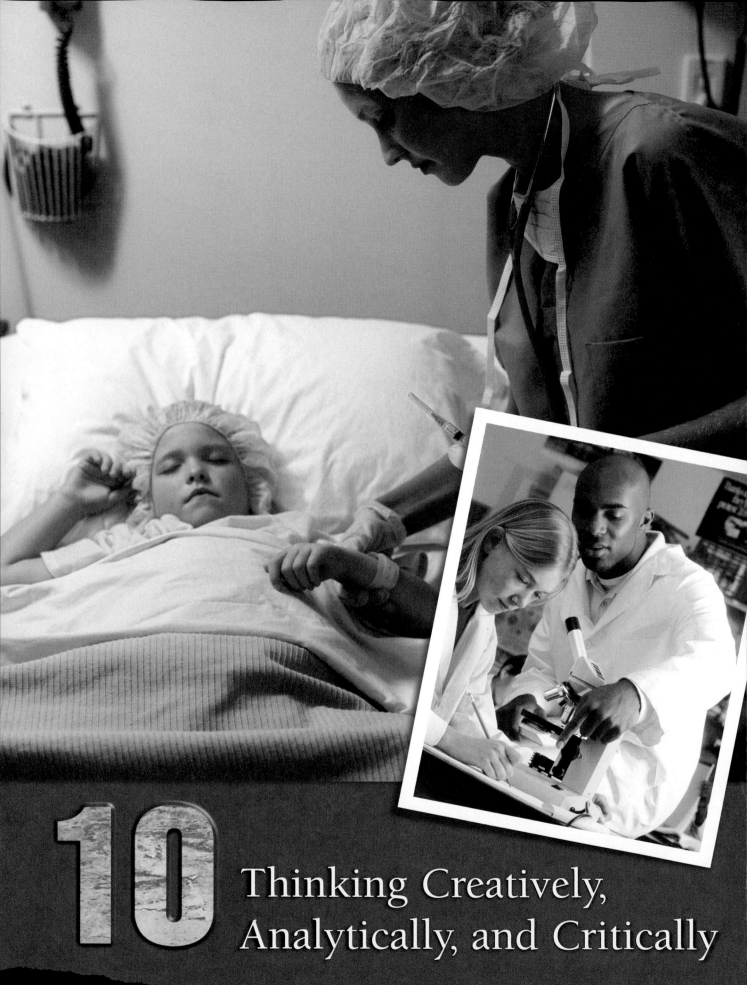

10 Thinking Creatively, Analytically, and Critically

manda uses a variety of methods to think creatively and critically in her classes, whether it is generating ideas for writing or evaluating other students' work. This chapter first teaches you how to think creatively, analytically, and critically in your classes and beyond. Then, the last part of the chapter focuses on using critical thinking to solve problems. Although Amanda may not be experiencing any problems so far in college, she can use the skills she learns in class to troubleshoot issues that arise as she completes her degree and enters the workforce. Cultivating strong critical thinking and problem-solving skills makes future choices easier as you complete a certificate or degree.

In this chapter, you will find answers to these questions:

- What is creative thinking and why is it important?

- How can I become more creative?

- What is analytical thinking and how will I use it in college?

- What is critical thinking and how is it connected to problem solving?

COMMUNITY · COLLEGE ·

Student Profile

NAME: *Amanda Ward*   AGE: *19*

MAJOR: *Journalism*

1. How do you use creative thinking in college?

   I have to come up with ideas for short stories and poems in my creative writing class, so I use different methods to create new ideas. I usually brainstorm or talk with my friends about ideas.

2. How do you use critical thinking in your college classes?

   Working with a variety of people in my creative writing class requires that I think critically. I have to evaluate and assess poems and short stories and explain how one piece of writing may be better than another.

3. What is your VARK?

   Kinesthetic.

Think About It

Think about it. You've heard those three simple words before, but have you ever thought about *how* you are thinking? The term for thinking about thinking is *metacognition,* or being aware of your own thought processes. Thus far, you have thought about what you value, how you learn, what college culture is, and how you relate to others. Throughout the chapters, you were asked to think about what you read and learn, whether it is through the reflection and critical thinking exercises or the end-of-chapter questions and ideas for further research. In fact, this book was designed so that you are actively engaged in thinking through information and creating knowledge.

The activities that brought you to this point are the same ones you currently practice in your classes. You are moving beyond taking information in only to send it back out in the same form for a test or paper. Instead, you are building creative, analytical, and critical thinking skills with each course. Strong critical thinking skills set you apart in the classroom and the workplace: You are better informed because you know to seek the information you need; you make better choices because you think through all the possibilities; and you continue to improve on your chosen solutions because you understand that evaluating your solution is key to making better future choices.

Bloom's Taxonomy

In 1956, Benjamin Bloom and his colleagues (Soto, 2005) described six levels of learning behavior that they considered part of the cognitive domain. These six levels are known as Bloom's Taxonomy. The first three levels are considered "lower-order" thinking skills because they require little more than recalling or using information in the same manner in which it was presented. Since the publication of Bloom's levels of thinking, instructors have used his theory to create course material and assignments that incorporate the higher levels: analysis, synthesis, and evaluation. These "higher-order" thinking skills are part of critical thinking because they involve breaking information apart, creating something new from the information, and assessing the information for reliability or usefulness. A majority of your classes in college focus on the last three levels.

Exhibit 10.1 contains each level of Bloom's Taxonomy as well as a list of actions connected to each level. You may recognize some of the verbs in your assignments or on your exams. Consider how you encounter the different actions in your course work. Do you have some classes that require more assignments at the knowledge

Reflection

EXERCISE 10.1

What levels of Bloom's Taxonomy do you find in most college assignments? Provide two examples of assignments you had at the three higher levels.

Companion
Website

EXHIBIT 10.1 *Bloom's taxonomy.*

LEVELS	ACTIONS
Knowledge	Describe, list, tell, locate, find, state, name, relate, identify
Comprehension	Explain, interpret, restate, compare, discuss, predict
Application	Solve, show, use, construct, complete, examine, classify, apply, compute, produce, solve
Analysis	Analyze, distinguish, examine, compare, contrast, separate, break down, diagram
Synthesis	Create, compose, plan, design, imagine, propose, rewrite, modify
Evaluation	Judge, select, choose, decide, justify, debate, argue, assess, rate, appraise, conclude

and comprehension levels? Do you have some classes that require you to synthesize and evaluate in most assignments? Just as knowing your learning style helps you make better decisions when you read, take notes, and study in college, understanding the different levels of Bloom's Taxonomy helps you see the purpose for the kinds of test questions and assignments you encounter. This awareness, like an appreciation for learning styles, helps you understand what kinds of thinking skills are necessary to be successful in college.

Critical Thinking

EXERCISE 10.2

Read the review questions at the end this chapter and determine the Bloom's Taxonomy level for each. (*Hint:* Compare the action verbs in Exhibit 10.1 with the verbs used in the review questions.)

Companion
Website

Creative Thinking

reative thinking, or the act of creating ideas for solving problems, is an integral part of education. Without creative thinking, there would be no inventions, new formulas, breakthroughs in technology and science, new art movements, advances in design and architecture—the list is endless. Without creative thinking, there would be no electricity, no indoor plumbing, no automobiles, and no zippers in our clothes. Just getting to your classes would be a totally different experience.

Harris (2002) contends that creative thinking is a skill, a process, and an attitude (pp. 1–2). In other words, creative thinkers are not born with special powers; they just use their imagination more regularly than others. The good news, though, is that you can learn to think creatively by following some basic guidelines.

Improve your imagination. Find ways to keep your mind sharp and your imagination flourishing. The puzzles that follow are just a sample of what you can do a few minutes a day to improve your thinking. Turning off the TV and picking up a book is another easy way to stimulate your imagination. If you enjoy kinesthetic activities, create something to get your mind active.

Creative thinking is a key part of science, art, technology, and any other discipline you can name.

Think in all directions. Thinking in all directions means you consider ideas that worked before, didn't work before, worked for other problems, and have not been paired with another idea. Some of the most creative ideas take ordinary solutions and reapply them to other problems. Creative thinking demands that all angles be considered as you generate ideas.

Suspend judgment. For creative thinking, evaluation is not necessary—save it for critical thinking and problem solving. The focus should be on getting ideas down, not on judging them for their practicality. "There is no wrong answer" is a common phrase at this point to keep you generating thoughts.

Keep it up. One main difference between people who think creatively and those who don't is perseverance, or the determination to see ideas through—and to keep generating them when the ones you come up with don't work.

Harris (2002) says, "Creative thinking creates the ideas with which critical thinking works" (p. 5). To improve your critical thinking and problem-solving abilities, consider these guidelines, find ways to practice them, and maintain your curiosity and a positive attitude.

Keeping Your Mind Limber

As stated earlier, a key to thinking creatively is to play games and complete puzzles designed to stretch your mind's muscles. Some of the activities for maintaining intellectual flexibility include word searches, jigsaw puzzles, crossword puzzles, and logic problems. You can find books that contain countless activities, like the ones that appear below, in stores or on the Internet. Some appear regularly in newspapers and magazines. You may also participate in games of strategy to keep your mind sharp. You can benefit from the mental workout of board games, such as checkers and chess, that involve strategy and thinking about the effects of future actions.

Critical Thinking   EXERCISE 10.3

How many different uses can you think of for a plastic straw?

Companion
Website

Cryptograms. Cryptograms are word puzzles that involve creating a "code" to be deciphered. Usually, a code, such as the following example, is given without any clues. The goal is to "break" the code by figuring out what letters have been replaced with other letters. For example, the letter A may appear as the letter T. Each time the letter T appears in the code, replace it with the letter A.

> *DECIPHERED CODE: HAPPY NEW YEAR*
>
> *CODE: LGKKM VJS PJGU*

Wordplays. Wordplays are combinations of letters, symbols, and numbers that create a visual wordplay. See how quickly you can figure out the common phrase or saying that is represented. The answer to the first one is "six feet under ground."

Practice

EXERCISE 10.4

Decipher this cryptogram:

SXXCRAZ DLMO BRAW TGXDRNGX YPA NX TMA.

GROUND ――― 6 FEET	MCE MCE MCE	R/E/A/D/I/N/G	OHOLENE

Wordplays are also found on vanity license plates. The next time you see a license plate with an unusual arrangement of numbers and letters, see if you can decode the message. Here are four examples:

10SNE1	4U2NV	BCNU2	2M8OS

Numberplays. The purpose of this activity is to get your mind thinking in terms of what you know about the number of things. The words associated with the numbers are abbreviated to their first letters only. For example, the numberplay "88 = K on a P" is "88 keys on a piano." The numberplay "365 = D in a Y" is "365 days in a year." See if you can solve these numberplays.

2 = W on a B	13 = S on an AF
4 = Q in a D	21 = D on a D
5 = D in a ZC	26 = L of the A
9 = P in the SS	52 = C in a D

Collaboration

EXERCISE 10.5

Working in a group, create five wordplay puzzles and five numberplay puzzles. Trade your puzzles with another group and see how well each group solves them.

Analytical Thinking

oth creative and analytical thinking are part of problem solving. While creative thinking involves the *creation* of ideas,

Famous People in History Logic Problem

Middle States Community College has many professors and students who look like famous people in history. They decided to hold a contest to see who looks most like a famous figure in history. Dr. Longhorn and four of her students entered the contest and won 1st through 5th places out of 22 entrants. Using the clues below, determine who looked like whom and what place they won.

1. Sandy placed one position ahead of the Eleanor Roosevelt look-alike, who placed one position higher than Ms. Goodman in the final judging.

2. Jenny and Ms. Judd also placed in the top five.

3. Amy finished one place ahead of the Hillary Clinton look-alike.

4. Kathryn, who isn't the Eleanor Roosevelt look-alike, and Ms. Kirby both want to be scientists.

5. Debbie finished immediately ahead of the Marie Curie look-alike and two places ahead of Ms. Judd in the final standings.

6. Ms. Kirby, Ms. Young, and the Imelda Marcos look-alike were featured in an article about the event in the college newspaper.

7. The Harriet Tubman look-alike placed just ahead of Kathryn in the judging.

8. Ms. Goodman isn't the student who appeared as Hillary Clinton.

From All-Star Puzzles' Star Look-Alikes logic puzzle at www.allstarpuzzles.com/logic/00161.html. Used with permission.

analytical thinking involves the *analysis,* or the breaking apart, of the problem and of the possible solutions to examine them fully. *Analytical thinking* is also defined by some disciplines as the scientific process of defining a problem, developing a hypothesis, gathering and examining facts, and proposing a solution. More recently, analytical and critical thinking were linked together as different parts of a process that ends with solving a problem. Analytical thinking is also found in such disciplines as literature, in which you break apart a poem and examine its parts, and computer science, in which you break apart a network and determine how each part comes together to create the whole.

To improve your analytical thinking skills, practice with basic logic problems that require you to break apart the problem and examine the different parts to arrive at an answer.

Practice

EXERCISE 10.6

Solve the logic problem in the box above.

Companion Website

Critical Thinking

The term *critical thinking* is difficult to define, but has a long tradition. Critical thinkers such as Socrates and Thomas Aquinas, to name only two, had a tremendous effect on the way we think about the world we live in. But what makes them critical thinkers? What is a critical thinker? Diestler (1998) defines a critical thinker as "someone who uses specific criteria to evaluate reasoning and make decisions" (p. 2). Someone who thinks critically does not take information at face value; instead, the information is reviewed for accuracy, authority, and logic before it is considered useable.

Chapter 7 discusses how to read critically—that is a start to making informed decisions about what you read, but you can also use critical thinking in other parts of your everyday life. There will be times when you have to make an important decision, and you should use critical thinking in order to make the best choice.

To illustrate the importance of using critical thinking skills, consider this scenario: You receive an e-mail from a friend who claims that she unknowingly sent you a virus. Her e-mail instructs you to search for the offending file and delete it immediately. Unaware of any problems usually associated with viruses, you nonetheless search for the file and find it, exactly where your friend said it would be on your computer. Your friend is a trustworthy person and you value her advice, so you delete the file. You get an e-mail from her the next day that says she is sorry she sent you a hoax, but you've already deleted a perfectly normal file from your computer.

Now, consider the next scenario: Your friend sends you a link to a pop-up blocker because he knows you hate those annoying intrusions while surfing the Internet. Because you have been deceived by free software before, you decide to search several reputable sites devoted to reviewing new software. You find that the pop-up blocker is a fraud; if you clicked on the link your friend sent, your computer would be overrun with pop-up advertisements of questionable origin.

In the first scenario, two people, at least, were deceived by what appeared to be legitimate, and helpful, information. Who doesn't want to rid his computer of a potentially dangerous virus? Unfortunately, you and your friend did not question the information. In the second scenario, however, you had encountered false claims before and realized that you should check every piece of information that comes to you, regardless of the friendly source. You became, in essence, a critical thinker. Thinking critically allowed you to review the information and search for authoritative sources that helped you make a decision about what action to take.

As the Information Age evolves, critical thinking skills are not just advantageous; they are essential to survival. Not only must you possess these skills, but others must also possess them so you do not have to evaluate every piece of information you receive. Can you imagine a world in which everything you read is suspect, and there is no sure way of determining what is true and accurate and what is not? For people who do not think critically, that imagined world is a reality.

Common Logical Fallacies

To evaluate information effectively (a part of critical thinking), familiarize yourself with some of the more common logical fallacies used when arguing a point. A *logical fallacy* is a mistake in reasoning. Although most people try to avoid fallacies when trying to persuade others, fallacies do appear even in the best of arguments. You should be aware of the many errors in reasoning that can lead to fallacies. Exhibit 10.2 summarizes common fallacies.

Critical Thinking PLUS*

Consider how understanding your personality style or learning preference can help you through challenging situations.

You read that left-brained people are better at analytical thinking and right-brained people are better at creative thinking. You consider yourself a left-brained thinker and your VARK learning style is kinesthetic. Your economics instructor asked the class to identify several ways the college economics club could earn money to send a group of students to Mexico for a week to study the impact of economic development. Your instructor said that the person who develops the most creative ideas will also go on the trip. You would like to go, but you don't think of yourself as creative. What can you do to generate creative ideas and go on the trip?

NOTES

*PERSONALITY + LEARNING STYLE = UNDERSTANDING SITUATIONS

Connection Between Critical Thinking and Problem Solving

Although not all critical thinking leads to solving a problem, problem solving relies on critical as well as creative and analytical thinking. In order to think critically to solve a problem, you have to go through a process. Remember, the more minds that work on a problem, the more likely all sides of the problem will be addressed, which may make the solution better. Although you may not always have an opportunity to work on a problem in a group, you can ask others for their advice during the process.

Here are the basic steps for using critical thinking to solve a problem:

- Clearly identify the problem.
- Brainstorm possible solutions to the problem.
- Analzye possible solutions for their viability.
- Think through each solution and determine the benefits and drawbacks of each.
- Choose the solution that potentially works best.
- Evaluate the solution after it is in place.

Step 1: Identify the Problem Sometimes we assume we know what the problem is and try to fix it only to discover that the solution doesn't work because we fixed the wrong problem. Consider a crying baby who last ate two hours ago. If faced with the problem of a crying baby, you may assume

EXHIBIT 10.2   *Common fallacies.*

LOGICAL FALLACY	DEFINITION	EXAMPLE
Ad hominem	Literally means "at the man." It happens when someone attacks the person who is making the argument rather than the argument itself	What does she know about the economy? She didn't report her taxes for two years.
Beg the question	Assumes that what is being argued is actually true	Taxing the American public is akin to stealing from them. Therefore, taxes should be abolished.
False analogy	Creates a comparison between two items that are not in fact similar	Adolph Hitler's treatment of Jews is very similar to Saddam Hussein's treatment of the people of Iraq.
Hasty generalization	Jumps too quickly to a conclusion about an issue based on very little proof	I did not do well in my online class, so I believe that online classes are not as good as on-campus classes.
Non sequitur	Does not make sense	If I am in Boston, then I am in Massachusetts. Since I am not in Boston, then I am not in Massachusetts.
Post hoc	Assumes that if something comes before an event, then it must have caused the event.	I packed my lunch today and I got a speeding ticket. Therefore, the speeding ticket was caused by packing my lunch.
Straw man	Makes out the opposing argument to be weaker than it is and then counters that weaker argument; also refers to creating a weak argument for the purpose of making your argument look stronger	The city council doesn't want to build the bridge because they think it is unattractive. We shouldn't make important transportation decisions based on aesthetics.

the baby is still hungry and wants more to eat. When you try to feed the baby, he rejects the food. Now what? Is the baby not hungry? Did you offer something the baby doesn't like? Is the baby sick, too hot, too cold, tired? You can imagine how much time and energy you might spend trying to find a solution to the problem.

Identifying a problem's cause is the first logical step before you can begin to solve it. If you do not correctly identify the cause—or at least eliminate possible causes—before starting the next step, either you won't solve the problem or you might create a whole new problem to solve.

Step 2: Brainstorm Ideas This is the step where creative thinking is used. When you generate ideas, there are no rules except don't eliminate any ideas because they are too far-fetched or too odd. The goal of this step is to get the ideas recorded, and the more you can think "outside the box," the more likely you are considering all possibilities.

Use brainstorming, freewriting, clustering, and role-playing (if you can work with another person) to get ideas flowing. This is a good time to use your learning style strength to stretch your imagination.

Critical thinking is an integral part of problem solving— identifying, analyzing, choosing, and evaluating solutions.

Step 3: Analyze the Possibilities Both creative and analytical thinking, or breaking down the different ideas, help you at this stage. What are the different parts of the possibilities? Are any impossible, impractical, or illogical? Identify the least viable solutions and remove them from the list.

Step 4: Think Through Solutions Thinking through each solution involves exploring their benefits and drawbacks. Consider the possibilities, but don't completely discard them after the next step. You may need them after you evaluate your final solution and find it to be ineffective.

Step 5: Choose the Best Solution When choosing the best solution, consider the effects of the solution. Will it cause another problem? What kind of emotional, physical, and financial investment will it take? What do you need to do to implement the solution correctly? Use creative thinking to consider all sides of the solution before you make a final decision. Analytical thinking can help you list all the possibilities in a table to examine the consequences.

Step 6: Evaluate the Solution The final stage of problem solving is also the highest level in Bloom's Taxonomy: evaluation. The ability to evaluate allows you to use what you learned in the problem-solving process to solve other problems. Ask yourself if the problem is resolved adequately. Did the solution only partly solve the problem or was it a complete solution? What, if anything, would you do differently if you experience the same problem?

Putting Critical Thinking into Practice

What do you do in the following situations?

- You have an exam at 9:00 A.M. You get into your car at 8:20 to get to class on time, and your car won't start.

- You need a math tutor to help you get through elementary algebra successfully. The tutoring center's hours are not convenient for you because you work every evening the center is open late.

- You are worried that you may not be able to purchase your textbooks for next semester because the bookstore's prices are higher than you anticipated.

If your car won't start and you have to get to an exam, would you give up and go back into the house, hoping that you can make up the exam? If you cannot find a tutor for elementary algebra, would you plod through the course and pray that you make it? If you can't afford textbooks next semester, would you see how far you can get without buying them? What are other possible solutions to these problems? If you use the critical thinking steps for problem solving, you may realize that there are other alternatives, or possible solutions, to your predicaments. Here are one student's problem-solving steps for the first scenario:

1. Clearly identify the problem. I have two problems. The first is that my car won't start, and the second is that I need to get to school to take an exam.

2. Brainstorm possible solutions to the problem. To address my more immediate problem, getting to school to take my test, I can do one or more of the following:

- Call a friend to pick me up.
- Call a cab to take me to school.
- Catch a bus.
- Call my instructor to ask about taking a makeup exam.
- Run to school.
- Walk to school.

3. Evaluate the possible solutions for their viability.

- *Call a friend:* I can get Jessica to pick me up, but she will then be late for work.
- *Call a cab:* It costs $20 and I won't get to school until 9:15 A.M.
- *Catch a bus:* I don't know the bus schedule and will have to walk 1.2 miles to the bus stop.
- *Call my instructor:* She may not allow me to make up the exam; I may not be able to get a message to her.
- *Run to school:* I am not in shape to make it all the way.
- *Walk to school:* The distance to school is 3.5 miles. It will take me at least an hour to get there, which will give me only 30 minutes to take my exam.

4. Think through each solution and determine the benefits and drawbacks to each. I eliminated walking or running to school and catching the bus. I am left with three possible solutions: (1) call my friend Jessica to pick me up; (2) call a cab; and (3) call my instructor about making up the exam.

- *Option 1:* The benefit of calling Jessica is that she is a friend and would help me out. I would also make it to the exam on time. A drawback to calling Jessica is that she would be late to work if she takes me to school.
- *Option 2:* The benefit of calling a cab is that I would definitely get to school. A drawback is that it costs $20, which I don't need to spend. Also, I wouldn't get to school until 9:15.
- *Option 3:* The benefit of calling my instructor is that I could explain why I can't make it to class, and she might be sympathetic to my dilemma. Another benefit is that she might allow me to make up the exam. The drawbacks are that I might not be able to get a message to her, and she might not allow me to make up the exam.

5. Choose the solution that potentially works the best. My solution is to call my friend Jessica because it is the easiest solution. I won't have to pay to get to school, and I can get there on time. She may, though, be irritated at me for asking for a favor at the last minute. Then again, she may be very glad to return a favor to me, or she may not want to take me because it will make her late for work.

6. Evaluate the solution after it is in place. After I have Jessica take me to school, I can evaluate whether or not the solution worked. If Jessica agrees to take me and can get me to school on time even though it makes her late, then the solution will be a success for me. If she has trouble picking me up or if she gets mad because I made her late, then I have to consider other solutions if I have car trouble again.

Collaboration

EXERCISE 10.8

Working in a group, discuss a student issue (e.g., parking, student events, or computer access) on your campus. Use the critical thinking process to develop a viable solution. Share your ideas with the class.

Companion
Website

Answers to Creative Thinking Puzzles

Cryptogram: KEEPING YOUR MIND FLEXIBLE CAN BE FUN.

Wordplays: (1) Three blind mice; (2) Reading between the lines; (3) A hole in one

License plates: (1) Tennis, anyone?; (2) For you to envy; (3) Be seeing you, too; (4) Tomatoes

Numberplays: 2 Wheels on a Bicycle; 4 Quarters in a Dollar; 5 Digits in a Zip Code; 9 Planets in the Solar System; 13 Stripes on an American Flag; 21 Dots on a Die; 26 Letters of the Alphabet; 52 Cards in a Deck

Logic puzzle.

First place: Sandy Longhorn as Imelda Marcos

Second place: Debbie Kirby as Eleanor Roosevelt

Third place: Jenny Goodman as Marie Curie

Fourth place: Amy Judd as Harriet Tubman

Fifth place: Katherine Young as Hillary Clinton

Reflection

EXERCISE 10.9

How is critical thinking essential to surviving in the 21st century?

Companion
Website

Learning Styles Application

This chart lists the four learning styles and tips based on the chapter's main ideas. Locate your learning style and read the corresponding tips to maximize your success in college.

VISUAL

Learners whose strength is visual need to see the causes of a problem and the consequences of possible solutions. You can use visual representations to determine what the best solution is.

AURAL

Aural learners can listen to or play music as a way to flex their creative muscles. Talking through or listening to possible solutions work better for you than writing down ideas.

READ/WRITE

Those who learn best by reading and writing can improve their creativity by reading books and articles about creative people and about creative solutions to problems. You also work through problem solving by brainstorming and writing out possible solutions.

KINESTHETIC

Kinesthetic learners can stretch their creative muscles by using their bodies. Exercise may clear your mind enough to think a little more clearly and creatively. Create physical models of possible solutions.

Path of Discovery

Journal Entry

How will practicing critical thinking steps affect future decisions? Do you think you will be better prepared to solve problems and make better choices, or do you think you will be more confused about the choices you have?

FROM COLLEGE TO UNIVERSITY

Higher-level thinking is the norm in upper-level classes

After you transfer to a university, you will continue to use creative, analytical, and critical thinking skills in upper-level classes because professors move away from the knowledge and comprehension levels of Bloom's Taxonomy to the higher levels of synthesis and evaluation. You will spend more time doing research and determining whether the sources you find are reliable and accurate. You will also use those sources to support your own new ideas, developed through creative thinking, about current issues in your major. You will be more responsible for the depth and breadth of your education, and strong thinking skills will help you deepen your learning.

FROM COLLEGE TO CAREER

How critical thinking is used at work

Critical thinking at work is essential to a rewarding and successful career. Your employer, no matter your position, will value your ability to think critically and solve problems, and you will value the work you do if you are allowed to use those skills to improve yourself and your environment.

How will you use critical thinking at work? There will be, no doubt, countless opportunities to think critically at work. For example, you may realize that the office does not run efficiently, so you evaluate ways to improve the flow of work. You may even be asked to think critically about a problem in order to solve it. No matter how you arrive at thinking critically on the job, keep the steps to problem solving handy.

As you read in this chapter, critical thinking is a process, not an end. Once you solve a problem, new ones will arise that require critical thinking. To improve yourself and your progress at work, be committed to thinking critically.

Chapter in Review

1. What kinds of thinking will you use in college?
2. Describe the critical thinking process for solving a problem.
3. Provide examples of uses for creative, analytical, and critical thinking.
4. Compare and contrast creative thinking and analytical thinking.
5. How effective is the critical thinking process? Would it be helpful in all situations? If not, describe the situations in which the critical thinking process might hinder a positive outcome. What other process would work better?

Case Scenarios

Read the following case scenarios and determine what each person should do. Refer to the information in this chapter as you write a description and plan of action for each student.

1. Joan was selected as a student ambassador for her college. One of her duties is to help prepare the fall orientation for new students. The advisors told the ambassadors that last year's new students rated orientation low because they had to wait in long lines to get registered and the information they received was too detailed and difficult to comprehend. Joan and her fellow ambassadors were asked to create a new way of providing orientation to students. What process should Joan and her fellow ambassadors follow to create a successful program for new students?

2. Sidra wants to earn money for college tuition next year, but she doesn't have the time to work 40 hours a week. If Sidra's creative thinking process results in the following ideas, explain what steps she should follow to determine the most viable solution: sell blood, tutor classmates, tattoo herself with a local company's logo and charge them for advertising, sell items on the Internet, work as a telemarketer, and house sit for friends and family members.

3. Kenya decided to apply for a loan forgiveness program that will pay all of her tuition as she completes a degree in computer networking. The loan forgiveness program requires that she find a job in networking within three months of graduation, or she will owe the full amount of her loans. After she completes a year of her degree program, she learns that the job market for networking specialists does not look promising for the next five years, which means she may have difficulty finding a job when she graduates in a year. What should Kenya do?

Research It Further

1. Using the keywords "critical thinking" and "creative thinking," search the Internet for tips on improving critical and creative thinking skills. Make a table of the different tips and present the information to your classmates.

2. Create a survey to distribute to fellow students that asks what the top concerns on campus are. Report your results to the class and choose one concern to solve using the critical thinking process.

3. Interview faculty members in different programs and ask them to provide a critical thinking scenario that a graduate in their programs would encounter at work. Ask them to work through the problem to a feasible solution. Share the different problem-solving scenarios with the class and ask them to compare and contrast the processes.

References

Diestler, S. (1998). *Becoming a critical thinker: A user friendly manual* (2nd ed.). Upper Saddle River, NJ: Prentice Hall.

Harris, R. (2002). *Creative problem solving: A step-by-step approach.* Los Angeles: Pyrczak Publishing.

Soto, M. (2005). "Bloom's Taxonomy." Retrieved Sept. 27, 2005, from www.officeport.com/edu/blooms/htm.

11 Information Literacy and Research Writing

Research and writing are two highly regarded activities in higher education. Even though community college instructors usually focus their careers on teaching, not researching, they still participate in research and writing as part of their professional enrichment and as part of improving their classes. Knowing how to find information and use it effectively will be integral components of your classes; these skills will also be important when you work on a four-year degree (and beyond) and later, enter the workforce. Most jobs require the ability to access information.

This chapter will help you become more adept at finding sources, assessing them for their worth and reliability, and using that information in your class assignments. Specifically, this chapter answers the following questions:

- *What is information literacy?*
- *How do I locate good sources?*
- *How do I evaluate the sources I find?*
- *What is the process of writing a research paper?*

COMMUNITY · COLLEGE ·

Student Profile

NAME: **Jeremy Rawn** AGE: **24**

MAJOR: **Undecided**

1. What is your experience with finding information for research assignments?

   I can usually find what I need on the Internet or in the library. If there is something I cannot find quickly, I usually move on to something else that will satisfy the assignment.

2. How often do you use the library and why?

   I use the on-campus library some, but I find a lot of stuff at the library's webpage. I like to use the webpage because I can access it from home.

3. What kinds of research papers have you written in college?

   I have only written two so far. One was for a sociology class and the other was a literature paper for my composition class.

4. What advice would you give other students about searching for information and using it in a paper?

   Definitely start early. Ask questions if you need help. The librarians can help you if you need anything.

5. What is your VARK?

   Aural and Kinesthetic.

Living in the Information Age

We are both lucky and cursed to be living in an age where so much information is at our fingertips. It doesn't seem that long ago that researching was limited to what was available on the shelves of our homes or our local libraries, the latter of which were not open at 2 A.M. Even then, we were limited to what we could access, and if we couldn't get the information we needed, then our research was not complete. Now, it seems that our access is boundless, and our ability to retrieve what we need—and what we don't—is only a click away.

With this shift in how we get information and how much information we can get comes a need to sharpen both our research and evaluation skills. No longer can we say that we didn't know something and no longer can we blindly believe everything we hear, see, and read. Instead, we have an obligation to learn how to find the available information and how to use it wisely.

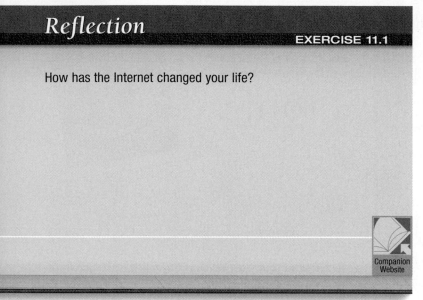

Reflection

EXERCISE 11.1

How has the Internet changed your life?

Companion
Website

Information Literacy

Even though we have more access to more material, we are not more informed. With so many choices, many of us get lost in all the possibilities. Developing a set of information literacy skills will help you navigate the sea of information now available. Information literacy is the ability to find, understand, evaluate, and incorporate information from a variety of sources or media. The American Library Association defines information literacy as "a set of skills needed to find, retrieve, analyze, and use information."

Locating Resources

When looking for sources to use for an assignment, where do you begin? Some students may go to the library and poke around the aisles and leaf through books and magazines. Others may log into the Internet and start entering keywords in a search engine. Some may look to friends and family for sources, especially if the assignment asks that they interview or survey people. As you can see, there are a variety of places you can go to locate sources for an assignment. The key to finding the sources you need is to decide where you should go first and what to do when you get there.

The first step to learning how to locate and use resources effectively is to go to the library early in the semester. If you have not already gone this semester, go soon, even if you do not have any assignments to be researched. Getting to know the layout, the resources, and the people who are there to help you are crucial to using the library and its sources well.

The first step to learning how to locate and use resources effectively is to go to the library early in the semester.

Also, familiarize yourself with the library's website. Many colleges put a number of library resources on the Web so students can access information both on and off campus. To access all of the available information on your library's website, you may have to get a log-in password, but your librarian can give you that information.

Browsing Versus Searching

Sherman and Price (2002) provide a useful comparison of browsing and searching:

> If you're familiar with a subject, it's often most useful to *browse* in the section [of the library] where books about the subject are shelved. . . . If you're unfamiliar with a subject, however, browsing is both inefficient and potentially futile if you fail to locate the section of the library where the material you're interested in is shelved. *Searching*, using the specialized tools offered by a library's catalog, is far more likely to provide satisfactory results. (p. 18)

INTEGRITY MATTERS

An important component of information literacy is the ethical and legal use of information once you find the source you need. The Association of College & Research Libraries specifies that "the information literate student follows laws, regulations, institutional policies, and etiquette related to the access and use of information resources" (www.acrl.org).

Although the authors make this analogy to help the reader understand how to use the Internet, it is still helpful to realize that both browsing and searching are useful activities if done appropriately. When you do not know much about a subject, searching is your best method of uncovering information. You can search the card catalog, scan a subject index, or ask a librarian directly. Once you are familiar with the location of sources on a particular topic, you can then browse the area just as you would browse the cereal aisle to find something to eat for breakfast.

Catalogs

What was once one of the most familiar sights in a library, the card catalog, is now a relic. Those wooden or metal file cabinets with the small drawers are more likely to be found in an antique store than a modern library. Even though the catalog in your library is probably online, you can still benefit from knowing how the card catalog works because many of the electronic programs provide the same information once available on a small card.

The original card catalog system was based on three types of cards: author, subject, and title. All of the cards were alphabetized. If you wanted to find the book on gardening by P. Allen Smith titled *Your Favorite Garden Spaces*, then you could look under "G" for gardening (subject card), "S" for "Smith" (author card), or "Y" for "*Your Favorite Garden Spaces*" (title card). Each card provided information about the book and where you could locate it in the library.

Now, you can access that information online if your college library has an online catalog system. Instead of pulling drawers and flipping through cards, you can type a word or words to find what you are looking for. Most catalog systems allow you to search by keyword, subject, author, and title. Once you type in a word, you get a list of possible matches to your query. It is your job, then, to look through the possibilities to find the one you want. After choosing a particular book, find the location information, called the "call number," and then look for the book on the shelf.

You should realize that using the online catalog is not the same as searching for something on the Internet. Most catalogs only provide information about the books housed in that library. If there are branches of the library, then it may tell you if the book is located elsewhere. Also, if your search for a keyword or subject is not productive, use keywords that are similar. For example, if you want to look for books on education, also search with words such as "learning" and "instruction."

Books

To search for and find books effectively, become familiar with the shelving system that libraries use. The Library of Congress Classification System, which is often used in college libraries, is a series of categories that correspond to the letters of the alphabet. Each letter represents a category or class and then is broken into subclasses (see the examples in Exhibits 11.1 and 11.2). For example, the letter "H" indicates Social Sciences. Subclasses for Social Sciences include "HG" for Finance, "HM" for Sociology, and "HQ" for

EXHIBIT 11.1 *Class Q—Books about science.*

CLASS Q—SCIENCE SUBCLASSES

Q	General Science	**QD**	Chemistry	**QL**	Zoology
QA	Mathematics	**QE**	Geology	**QM**	Human anatomy
QB	Astronomy	**QH**	Natural history—biology	**QP**	Physiology
QC	Physics	**QK**	Botany	**QM**	Microbiology

Family, women, and marriage. The classification goes even further to include a combination of letters and numbers. Knowing how the classification works not only helps you search for sources more easily, but it also helps you browse more effectively. If you know that the section "QD" contains books on chemistry, then you can go to that section when you want to see what kinds of books your library has on that subject.

In addition to knowing where books on a particular subject are located, become familiar with how you can use books in research. Books are often considered good sources for authoritative information. Because authors go through a lengthy process before their books are published—the books are reviewed and edited, usually by respected authorities on the subject—those books are more likely to contain accurate and reliable information. Moreover, book authors take the time to reflect on an event or issue rather than react quickly, which often means a more thoughtful presentation of ideas.

On the other hand, information presented in books is quickly outdated, especially in fields that rely on cutting-edge ideas. Some books about computers and medicine become obsolete as new developments and theories emerge. Despite the safeguards in place for publishing books, not all of them contain reliable, accurate, and authoritative information. You still have to think critically when you read books and use the information in your research.

E-books are becoming increasingly popular with libraries that have limited space or money to purchase hard copies of texts. E-books can be downloaded to handheld readers, or they can be checked out through your library's online catalog. Often, you can browse the e-book's table of contents before electronically checking the book out. Once you check it out, you can access the full book online, usually for a few days. If your library does not offer e-books, but you would like to browse a book's table of contents and sample pages, you may find what you are looking for on www.amazon.com. Although Amazon.com sells books, it does allow you to look through some of the books much as you would flip through a physical book to determine whether it will help you in your research.

EXHIBIT 11.2 *Catalog information for books on chemistry.*

Call Number: QD31.2 .B78 1994	*Chemistry :* *The central science*	Theodore L. Brown; H. Eugene LeMay, Jr.; Bruce E. Bursten	1994
Call Number: QD181 .H1 R54 2002	*Hydrogen :* *The essential element*	John S. Rigden	2002

Databases

Like the card catalog, databases are used to find resources. Typically, databases contain information about articles rather than entire books, although some databases do provide such access. Most databases provide access to newspapers, magazines, and journal articles, either an abstract of an article or the full text. Databases can reside on a single computer, on a network that is accessed outside the library, or on a CD-ROM. The growing trend is to provide database access to students who live off campus. In order to gain access, you must use a username and password, which you get from a librarian.

To use a database effectively, you have to know what you are looking for—have a keyword in mind. Because most databases are discipline specific, choose one that relates to your topic. For instance, if you want to search for legal cases in which the death penalty was overturned, use a database such as FindLaw, which provides access to articles in the legal profession. If you want to search for recent trends in high-school teaching, use the database ERIC, which stands for Educational Resource Information Center. As with the catalog, experiment with different keywords and phrases until you find what you are looking for.

Magazines, Journals, and Newspapers

Unlike books, periodicals such as magazines, journals, and newspapers are published more frequently, hence the name periodical. They are also different from books in that they contain the most recent information. For example, daily newspapers provide access to the most up-to-date stories even though the facts may be revised with each passing day. Magazines, which are usually published weekly, monthly, or bimonthly, may be less current, but can provide information about hot topics. Journals, which are published less frequently than newspapers and magazines, provide information about current trends while still taking the time to check the facts and theories presented. Often, journals are "peer reviewed," which means they go through an extra step of having experts in the field review the information's validity before it is published.

To illustrate how each type of source handles current topics, think about the time line for the events of September 11, 2001. Newspapers were the first print sources to report the events. However, the news stories of the first few days did not contain much solid information; rather, they raised many questions as to why it happened. Weeks later, magazine articles provided more pieces of the puzzle and filled in the gaps that the earlier newspaper articles created. Months later, even years later, peer-reviewed journal articles help us see the larger picture and how the event fits into the historical landscape of the early 21st century. As you can see, each type of periodical has different benefits depending on what kind of information you need.

Reference Materials

Encyclopedias, dictionaries, atlases, almanacs, maps, and directories are just a few of the reference materials found in your library or on your library's website. Because of their inherent usefulness, they should be considered as authoritative sources when starting your research project. In your library's reference section, you may find specific encyclopedias—ones that focus on medieval history or Greek mythology, for example—and specialized dictionaries—ones that focus on medical terms, for example. Reference materials are best used in the beginning stages of research instead of as sources for academic arguments.

Other Services

Your library and its staff are excellent resources for anything you may need during your college career. They provide a variety of services to help you find resources more easily. One of the easiest ways to take advantage of the library's services is by asking a librarian directly for help. You may ask in person or online—if they provide a library e-mail address. Your library may also provide interlibrary loans, which is a service that allows you to borrow books and materials from other libraries. Just determine which book or material you need and complete an interlibrary loan form obtained from the library staff.

Other methods of obtaining what you need may (depending on the range of services your library offers) include an academic library card that can be used at other area college libraries; library instruction for classes; library tours for individuals or groups of new students; and additional online resources that strengthen information literacy skills. To make full use of your library's resources and services, consider getting to know both their physical space on campus and their presence online.

Evaluating Web Sources

Website evaluation is a necessity for anyone who wants to use the information found on the Internet. Unlike books and peer-reviewed journals, anyone with an Internet connection can post information about any topic no matter how inaccurate or non-objective. With so much information available, it is essential to determine what information is reliable and useable.

In order to use websites effectively in your research, consider the following criteria used to evaluate websites.

Authority

When you visit a website, one of your first considerations should be the site's authority. Make a judgment early in your research as to whether or not the website is authoritative. How do you determine authority? To be honest, it

Critical Thinking PLUS*

Consider how understanding your personality style or learning preference can help you through challeging situations.

Your learning style preference is aural, and you consider yourself more logical, or left-brained, than creative, or right-brained. You have a major research paper due at the end of the semester, and part of the assignment is a required 10-minute class presentation of your paper. Your professor said that those projects that are well researched, logically written, and creatively presented will receive an A for the assignment. You really want to make an A on the assignment, but you are not sure if you can meet all the criteria. What can you do, considering your learning style preferences, to research, write, and present an excellent paper?

NOTES

* PERSONALITY + LEARNING STYLE = UNDERSTANDING SITUATIONS

can be difficult to determine a site's affiliation or who is ultimately responsible for the content. However, there are a few signs that can help you determine reliability. First, does the site's address end in "com," "org," or "edu"? If the site is a commercial site ("com"), then it is likely that the site is less reliable for scholarly information.

If, however, you are researching commercial sites and their marketing practices, a "com" site may be appropriate. If you are looking for a review of *Jane Eyre*, a site such as www.amazon.com will not necessarily provide you with an unbiased review; because Amazon.com's purpose is to sell the book, then you may not read a bad review.

Authority can also be evident in the site's affiliation. If you are looking for the latest respiratory therapies, then a site sponsored by the American Medical Association or endorsed by the *Journal of the American Medical Association* is considered reliable and authoritative. Likewise, a site sponsored by the government is a trustworthy source for statistics on federal issues.

Accuracy

If you are unsure of the site's authority or affiliation, you may be able to judge the information's reliability by determining its accuracy. Some easy telltale signs of inaccuracy include numerous grammatical and punctuation errors as well as misspelled words. Also, if the site does not list the person responsible for content, the site may not be dependable.

Another way to check information accuracy is to fact check some of the statements by searching for other sources that contain the same information. For example, if the site states that the government spent $38 billion on defense in 2002, then check other sites and sources by using "defense spending" or similar keywords in your search. You can also check print sources, such as government publications, in your library. If the website provides a bibliography or a list of sources used to present the information, then you have a great place to start looking at the information's accuracy.

Objectivity

As you become more familiar with the characteristics of a reliable website, you will be able to judge its objectivity. Simply stated, an objective website presents information fairly and without bias. How can you determine whether a site is biased? Sometimes it is hard to tell, but you can start by looking for context clues such as particular language and logical fallacies. If a site uses terms such as "draft dodger" to describe President Clinton, then you can assume that the site has some bias. Likewise, if a site refers to Republicans as "callous statesmen," then you can bet the information is slanted.

Timeliness

The timeliness, or currency, of the site's information is equally important. If the site has not been updated in five years, you may want to move to another source. Of course, the importance of timeliness depends on the subject matter. If, for instance, you are researching information about the events surrounding the beginning of the Civil War, you may not be as concerned with the information's timeliness as you would be if you are looking for information about Alzheimer's.

To locate the copyright date or the "last updated" statement, look at the bottom of the homepage. Often, there is also a copyright date that shows whether the page is still current. If there is no date, you cannot be sure when the site was uploaded and if any significant changes have occurred recently. When working with an undated, unknown source, be sure the information meets the other criteria first before deciding to use it in your research.

EXERCISE 11.4   *Critical Thinking*

Do you think all websites should be reviewed by a group of people whose job is to decide whether each site is reliable and authoritative? Should this group have the authority to ban sites that do not meet certain reliability standards? Why or why not?

Companion Website

Research Writing

College research assignments are designed to make students think critically about an issue; however, a common misconception about these assignments is that many students believe they must not include their own ideas about a topic. On the contrary, the purpose of such an assignment is to allow you to develop your own position about an issue along with providing authoritative support for your own ideas.

Understanding the Assignment

When assigned a research paper, pay special attention to the requirements. Here are just a few considerations that may be part of the assignment:

Topic. Is one assigned or do you choose your own? Are there any "off limits" topics?

If you are assigned a topic, then some of your work is done. You may get a broad topic, such as pre-kindergarten classroom management, or one that is more specific: "What has been the impact of the Internet on the American economy?" There are benefits to a broad topic: You can narrow it to something you are interested in and you have some leeway to change it if you cannot find enough sources.

However, there are also some drawbacks: Broad topics are sometimes difficult to narrow, and some students tend to write papers that are too general. Narrow topics can be easier to work with because you won't spend time deciding what to write about; however, a narrow topic can limit the number of sources you can use.

If you are allowed to choose a topic, make sure that none is off limits. Some professors prohibit students from writing about overused issues such as the death penalty, abortion, and gun control. Even if your instructor does not mind if you choose one of those topics, try to avoid them anyway because they are difficult to write about in a fresh, interesting way.

Before you begin your research, spend some time brainstorming (see Chapter 9) and narrowing your focus. Have your professor review your topic before beginning because she may provide a new direction or similar advice. Writing about what you know, if you have the choice, is an effective way to complete a research assignment. On the other hand, you may want to choose a topic you are not familiar with, but want to learn more about.

Sources. Another requirement to consider is the sources you are allowed to use. Can you use websites? Do you have to include a journal article? Should you avoid encyclopedias?

If you are given clear instructions as to what types of sources you should use, then use only those sources. However, if you are not given any guidelines, do your best to use sources that are appropriate to the discipline and the assignment. For example, which is a better source for a psychology paper on autism—an article from *People* magazine in which a celebrity talks about his autistic child or an article from the *Journal of the American Medical Association*? If the assignment is to research scientific developments in the area of autism, then the better source is the journal article.

Other requirements. Do you have to use a certain documentation style? Are other parts required such as an abstract, outline, or list of references? How long should the paper be?

These minor details are just as important as the topic and sources. Pay close attention to requirements for length, format, and documentation style. If your

professor asks for a 10-page paper, do not turn in a 3-page paper. If your instructor asks for 1-inch margins and 12-point font, do not turn in a paper that has 2-inch margins and 14-point font. If your professor requires APA documentation, do not use MLA.

Attention to detail is very important because it reflects the quality of the work you did. If the paper looks sloppy, the research may also be sloppy. A neat research paper that meets the assignment guidelines gives a good impression that is reinforced by the good work you did writing the paper.

Developing a Thesis

Once you determine the assignment's parameters and narrow your topic, creating a thesis is your next step—*before* you set foot in the library or access the first database. Asking yourself questions about the topic is one way to create a working thesis—a statement that helps you focus your research but may be revised as you develop your paper. As you list questions, see how many you can answer with the knowledge you currently have about the topic. If you know something about the topic or are interested in some aspect of the topic, you are more likely to use your research time efficiently.

Companion Website

Reflection

EXERCISE 11.5

What experience do you have with research writing? How did you complete research assignments in the past?

Taking Notes

One of the best ways to stay organized when doing research is to use note cards, 3 × 5 for the notes and 4 × 6 for the source information. If you want

Developing a Thesis by Asking Questions

Topic: Current trends in early childhood education

- What are the current trends?
- What education trends are geared toward toddlers?
- Do any trends focus on physical development?
- What kinds of physical skills do the new trends develop?
- Why were these new trends developed to improve physical development in toddlers?

Working thesis: Some of the current trends in early childhood education focus on the physical development of toddlers because experts found that a well-developed sense of balance helps toddlers learn more effectively.

When taking research notes, record the source information accurately and completely.

to be even more organized, buy colored cards, place all your research questions on one color, and assign each source a different color. If you do not want to buy note cards, cut 8½ × 11 paper into smaller pieces. Either way, the smaller pieces of paper are essential to keeping your research organized and manageable. Why do smaller pieces of paper make taking notes easier? First, they prevent you from writing too much information down from one source. Moreover, note cards are easier to organize than information on sheets of paper. You can easily shuffle cards around or lay them out on the table to arrange them in a certain order.

When taking notes, whether on note cards or in a notebook, be sure to write down the source you are using. Cards that do not have any source information are useless—you have the ideas or words, but you won't know from where they came. Also, when you write information on the note card, limit yourself to only a few sentences. If you put too much information on a card, not only will you run out of room, but you will also write down too much of someone else's idea, which stifles your own creative thoughts. Use the examples in Exhibit 11.3 regardless of your paper's topic or the discipline.

EXHIBIT 11.3   *Sample note cards.*

FOR QUOTE:

Source: Sherman and Price,
The Invisible Web (2002)

Q [for quote]
"Targeted directories and focused crawlers, as their names imply, focus on a specific subject area or domain of knowledge." (p. 38)

FOR PARAPHRASE:

Source: Baldwin, *The Community
College Experience* PLUS (2007)

P [for paraphrase]
Creating outlines and writing down questions and key phrases in your textbook are two ways of taking notes (pp. 89–90).

Organizing Your Paper

Once you finish your research, start thinking about the paper's organization. Why organize first? If the research assignment is longer than a few pages, then you have to determine how you want to structure it before you begin. Think about this book: If it wasn't organized in chapters, then it would be difficult to understand how all the information fits together. Organizing first not only saves you time, but it also helps you convey your ideas clearly.

Before beginning, look through your note cards to determine what kind of information you have. You may even want to sort the note cards into categories. For example, if you have five cards on the start of the Internet, place those together.

Another important activity to help you organize the paper is to create an outline. Some instructors require one, and they do so to help you keep your argument focused. The following is an example of an outline:

Practice

EXERCISE 11.6

Choose two different passages from this chapter and create a quotation card and a paraphrase card like the ones in Exhibit 11.3.

Companion Website

I. Introduction

    A. Topic background

        1. First point

        2. Second point

    B. Topic thesis

II. First main point

    A. Supporting evidence #1

        1. First point about supporting evidence #1

        2. Second point about supporting evidence #1

    B. Supporting evidence #2

    C. Supporting evidence #3

III. Second main point

    A. Supporting evidence #1

    B. Supporting evidence #2

    C. Supporting evidence #3

IV. Third main point

    A. Supporting evidence #1

    B. Supporting evidence #2

    C. Supporting evidence #3

V. Conclusion

    A. Review of the supporting evidence

    B. Restatement of the thesis

Collaboration

EXERCISE 11.7

Working in a group, list four possible research topics on which a student taking a college survival course might write a paper. Choose one topic and provide ideas of where and how the student would find sources.

Companion Website

Using Sources Appropriately

As you become comfortable using sources, you will find that there are many ways to avoid plagiarism. Chapter 9 includes basic information about avoiding plagiarism, but it is worth emphasizing again. Even though the word "plagiarism" gets students' attention, the heart of the issue is using sources appropriately. When researching, focus on what you are doing, whether choosing sources or taking notes from them, and be organized as you work through the research process. Plagiarism is sometimes the result of sloppy work such as forgetting to document sources properly; however, sloppiness is not an excuse in college, nor is it an excuse in the workplace.

The following are a few tips for avoiding unintentional plagiarism when writing a research paper:

- Write down the name of every source you use. Keep that list, which will form your references or works cited page, in a safe place.
- Photocopy the materials you use and note the sources from which they come.
- Label each note with the source name.
- Write your original ideas on separate note cards or sheets of paper. Clearly label the notes "My Ideas."
- Whenever you quote a source, be sure to use quotation marks around the original wording and write the page number down. Also, write "Q" for "quote" at the top of the card or sheet of paper.
- Whenever you put a source's information into your own words, be sure to write the page number down and write a "P" at the top of the card or paper for "paraphrase." Double check your paraphrase with the original to ensure you have not copied word for word.

Be especially careful to avoid behaviors that lead to plagiarism. Professors are now more likely to require you to provide evidence of your work, and they may check your work when you use sources. When in doubt, about the instructor's expectations or the process of research writing, be sure to ask. One final tip: Keep copies of your paper, sources, and notes until the semester is over and the grade is posted in case any question arises about the originality of your work. There is an added benefit to keeping copies of your papers: you can see the progress you make as a thinker and writer.

Drafting, Revising, and Editing

Now, you can start drafting your paper. Let your own ideas about the topic dominate the paper. Your sources are only for support and should not overshadow what you have to say about the topic. Remember, the purpose of college research writing is not to restate what others have said; rather, it is to present the information in a new, unique way with your thoughts in the forefront. Don't discount your perspective on the subject.

Once you have a draft, give yourself time to revise and rewrite. Students sometimes overlook the benefits of writing more than one draft.

EXHIBIT 11.4   *Documentation styles.*

DISCIPLINE	STYLE	STYLE MANUAL
English and Humanities	Modern Language Association (MLA)	*MLA Handbook for Writers of Research* (6th ed.), Joseph Gibaldi, MLA, 2003.
Social Sciences	American Psychological Association (APA)	*Publication Manual of the American Psychological Association* (5th ed.), APA, 2001.
Biology	Council of Biology Editors (CBE)	*Scientific Style and Format: The CBE Manual for Authors, Editors, and Publishers,* Edward J. Huth, Cambridge University Press, 1994.
Journalism	Associated Press (AP)	*Associated Press Style Book,* Associated Press, Basic Books, 2004.
History	Chicago	*The Chicago Manual of Style* (15th ed.), University of Chicago, 2003.
Business	American Management Association (AMA)	*The AMA Style Guide for Business Writing,* American Management Association, 1996.

If the assignment is long—more than seven pages—then it's necessary to prepare a few drafts. Make sure your ideas all fit together and the paragraphs flow from one to another. If you have several days before the assignment is due, put the paper away for a day and return to it when you are rested. Sometimes "fresh eyes" see problems that tired eyes overlook.

Two of the final activities are proofreading and editing. Be sure to allow time to correct typographical errors and improve your grammar and punctuation. Before turning the paper in, check it over to ensure you have met the assignment's requirements and that all parts and pages are attached and in order. You don't want to lose points on errors or omissions that are easily fixed.

Style Manuals

An important part of putting the finishing touches on your paper is to know which documentation style you are required to use. Each discipline, such as literature and biology, has its own guidelines for citing sources, and your instructors will tell you which style you should use for their assignments (see the summary of information in Exhibit 11.4). You may find yourself writing three different research papers, using three different styles—all in the same semester.

Reflection

EXERCISE 11.8

What did you learn from this chapter that will help you with the next research assignment?

Companion Website

Other Research Assignments

lthough you may not write a research paper for every college class, you may be required to complete other types of writing assignments that involve research. Chapter 9 discusses two types of writing assignments that involve finding and using a source: summary and critique papers. Other types of assignments may be part of a larger research assignment. An annotated bibliography is often assigned during the research process as a way for you to demonstrate that you found, read, and evaluated potential sources for your paper. An annotated bibliography contains the works cited or reference information for each source as well as a summary of the source (see the box below). In some cases, annotated bibliographies contain both a summary and critique of the source.

Critical Thinking
EXERCISE 11.9

What research skills will you use at work?

Companion Website

Final Words on Research Writing

ne of the hardest parts of research writing is taking the time to do it. Good research is not quick and easy; instead, it takes time and effort to decide what you want to learn more about and to find good sources you can rely on for accurate information. Then, it takes more time to read and digest the information. Taking the time to think about what you are writing pays off with a wonderful experience and a better product: the paper.

Example of Annotated Bibliography Entry

Sherman, C., & Price, G. (2002). *The invisible Web: Uncovering information sources search engines can't see.* Bedford, NJ: Information Today, Inc.

This book provides information about how to find information on the "deep Web" where many sites and pages are hidden from typical searches.

Learning Styles Application

This chart lists the four learning styles and tips based on the chapter's main ideas. Locate your learning style and read the corresponding tips to maximize your success in college.

VISUAL

Visual learners find that drafting an outline helps them understand better how all the research pieces fit together. Use images to help you with the research process. Be careful in your research: you may put too much trust in the look of a website if it appears reliable.

AURAL

Those who learn best by listening often find talking to librarians or other students is the best way to get help with research projects. You may also find it easier to read text aloud to determine if the writer's argument is logical and the details to support his thesis are sound.

READ/WRITE

Read/write learners enjoy reading texts and incorporating others' ideas into their own writing. However, spend time thinking about what you read before writing about it.

KINESTHETIC

Kinesthetic learners like the physical activity involved with locating sources. Incorporate movement while working on research assignments to ease the stress of sitting for long periods reading and writing.

Path of Discovery

Journal Entry

How can research contribute to lifelong learning and a better life?

FROM COLLEGE TO UNIVERSITY

How information literacy will be used in future classes

Being an information literate student is essential to your success when you transfer to complete a four-year degree. As you read in earlier chapters, you will be expected to read more and to think critically about the readings. Therefore, being information literate is crucial to your ability to handle these additional responsibilities.

As you do more research for classes in your major field, you will become more familiar, and information literate, with those sources that are highly regarded by experts in the field. For instance, you may notice your professors require reading certain journals or certain authors; they may also refer to certain studies or theories they regard as authoritative. Being aware of the names of authors, researchers, and publications that are highly regarded in your field makes it easier to select appropriate sources.

You will also be required to hone your critical thinking skills. You have to read actively and question arguments, because upper-level classes are based primarily on questioning the current scholarship.

FROM COLLEGE TO CAREER

The new workforce demands strong research skills

Not only is your college experience dramatically different because we live in an age of information, but the workforce also continues to change. Regardless of your career path, determining a need for information, finding that information, and using it appropriately—information literacy skills— will be a part of your job. There will always be opportunities to improve your skills or improve how well you work for your clients. The emphasis in the workplace is on getting information quickly and accessing authoritative sources. What good are the sales figures from a competing firm if they are not reliable? Another important part of researching information in the workplace is to acknowledge your sources of information—it gives you credibility and shows others you can and do research effectively.

Chapter in Review

1. List several ways you can improve your life by using the research techniques discussed in this chapter.

2. Describe the different library resources new students should learn to use.

3. Have you researched something recently? If so, why did you do the research and what did you find?

4. Describe your experience with research writing. How did you complete research assignments in the past?

5. What did you learn from this chapter that will be useful for the next research assignment?

Case Scenarios

Read the following case scenarios and determine what each person should do. Refer to the information in this chapter as you write a description and plan of action for each student.

1. Jane has a research paper due in two weeks. Her assignment is to search the Internet and find sources on obesity in children. She can use any sources, but they must be "authoritative." What advice can you give Jane so she uses only quality sources?

2. Aude found the perfect paper online at a "free college essays" website. Because he is running out of time, Aude decides to cut and paste parts of the paper into what he has already. What advice would you give Aude before he turns in his paper?

3. Lindy has never stepped foot in a library. She was assigned a 20-page research paper, but doesn't know where to begin. She is considering going to the library about a week before her paper is due and wandering around until she thinks of a topic. What advice can you give her before she wastes too much of her time?

Research It Further

1. Check out a student success video/DVD from your library and watch it outside class. Write a review. What information was helpful? What information was difficult to understand? What information was left out? Was the video fun or boring to watch? Present your review to the class. If your instructor has access to a television and VCR or DVD player, play parts of the video or DVD to prove your conclusions about it.

2. Type the words "college survival" or "student success" into an Internet search engine such as www.yahoo.com or www.google.com. Look at the websites that are found and choose one to review. Print the website and write a review of it: What information was helpful? What information was difficult to understand? What information was left out? Was the site easy to read and navigate? Present your review to the class and make an overall recommendation.

3. Using the term "college scholarships," search the Web for sites that contain information for students who want to learn about college scholarships. Using the criteria in this chapter for evaluating Web sources, determine which site provides the most accurate information.

References

American Library Association. (2005). "Introduction to Information Literacy." Retrieved August 16, 2005, from www.ala.org/ala/acrl/acrlissues/acrlinfolit/ infolitoverview/introtoinfolit/introinfolit.htm#what.

Sherman, C., & Price, G. (2002). *The invisible Web: Uncovering information sources search engines can't see.* Bedford, NJ: Information Today, Inc.

12 Staying Healthy

For most of us, good health is a matter of making appropriate choices. What to eat, how much to exercise, and how to reconnect with ourselves are choices we make every day, yet so many of us make inappropriate choices. The choices we make now are the ones that we will have to literally live with for the next few decades. We will live longer than our ancestors did, but will our lives and our health be better? Some experts are seriously worried that we are making decisions about our health without thinking through the consequences.

This chapter provides you with information to help you make better choices about your physical, mental, and sexual health. Specifically, this chapter answers the following questions:

- What physical health issues should I be concerned about?

- What are stress-related illnesses and how do I avoid them?

- What effects do drugs and alcohol have on a person's ability to function?

- What are the risks of unhealthy relationships?

- What can I do to make better choices about my health?

COMMUNITY · COLLEGE ·

Student Profile

NAME: **Alecia Williams**   AGE: **18**

MAJOR: **Psychology**

1. Why do you think health is an important part of success in college?

   Health is important so that all of your focus is on school and not on being sick or tired.

2. What do you do to stay healthy during the semester?

   I try to get enough sleep at night, eat three meals a day, and dress for the weather.

3. What advice would you give other students regarding the health choices they make?

   Eat healthy and get enough rest. Don't party too much during the semester.

4. What is your VARK?

   Aural.

What's Good for You

Think about this scenario: You just bought a brand-new car and are about to drive it off the lot. Before you do, the salesperson refers you to the owner's manual and begins to tell you how often you should fill the tank, replace the oil, check the brakes, and rotate the tires. You tell the salesperson you don't need to know any of that stuff and drive off. You know that the gas tank should be filled whenever the light on the dashboard comes on—what else is there to know?

For those who own cars, you can imagine what will happen next. One day, in a few months or a few years, the car stops working regularly or stops working at all. In some cases, the repairs are minimal; in other cases, major repairs must be made to get the car into shape. The costs could be astronomical, so much so that you find yourself without a car and without a way to get another one any time soon.

Now, consider that the car is your body. You know when you are hungry and when you are tired, when you feel happy and when you are stressed, but do you know how to take care of yourself? Maybe you know that exercising improves your health and helps you manage stress, but you don't take time to include fitness in your weekly routine. A car may function for a while without receiving regularly scheduled maintenance, but the neglect will eventually take its toll. The same is true with your health.

Learning to take care of your physical and mental health is crucial to getting where you want to go—you won't arrive at your destination if your "vehicle" is not in proper working order. One of the benefits of higher education, as stated previously, is that you learn to make better choices, including making better choices about your health. You do that by understanding what you can control and getting information to help you stay physically and mentally healthy.

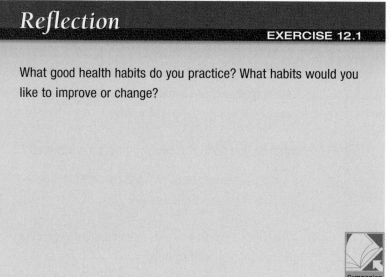

Reflection

EXERCISE 12.1

What good health habits do you practice? What habits would you like to improve or change?

Companion
Website

Healthy Eating

One key to living a healthy life is making it a priority to eat nutritious food. Getting the recommended daily allowances of fruits, vegetables, whole grains, proteins, and fats is a commonsense approach to healthy eating. However, as a society, we choose less healthy foods that are quick and easy—and loaded with calories, fat, salt, and sugar. The reasons for poor nutritional choices include lack of time, information, and access to healthy alternatives. Increased stress is another reason that students make poor food choices; they may choose comfort food over nutritious alternatives.

To make healthier choices, arm yourself with information. As with any aspect of your health, the more you know, the better choices you can make.

Learn what healthy foods are and seek them out. Read about and pay attention to portion sizes; too much of even a healthy food adds unneeded calories and contributes to weight gain. Learn to interpret the food labels and ingredient lists that provide information about what is in the food and how much of it represents recommended daily values. The U.S. Food and Drug Administration's Web page "How to Understand and Use the Nutrition Facts Label" provides detailed information.

Another way to get information is to talk with a physician or a nutritionist to learn what kinds of food are best for you to consume. Regular doctor's visits will determine if you have any potential health risks (e.g., high blood pressure or diabetes) that make your food decisions even more crucial to good health. Keeping chronic illnesses in check with monitoring and medication not only helps you feel better, but also keeps you healthy over the long term.

Eating healthy means eating regularly. Most experts recommend eating smaller meals more frequently rather than heavy meals five to seven hours apart. At the very least, start the day with a healthy breakfast, even if you don't have enough time to sit down and eat a full meal. You will be more alert and energized throughout the early morning. However, what you eat for breakfast is just as important as eating something. Powdered doughnuts and a sugary, caffeinated soda do not provide you with the nutrients you need to be at your best. A piece of fruit and a cup of yogurt, for example, is a better choice if you have to eat on the run. In addition to eating small, frequent nutritious meals, drinking plenty of water throughout the day has numerous health benefits, including regulating body temperature and assisting digestion.

Eating healthy means eating regularly—several smaller meals rather than few heavy meals.

Avoiding fad diets is another strategy for staying healthy. Although they promise increased energy and weight loss, the results are usually short lived and may be harmful. A better approach is to stick to the recommended guidelines from the Food and Drug Administration or a health expert. Be aware, too, of the potential for eating disorders such as anorexia and bulimia. *Anorexia*, a condition in which people strictly control how much food they eat, and *bulimia*, a condition in which people cycle between overeating (binge eating) in a short amount of time and then purging (through vomiting or abusing laxatives), are two eating disorders that can cause serious physical and psychological harm. Students who suffer from anorexia or bulimia, or believe they do, should see a health professional as soon as possible.

Why should you be concerned about what you eat and how much? One benefit of eating healthy is that it improves your body's functions. You may find that eating better improves your ability to sleep or reduces the fatigue you feel by the end of the day. Eating well also improves your mental abilities. Studies show that eating certain foods, such as fish, improves your test-taking abilities. Finally, healthy eating helps keep stress under control, which in turn keeps stress-related illnesses at a minimum.

TIPS FOR EATING HEALTHY IN COLLEGE

- Find and read reliable information about health issues.
- Eat consciously and take time to appreciate the nourishment you receive from healthy foods.
- Plan your meals *and* snacks ahead of time so you are not susceptible to last-minute, poor choices.
- Put bottled water in your backpack and drink it throughout the day.
- Take healthy snacks with you to eat between classes to avoid making unhealthy choices at the vending machines or at the student union.
- Pay attention to portion sizes and eat what you need to stay healthy, not the amount you want to eat.
- Make wise choices at vending machines by avoiding food that is high in fat, caffeine, sugar, or salt.
- Make any changes gradually. Think long-term health, not short-term results.

Critical Thinking
EXERCISE 12.2

What are the challenges to eating healthy for students who juggle multiple responsibilities while going to college?

Companion
Website

Exercise

We all know that making good choices about nutrition and exercise is part of a healthy lifestyle, but busy students often find it difficult to squeeze in time to work out. As a student, you will spend many hours sitting while you study or work on the computer. Even if you have a regular exercise routine, you may find you have to make studying a higher priority.

Because you have less time for exercise, it is even more important that you find time to include exercise in your busy schedule. At the very least, regular exercise helps relieve stress, which will be important as you juggle the demands of college.

Regular exercise also lowers blood pressure, increases metabolism, improves muscle tone, and lessens the risk of suffering from those diseases directly related to a sedentary lifestyle. It also improves your mood and self-confidence. Experts vary on how much exercise is ideal, but most agree 30 minutes of sustained activity 3 or 4 times a week will provide you with health benefits.

If you have trouble beginning or staying in an exercise routine, consider setting fitness goals that are reasonable and achievable. Reward yourself whenever you meet your goals, and don't get discouraged if you fall short now and then. Exercising regularly should be a lifestyle, not a short-term activity, so think of your progress as part of a long-term plan to live better. As with any exercise program, see a doctor before you begin and start gradually if you are not usually physically active.

Practice

EXERCISE 12.3

List two nutrition and exercise goals you believe you can meet this week.

Companion Website

TIPS FOR EXERCISING WHILE IN COLLEGE

- Take a physical education class.
- Use the exercise facilities and equipment on campus.
- Take advantage of walking trails or paved walkways on campus.
- Park away from the buildings and walk to class.
- Join a gym and go regularly.
- Ask a friend to exercise with you.
- Incorporate short exercise sessions into your study routine by taking walking or stretching breaks in between reading or writing papers.
- Learn how to play a new sport or investigate a new form of exercise.

Sleep Deprivation

Getting an adequate amount of sleep each night is as important to maintaining good health as what you eat and how often you exercise, but most Americans, especially college students, do not get enough. Experts say that adults should get seven to nine hours of sleep a night to function normally throughout the day, but millions regularly get six hours or less. While you are in college, you may think six hours a night is a luxury as you juggle multiple responsibilities. Although there will be times that, because of circumstances, you won't get enough sleep, those times should be few and far between. Maintain a regular sleeping and waking schedule so you get the amount of sleep you need. Despite the stories of what college life is like, pulling "all-nighters" to study for tests or complete assignments is strongly discouraged because it makes you less likely to perform well the next day.

For some students, the idea of keeping a regular sleeping and waking schedule seems impossible because other factors impede their ability to sleep. The reasons for their sleep deprivation are varied, but include health

Critical Thinking PLUS*

Consider how understanding your personality style or learning preference can help you through challenging situations.

After not exercising the first part of the semester, you know you need to start moving more each day. You aren't athletically inclined and often start ambitious exercise plans only to drop them completely when you miss a few days in a row. You have an aural learning preference and consider yourself an extrovert who needs to be around people to get energized. The only time you have to work out is early in the morning, usually before dawn. What can you do to start a plan you can stick to throughout the semester and beyond?

NOTES

*PERSONALITY + LEARNING STYLE = UNDERSTANDING SITUATIONS

problems such as breathing obstructions and stress. If you believe your lack of sleep is the result of medical problems, consider seeing a health care professional. For stress-related sleep problems, practice the stress-relieving strategies in Chapter 3 to alleviate the symptoms; however, if you find the relaxation techniques do not improve your ability to sleep well, consider seeing a general practitioner or mental health professional for issues regarding stress.

What you put into your body can affect your sleeping habits. Eating high-fat and high-sugar foods near bedtime can play havoc with your body rhythms and affect your sleep. Restful sleep can also elude you if you consume alcohol or caffeine—even in small amounts—close to bedtime. Drugs, including medications for common illnesses, can deprive you of sleep or make you feel sluggish after taking them. Avoid consuming food, drink, or medications that overstimulate or make you drowsy right before bedtime. Never abuse prescription or over-the-counter medications or illegal drugs to stay awake.

In addition to what you *put into* your body, what you *do to* it affects your ability to get a good night's rest. Exercising too close to bedtime makes it harder to fall asleep. However, too little physical exertion during the day can also cause difficulty falling and staying asleep. Experts suggest exercising early in the day—an activity as easy as walking for 30 minutes will suffice—in order to sleep more productively at night. Regular exercise also alleviates the negative effects of stress. If you find, though, that you cannot "shut off" your mind because thoughts overwhelm you, consider noting your worries—anything you may stay up thinking about after the light is off—in a journal to help you unwind and put away your day's thoughts.

Because sleep deprivation contributes to irritability, depression, and physical health problems, it is important to get enough sleep throughout the semester. If you find it difficult to stick to a regular sleep schedule, treat it like any other goal and write down what you want to do. Make it easier to achieve your goal—keep your bed and bedroom free of clutter and avoid using your bed as a place to do homework or watch television. Create a sanctuary in your bedroom; a place where you can truly relax may alleviate the stress and anxiety that contribute to sleeplessness. Finally, avoid taking naps during the day, even on weekends, as they disrupt your sleep schedule. If you have an irregular schedule each day, find a system that is relatively regular and works for you. You may have to be creative about how you get enough sleep each day.

The bottom line is that sleep deprivation can be dangerous and deadly. How little sleep you get should not be a medal of honor that demonstrates how much you work or how dedicated you are to meeting your goals. Getting enough sleep is a necessary part of living well, enjoying what you *do* accomplish, and being enjoyable to be around when you are awake.

EFFECTS OF SLEEP DEPRIVATION

- High blood pressure
- Memory loss
- Weight gain
- Depression
- Headaches
- Clumsiness
- Anxiety
- Decreased energy
- Increased mistakes
- Motor vehicle accidents

Reflection

EXERCISE 12.5

What are your sleeping habits? When do you get "off schedule"? How do you get back into your sleeping schedule?

Companion Website

Stress-Related Illnesses

Stress can cause a variety of health-related problems. Stress-related illnesses vary from person to person, but there is one common denominator: Using stress-reducing techniques decreases its negative health effects. Although some of the following illnesses can be caused by heredity and environment, they can be signs that stress is making you ill:

- Digestive problems including upset stomach, heartburn, constipation, diarrhea, and ulcers
- Severe headaches and migraines
- High blood pressure, heart attack, and stroke
- Muscle and joint pain
- Cold, flu, respiratory, and sinus infections

Eating well, exercising, and getting adequate sleep are all ways to help prevent stress-related illnesses. Be careful, especially at stressful times such as the beginning and end of the semester, that you do not neglect both your physical and mental health, for you will be more susceptible to stress-related illnesses that could keep you from doing well in college.

Drugs and Alcohol

We know some habits are potentially hazardous to our health, yet some people still do them. Smoking and using tobacco products, taking drugs, and consuming too much alcohol are known risks, but college students sometimes pick up these poor health habits because of peer pressure, a desire to fit in, and a need to find a way to relax or escape.

According to the American Heart Association (2005), about a quarter of Americans smoke; people with the least education (9–11 years in school) are more likely to smoke than people with more education (more than 16 years in school). Smoking or chewing tobacco carries with it increased risks of heart disease, stroke, high blood pressure, cancer, and emphysema. The more educated you become about the health risks associated with smoking and using smokeless tobacco, the more obvious it becomes that using tobacco products causes serious health consequences. Although there are many methods of quitting, it is worth investigating what your college and community offer if you are a smoker or a user of smokeless tobacco. Your college may provide information, support groups, or physician referrals to students who want to quit.

Alcohol and drugs are two other health issues that affect college students—sometimes even before they get to college. Having parents, partners, or friends who abuse drugs or alcohol is one way students are affected. They may feel they have to take care of others who drink too much or take drugs, which takes a toll on their time and emotional well-being. Students may abuse drugs and alcohol while in college—and the effects can be far-reaching. According to Facts on Tap, a website that offers drug and alcohol education and prevention information, 159,000 first-year college students will drop out because of issues related to drug and alcohol abuse.

Being drunk or high can have grave consequences, the least of which is that you may do something you later regret. You increase your risk of having an unwanted sexual experience or causing physical harm to yourself and others. Death from overdose happens even to those who are first-time users. Whether consumed for recreational purposes or other, more serious health reasons, drugs and alcohol should not be part of your college experience.

In addition to abusing alcohol and illegal substances, using medications for purposes other than for which they were prescribed can have grave consequences, including death. The excessive use of medications that contain amphetamines and narcotics may seem like a good idea at first if you have trouble staying awake or going to sleep, but using them for longer than prescribed can lead to dependency.

TIPS FOR AVOIDING DRUGS AND ALCOHOL IN COLLEGE

- Educate yourself about the effects of abusing drugs and alcohol.
- Cultivate relationships with people who have healthy habits.
- Avoid situations in which you know drugs and alcohol will be present.
- Take walking breaks instead of smoking breaks.
- Find other ways to relax that are healthy, free, and legal.
- Talk with a counselor or health care professional if you feel you are about to make a poor decision regarding the use of drugs and alcohol.
- Appeal to your vanity: Drugs, alcohol, and tobacco make you look and smell bad.

Depression

The pressures to succeed and juggle multiple priorities often cause negative stress and feelings of being overwhelmed. Many times, feeling a little stressed during the semester is normal, but there are times that some students feel they are in over their heads, with no hope of getting out. It is no wonder then that one of the most common mental health issues on college campuses is depression.

In an online article about college students and depression, Schoenherr (2004) quotes Alan Glass, M.D., the director of Student Health and Counseling at Washington University–St. Louis, who believes the problems student face often start before they enroll in college: "Students arrive already having started various medications for depression, anxiety and attention deficit disorders."

SIGNS OF DEPRESSION

- Loss of pleasure in activities
- Feelings of hopelessness
- Inability to get out of bed
- Increased use of alcohol or drugs
- Changes in appetite or weight (gain or loss)
- Changes in sleep patterns (sleeping too little or too much)
- Extreme sensitivity, excessive crying
- Lack of energy or interest in participating in activities
- Lack of interest in taking care of oneself

Suicide

Suicide is mental health issue associated with depression. Because of the startling estimate that 25 percent of college students have contemplated suicide, it is no wonder that college health and counseling centers strive to educate students about the signs of severe depression and potential suicide attempts. Thoughts of suicide should always be taken seriously—seek help

immediately. Call a college counselor, an advisor, a hospital emergency room, or 911 if you are thinking about committing suicide.

Sexual Health Issues

 discussion of health issues is not complete without talking about sexual health. Most colleges and universities strive to educate their students, especially those who are recently out of high school, about sexual responsibility and common sexually transmitted diseases (STDs). Gately (2003) reports that many experts and college officials are alarmed by recent statistics that show 73 percent of students report having unprotected sex while in college. More disturbing is that 68 percent of those having unprotected sex do not consider themselves at risk (Gately, 2003). This last statistic points to a major reason that students, despite sex education in high school or elsewhere, continue to engage in risky sexual behavior: Students, especially those between 18 and 24 years of age, believe they are immortal and that nothing they do will have negative consequences. Because most STDs don't cause immediate visible or physiological symptoms, students at risk for contracting an STD rarely ask to be screened for signs of infection.

Risky behavior, which includes having sex with multiple partners and having unprotected sex, opens the door to various infections and illnesses, including chlamydia, gonorrhea, genital herpes, HIV, and AIDS. Some diseases can be transmitted in ways other than sexual intercourse. Hepatitis B and C are both diseases that can be contracted through shared razors and toothbrushes, body piercing, and tattooing. Exhibit 12.1 summarizes information about prevalent STDs.

If you are sexually active, get screened regularly for STDs even if you do not have symptoms. Your long-term health and the health of those you come in contact with are at risk if you do not. As with any health issue, educate yourself with the facts about risk factors and symptoms. Then, monitor your behavior, practice safe sex, and see a doctor regularly to maintain good health.

Collaboration
EXERCISE 12.6

Working in a group, list the different signs of depression. Then, discuss the resources your college provides for students suffering from depression.

Companion
Website

Collaboration
EXERCISE 12.7

Working in a group, discuss the different obstacles students may face to maintaining good sexual health. Determine what your college can do to help students get the information and help they need.

Companion
Website

Healthy Relationships

aintaining healthy relationships is as much a part of your good health as eating nutritious foods and exercising. Chapter 5 discusses the types of relationships you will have in college and how to relate

EXHIBIT 12.1   *Common STDs.*

STD	SYMPTOMS	TREATMENT
HIV and AIDS	May have no symptoms; extreme fatigue, rapid weight loss	No cure, but prescribed medication can keep the virus from replicating
Chlamydia	May have no symptoms; abnormal discharge, burning during urination	Antibiotics
Genital herpes	May have no symptoms; itching, burning, bumps in the genital area	No cure, but prescribed medication can help treat outbreaks
Gonorrhea	Pain or burning during urination; yellowish or bloody discharge; men may have no symptoms	Antibiotics
Hepatitis B	Headache, muscle ache, fatigue, low-grade fever, skin and whites of eyes have yellowish tint	No cure, but prescribed medication can help guard against liver damage

better with others, but there are some issues that signal unhealthy, even dangerous, relationships. One issue is abuse: physical, mental, verbal, and sexual. Being in a relationship with someone who is abusive is not healthy. Although the previous statement seems like common sense, it bears taking time to think about. No one deserves to be hit, controlled, or humiliated *ever*.

Although we know that someone who makes us feel bad physically or emotionally prevents us from being our best, studies indicate that abused men and women find it difficult to get out of abusive relationships. One reason people stay with abusive partners is that the abusers are initially charming, attentive, and loving. Usually, abusers begin to show subtle signs that something is not right; they may be extremely jealous, verbally insulting, or focused on your every move. Victims may also be financially or emotionally dependent on their abusers, which makes eliminating their influence difficult at best.

One particular type of unhealthy relationship that occurs frequently among traditional college students is date or acquaintance rape. Simply defined, *date rape* is a forced sexual act in which one party does not actively consent; oftentimes, the two people involved are not complete strangers—hence the terms date rape and acquaintance rape. Both men and women can be victims of date rape, although women are more often the victims. Alcohol or a date rape drug such as Rohypnol may be involved. College-age women and men should know who they are going out with, not get intoxicated, make sure their food or drinks are not handled by others, and communicate loud and clear if they find themselves in an uncomfortable situation.

TIPS FOR MAINTAINING HEALTHY RELATIONSHIPS

- Get to know people well before spending time alone with them.
- Learn to communicate your wants and needs effectively. Say "no" loud and clear when you do not want something to happen.
- Watch for signs of abuse; sometimes, these signs appear in subtle ways early in a relationship.

- If a situation makes you uncomfortable, get out of it immediately.
- Do not abuse alcohol and drugs, which can impair your ability to judge situations.
- Seek professional help if necessary to remove yourself from an abusive relationship.

Critical Thinking
EXERCISE 12.8

Why do you think men and women between 19 and 24 years of age are more likely to be in an abusive relationship? What can students do to prevent being victims of abuse?

Companion
Website

Communication Challenges

Sometimes, one of the most important activities to promote good mental health is communication. Keeping feelings bottled up inside can lead to unhealthy thoughts and expectations. Learning to express fear, anger, and disappointment lessens the negative stress caused by carrying those feelings inside. If you do not feel comfortable expressing what is on your mind to family and friends, talk with a counselor or therapist who can help you learn to communicate more openly with others. You can also learn effective communication techniques and conflict management methods by reading books and articles and watching others who model effective behavior.

Living a Balanced Life

Living a balanced life means paying attention to and improving all areas of your life—from relationships to cardiovascular health to your inner peace. If one area is overdeveloped, then other areas suffer from a lack of balance. There will be times that you have to put in more hours at work and school, throwing the balance off slightly, but be careful to make time for those areas that were neglected.

A great way to stay balanced is to create relationships with people on campus. Having healthy relationships with professors, advisors, and classmates not only enables you to stay connected with your college work, but it also provides a personal support network in case you need help with the stresses of being in college.

Balancing your life to eliminate stress also entails evaluating your values and priorities whenever you begin to feel stressed. Identify those areas in your life that are out of balance and give them higher priority. For example, if you value exercise and are stressed because

Reflection
EXERCISE 12.9

How do you keep relationships healthy?

Companion
Website

you spend most of your time at work or at school, make working out a higher priority, creating better balance in your life.

Having healthy relationships provides a personal support network for you should you need help.

Getting Help

To make good choices and stay healthy, it is important to get regular checkups and see a health professional whenever you experience pain, difficulty, or even uncertainty about a health issue. Your college may provide access to a health clinic or health fairs. The college clinic may offer free screenings, health seminars, and over-the-counter medications. Take advantage of such services as blood pressure checks or information about handling diabetes because they may provide you with life-improving, or life-saving, information. If your college provides only limited access to health services, then you should find other ways to monitor your health. Regular checkups are part of taking care of yourself both in the short-term and the long-term.

Part of staying healthy is staying informed about health issues. Use what you learned about finding reliable sources and determining their credibility when searching for information about your physical, mental, and psychological health. Never use information from the Internet to diagnose and treat yourself. Instead, if you find information that seems to pertain to your health issue, consider making an appointment with a doctor and provide her with your findings. Your doctor, or health professional, can help determine the best course of action for you.

Learning Styles Application

This chart lists the four learning styles and tips based on the chapter's main ideas. Locate your learning style and read the corresponding tips to maximize your success in college.

VISUAL

Students with visual learning preferences, just as those with read/write learning preferences, may find reading about the consequences of poor health choices an effective way to take in information. You may also find visual representations of the effects of poor health choices particularly motivating to make better choices.

AURAL

Those with aural learning preferences may benefit from listening to speakers talk about how to incorporate healthy practices into their already busy schedules. You may also find talking with a counselor a good means of getting information to help you make better choices.

READ/WRITE

Students with read/write learning preferences may find reading about the effects of poor health choices a way to motivate them to make better choices. Look for statistics and articles about how to improve your health and write down your goals.

KINESTHETIC

Students who prefer to learn kinesthetically often make physical activity a priority in their schedules. However, you should also continue to read about the benefits of living a healthy lifestyle.

Path of Discovery

Journal Entry

After reading this chapter, what changes will you make to improve your health?

FROM COLLEGE TO UNIVERSITY

Maintaining healthy habits helps you effectively deal with stress

The good habits you form now will keep you healthy as you move from your community college to the university. If you incorporate regular exercise into your daily or weekly routine, work to maintain your schedule despite the extra work and stress you may experience. You will find more demands on your time and more stress as you begin to think about life beyond your degree. Eating well, exercising, getting plenty of sleep, and taking care of yourself will decrease your anxiety and feelings of being overwhelmed. Practicing good health habits makes them a permanent part of your schedule. Living healthy is more than what you do in college—it also contributes to a better life as you age.

FROM COLLEGE TO CAREER

Making healthy lifestyle changes is a good long-term strategy

Making healthy choices in college certainly has short-term results—you feel better and handle the negative effects of stress more effectively. However, making better choices should be a long-term strategy to create a better life for you and your family. Therefore, when you complete your certificate or degree and enter into or back into the workforce, you may need to revise or reinforce your health goals. For example, you may have had time after classes to work out or play a sport as part of your exercise routine, but after graduation, you may have to change the time, place, or exercise type.

In addition to finding time to continue your positive health choices from college, you should consider making mental health a part of your overall health plan. Maintaining healthy relationships with those who have positive influences on your life is one way to keep stress levels low and create a safety net of friends and family for times when you need them. Avoiding drugs, alcohol, and other poor health choices is crucial to performing your best at work. Some employers have strict policies about the use of drugs and alcohol on or off the job.

Because of the importance of good health, some employers make keeping their employees healthy a top priority—it saves time and money in the long run when employees miss less work due to illness. Talk with the human resources department about what your company offers to support healthy habits. They may offer free screening, free or reduced-cost vaccinations, time off for doctors' appointments, health insurance, discounted gym memberships, and planned physical activities such as softball or basketball games.

Chapter in Review

1. What are the different ways a student can incorporate exercise into a busy schedule?
2. What are the major health issues college students face?
3. What can students do if they find themselves in an unhealthy relationship?
4. Predict what the effects will be for a student who makes poor health choices during a semester.
5. According the chapter's discussion, evaluate how well you are improving or maintaining healthy habits.

Case Scenarios

Read the following case scenarios and determine what each person should do. Refer to the information in this chapter as you write a description and plan of action for each student.

1. Vin-Singh has had trouble sleeping since he started college. He shares an apartment with another student who likes to stay up late and play loud music. Vin-Singh eats well and avoids caffeinated drinks, but he does not exercise regularly and often feels anxious when he tries to sleep. What advice can you give him to improve his sleep?

2. Wanda has not exercised since she was in high school, and 20 years later, she sees the importance of improving her health. In fact, she wonders if the 30 pounds she gained since high school is keeping her from feeling her best when she juggles the demands of college. She is about to start her last year, one that will be stressful as she takes classes to help her pass a licensing exam and get a good job. She also wants to lose weight and start an aggressive exercise program. In light of what she is about to face, what advice can you give her?

3. Ever since D. J. started college, he focused on his studies and cut out all activities that do not help him achieve his education goals. He told his friends that he can't hang out with them; he cut back on his hours at work; he stopped playing basketball and running; he even stopped attending religious services so he has time to take as many hours as possible each semester. He wants to graduate with a degree as fast as he can and start working, and his grades are good. However, after a few semesters, he feels depressed and isolated, but he is not sure why. What advice can you give him?

Research It Further

1. Interview three people about their health habits. Find out what they do to maintain good health. Note your findings and present them to your class.

2. Search the Internet for national statistics regarding violence against women. Determine which groups are more likely to experience physical and sexual abuse. Inform your class of your findings.

3. What does your college offer in terms of health care for students? Create a list of services and events along with contact numbers for community services that students may need. Present your list to your classmates.

References

American Heart Association. (2005). "Cigarette smoking statistics." Retrieved September 3, 2005, from www.americanheart.org/presenter.jhtml?identifier= 4559.

Facts on Tap. "The College Experience?" Retrieved September 3, 2005, from www.factsontap.org/collexp/Collexp.htm.

Gately, G. (2003, August 23). College students ignoring risks of unprotected sex. *Health Day News*. Retrieved August 29, 2005, from http://www.hon.ch/ News/HSN/514963.html.

Schoenherr, N. (2004). Depression, suicide are the major health issues facing college students, says student health director. *News & Information*. Washington University–St. Louis, MO. Retrieved August 24, 2005, from http://news-info.wustl.edu/tips/page/normal/4198.html.

U.S. Food and Drug Administration. (2004). "How to understand and use the nutrition food label." Retrieved August 29, 2005, from www.cfsan.fda.gov/~dms/foodlab.html.

13 Taking the Next Steps

After reading this chapter, you will have a better understanding of your choices after community college. Even though you just started your journey toward a certificate or a degree, you may want to keep in mind your options and the different paths you can take. Ideally, you should read this chapter thoroughly and then refer to it as you complete each semester to ensure that you are on the right track and to remind yourself of the different choices you have. At the very least, you will be able to say, at the end of this semester, "I did it!"

After you complete this chapter, you should be able to answer the following questions:

- How should I begin to prepare for the end of the semester? What should I expect?

- How should I plan for next semester? What classes should I take?

- How will I continue paying for college? What help is out there for me?

- How will my long-term goals change once I achieve my short-term goals?

- What am I going to do once I finish my degree?

COMMUNITY · COLLEGE ·

Student Profile

NAME: **Dorothy Martin** AGE: **37**

MAJOR: **Associate of Arts in Teaching, Bachelor of Arts in Secondary Education with emphasis on math and science**

1. What is the best part of finishing your degree at your community college?

   The best part is the accomplishment, to say, "I did this." Having kids and grandkids at home, I was able to show them how important education is, and it made an impact on them.

2. What was the most challenging part of completing an associate's degree?

   Getting classes at a time I needed them, figuring out my schedule and juggling children, work, and my college classes.

3. What advice would you give community college students?

   Talk to a counselor and plan your schedule. Don't just look for classes without researching them. You may end up taking classes you don't need. Talk to someone—an instructor, a counselor. Plan ahead. You don't want to get down to your last semester and find out you don't meet the degree requirements. You will have hours, but no degree.

4. Any additional advice?

   Don't worry about what you want to "be" yet; just get your basic courses first, then plan for a degree.

5. What is your VARK?

   Aural and Read/Write.

Endings and Beginnings

B y the time you start reading this chapter, most of the semester should be over. That means you should already be thinking about next semester and beyond. The end of the semester is a good time to start assessing how you did and where you want to go. First, however, there are some issues to consider before you are ready to move on.

Before planning for next semester, there are some loose ends to tie up in the current semester. You now know what to expect at the beginning of next semester, and with that additional information, you can make better choices and prepare yourself for what lies ahead.

Student Evaluations

Student evaluations are an integral part of taking a college class. Each semester, you may be asked to complete an evaluation form by your instructor. The evaluations are anonymous and are not given to the instructor until the grades are posted; thus, you should feel comfortable being open and honest about the course when completing the form.

The purpose of student evaluations is to provide the instructor as well as the administration with feedback on how the students feel about the instruction they received. Some colleges look very closely at student evaluations and determine raises and promotions based in part on the scores instructors receive. Other colleges merely use the evaluations as a discussion tool to improve the instructors' teaching. No matter how your college uses the information, try to be honest about your instructors' abilities. Providing constructive criticism, rather than general comments, is the most helpful to the instructor.

Phrases such as "He stinks" or "He is perfect" do not provide specific information to help your professor improve or continue doing what you think works very well. Instead, offer suggestions such as "The instructor graded fairly and handed back exams in a timely manner" or "The professor never explained the assignments." These statements allow your instructors to pinpoint exactly what worked and what didn't.

Most student evaluation forms contain questions you answer by filling in a bubble and questions you answer by writing a narrative response. Here are examples of questions you may see on a student evaluation form:

1. My instructor uses class time effectively.

    A. Strongly Agree   B. Agree   C. Strongly Disagree

2. My instructor grades fairly.

    A. Strongly Agree   B. Agree   C. Strongly Disagree

3. What can your instructor do to improve the course?

4. What does you instructor do well?

When answering questions such as these, take your time to reflect on the instructor's performance during the semester. If you have the room, create a list of activities you did in class during the semester and think about them. Then, consider the overall performance of your instructor. Did he come to class on time? Was she easy to contact when you needed her? Did he act professionally? Did she seem to have a good knowledge of the subject matter? Remember that the objective of student evaluations is to provide feedback to help instructors improve.

Preparing for Finals

Another traditional "ending" to a semester is the final exam. Surviving finals week is a well-earned badge of a college student. The reasons that finals are so stressful for some college students are that they often carry more weight than any other exam during the semester, they contain questions about material from the entire semester, and they are all scheduled around the same time. In order to survive your finals, go back to Chapter 8 and review the material about taking tests. Hopefully, you have already started preparing for your finals. If not, there are some steps you can follow to get ready quickly:

- Note the day, place, and time of each final on your calendar.
- Start getting prepared today. Cramming only adds to your anxiety and stress levels. If you study a little at a time each day for a few weeks before the exam, you are more likely to retain the information.
- Ask questions about the exam. What will you be allowed to use? What do you need to bring? What should you study?
- Mentally walk through the exam. Imagine yourself arriving on time, feeling comfortable, and taking the final with ease.
- Get plenty of rest during the days leading up to the exam. Go to bed early the night before and set your alarm. Have a backup plan in case you sleep through your alarm. For example, have a friend call you to make sure you are awake.

- Leave early for the exam. Plan on getting there 20 minutes before the exam starts in case there are troubles along the way.
- Use your time wisely. Final exams usually take longer to complete than regular tests, so be sure you use the entire time you have (one to three hours).
- Some colleges require photo identification to take exams, especially if they are high-stakes such as licensing exams. Just in case, bring two forms of photo identification with you.
- Be prepared, as the Boy Scouts motto states. Bring writing supplies and any preapproved items such as a calculator or dictionary.

Because many instructors place greater emphasis on the final exam, you should also take them seriously. Take the time to finish out the semester on a high note.

Reflection

EXERCISE 13.1

How do you feel about preparing for final exams? What have you done so far to prepare?

Companion
Website

Mapping a Plan for Your Educational Future

Choosing Classes for Next Semester

Even if you have not completed your classes this semester, you can start planning for next semester. By now, you should be familiar with the college catalog and be able to identify the courses you may want to take. In addition, thinking about what degree you want to complete makes it easier to decide which courses you need to take.

Exhibit 13.1 is an example of a degree program that a student named Marsha is considering.

This degree plan is relatively simple to follow. However, Marsha may become confused if she has to take prerequisites before she can take some of the courses. For example, when Marsha entered college, her ACT test scores placed her below college entrance requirements. Thus, she had to complete her developmental courses before she could take some of the college-level courses that are part of her degree program.

So, how does Marsha plan for next semester? If Marsha is completing her first semester and took Introduction to College (a three-hour credit course), Developmental Reading (receives no college-level credit), Developmental Writing (receives no college-level credit), Introduction to Sociology (a three-hour credit course), and Psychology and the Human Experience (a three-hour credit course), then she has already met two of the requirements for an Associate of Applied Science in Early Childhood Education. She can check those courses off her degree plan and start working toward the remaining courses as long as she meets the developmental requirements for them.

An example of Marsha's schedule for next semester might look like the following:

ENGL 1311	English Composition I	3 Hours
ECD 1103	Child Development	3 Hours
ECD 1003	Foundations of Early Childhood Education	3 Hours
Music 2300	Introduction to Music	3 Hours
ECD 1203	Healthy, Safe Learning Environment	3 Hours
		15 Hours

If Marsha takes 15 hours her second semester and 15 hours each semester after that, she still needs to take an extra semester because the first one only gave her 6 hours toward her degree. Even though a degree plan maps out each semester, it may take longer to complete if you need to take fewer hours each semester or if you have to complete developmental classes.

Choosing Professors for Next Semester

Just as important as what you take is *whom* you take it from. By now, you should realize that choosing the right instructor can make the difference in how much you enjoy and learn in a class. If you have the option of choosing an instructor, then start talking to other students about her. Ask specific questions and ask a variety of people. Remember that each student has her

EXHIBIT 13.1 *Sample degree program.*

[Department] **Early Childhood Development**

[Type of degree—usually completed in four semesters] **Associate of Applied Science**

[Emphasis within the degree] **Option: Early Childhood Education**

[Description of how this degree will benefit you] This option is for early childhood caregivers and paraprofessionals who wish to improve their skills and credentials. Early childhood curriculum is the focus. This option is also appropriate for supervisors, curriculum coordinators, and for CDA renewal.

[Suggested schedule for each semester. It usually is not mandatory that you take the courses in the order suggested.]

FIRST SEMESTER		CREDIT HOURS
ECD 1003	Foundations of Early Childhood Education	3
ECD 1103	Child Development	3
ECD 1203	Healthy, Safe Learning Environment	3
ECD 1303	Practicum I	3
ENGL 1311	English Composition I	3
	Total Credit Hours	15

SECOND SEMESTER		
ECD 2003	Child Behavior	3
ECD 2103	Preschool Curriculum	
OR		
ECD 2403	Infant/Toddler Curriculum	3
ECD 2503	Nutrition for the Young Child	3
ECD 2303	Practicum II	3
MATH 1301	College Business Mathematics	3
	Total Credit Hours	15

THIRD SEMESTER		
ECD 2703	Language Arts	3
ECD 2803	Special Needs	3
ENGL 1312	English Composition II	3
PSYC 2300	Psychology and the Human Experience	3
HLSC 1304	Concepts of Lifetime Health and Wellness	
OR		
MUSC 2300	Introduction to Music	
OR		
ARTS 2300	Introduction to Visual Arts	3
	Total Credit Hours	15

FOURTH SEMESTER		
ECD 2903	Trends in Curriculum	3
BUS 1303	Introduction to Computers or higher level computer course	3
SOCI 2300	Introduction to Sociology	3
SPCH 1300	Speech Communication	3
ANTH 2310	Cultural Anthropology	
OR		
PSYC 2301	Developmental Psychology	3
	Total Credit Hours	15
	Total Hours for A.A.S.	**60**

own view of what makes a good instructor, a view that might not match your own. The questions you should ask must move beyond the vague "Is she a good teacher?" Instead, ask about her teaching style, the types of assignments she gives, and how available she is during office hours.

An even better way to determine which instructors are the best for you is to talk to them before you enroll in their classes. Make an appointment with a potential instructor and ask the questions you want to know the answers to: How much reading is involved? How do you teach the course? Do you require a research paper? What do you expect students to know when they complete the course? The benefits of interviewing your instructor before you sign up for the class are many: You can determine if the instructor is a good fit with your learning style, and you can impress your instructor with your maturity and interest in your education.

Building Your Schedule

What worked this semester? What didn't? Why? What will change for you next semester? Did you have enough time in between classes? Did you waste time that could have been spent more productively? All of these questions should be answered, and now that you know more about college, you should be able to make educated decisions about next semester.

When planning the next semester, consider four factors: how many hours you need to take, how many hours you need to work, the other obligations (e.g., planned trips for work or with family) you have, and how much stress the other three factors will cause.

Number of Credit Hours

In order to determine how many credit hours you can take, review your financial aid, scholarship, and insurance as well as the degree plan information. If you are receiving financial aid, you may be required to take a full load, which often means at least 12 hours. Likewise, many insurance companies give discounts to young adults who take a certain number of hours each semester while maintaining a good GPA.

Number of Work Hours

If you will not be working next semester, skip this section. However, even if you are only working 10 hours a week, you have to schedule your work hours so they do not overlap the times you are in class. You also need plenty of time to get to and from work and school. Cutting it too close can cause problems for employers and instructors. For example, do not register for a class that meets from 2:00 to 3:00 if you must be at work at 3:00.

Asking to leave class early so that you can make it to work on time is not appropriate. Although you may have an instructor who allows you to do so, you will miss valuable information and may not succeed in the class. Likewise, if you are scheduled to work an 8-hour day and you leave early without permission or without making up the time lost, then you will not be successful on the job. Therefore, you must work out any potential problems ahead of time. Now is a good time to start thinking about possible solutions.

Other Obligations

Working, going to school, taking care of a family, and participating in social and community activities all require your time and energy; to balance all of your activities, keep an eye on upcoming events and plan accordingly. For example, if you are thinking about registering for the fall semester and you know you must take a week-long trip for work in October, contact potential instructors to see what their policies are for missing class. Likewise, if you like to participate in your child's school activities, consider how much time you can give if you are also studying for classes. You may find that you have to cut back on social and volunteer commitments or at least postpone them until after the semester.

Stress Levels

Just as important as your work schedule and course load is your ability to handle all of your responsibilities. If you have to take 15 hours to maintain your financial aid and you have to work 40 hours to pay your bills, but you feel overwhelmed and anxious about balancing it all, then you are not likely to handle both well. If you find yourself in this situation, reconsider your plans before you get in over your head. Getting locked into a rigid schedule that doesn't allow you to drop a course that is too difficult or to decrease your hours at work will lead to frustration and high levels of negative stress.

On the other hand, you may thrive with such a schedule because you work better when you have to manage your time carefully. You may be the type of person who cannot study well if you have unlimited amounts of time to do it. If this is the case, then you may feel excited about having so much activity in your schedule. Still, you could encounter a problem in which having flexibility (being able to drop a class or reduce your work hours) will help you cope. If not, pay extra attention to staying on top of your work. For example, if you find on the first day of the semester that one of your classes will be much more demanding than you had anticipated, you have to be more careful about keeping up with assignments and managing your stress effectively. Planning ahead and managing your time will help you cope with a stressful schedule.

EXERCISE 13.2   *Collaboration*

Working with another classmate or in a group, write a description of an ideal class and instructor. What would a typical class period be like? What would students know after this ideal experience?

Companion
Website

Troubleshooting Your Schedule

What should you do if you cannot work your schedule out despite your efforts to make it all fit together? There may be a semester that a course you need is not offered or the class is filled before you can register. Should you throw up your hands and quit when faced with these problems? Of course not. Instead, take advantage of the relationships you have cultivated in school. Now is the time to talk to other students, instructors, and advisors. They may be able to offer solutions you have not considered. Although pleading to get into courses that are filled is not recommended, asking politely is an option. If you have a good relationship with an administrator and you are a good student, you may be more likely to get what you need.

If, though, there is an academic need for you to get into a class or rearrange your schedule, point that out when you ask. Some college officials are willing to bend the rules if your graduation depends on it. For example, if you need one more class to complete your degree and transfer on time, you may be more persuasive about getting into a class that is closed. However, even if you don't get what you want from your relationships with people at the college, always be considerate and polite. Although they may not be able to help you this time, they will be more likely to help you when they can if you act in a mature manner.

Deadlines and Dates

Once you decide on your schedule and the classes you want to take, take advantage of early registration periods and due dates. Even if not returning next semester is a possibility, you should consider registering for courses just in case. You should be able to drop them by a certain date without penalty, and it is easier to drop the classes than to build a schedule from classes that are still open. In addition to being aware of registration periods, take note of payment due dates. Some colleges require that you pay soon after registering, even if that means paying for tuition and fees a few months in advance. If you do not pay on time, your classes may be dropped—then you have to start all over and you may not get the classes you want.

Discovering Your Dream

Throughout this book, you listed your goals, both short- and long-term, and filled pages with time management, reading, writing, and personal goals. But what are your dreams? What do you want to do that you have not written down because you feel it is too far-fetched? There are many stories out there of people who denied their passions and took jobs that provided them financial security and prestige, only to discover that those were not their values and their lives were not fulfilling.

Why don't more people follow their dreams? First, they may not know what they are. To realize your dreams, you must write them down and specify what you want. You may have to brainstorm for a while before you get to the real desire you have. Second, they may be scared. Following what your heart wants you to do often contradicts what your head is saying. Third, some people need to make the "safe" choice first before they feel confident that they can fulfill their dreams. They may have to take a job that pays well so that they can save money to fulfill their dreams at a later date.

As you begin to consider what you really want out of life, answer these questions:

- What activities do I find the most pleasure in?
- What do I do in my spare time?
- What are my hobbies?
- If I didn't have to worry about money, what would I be doing?

- What do I fantasize about doing with my life?
- If I had only one more year to live, what would I do differently?

Although you may not be able to drop everything right now and follow your heart, at least start thinking about what you really want to do with your life as you plan your college degree.

Paying for College

When thinking about your financial future, no doubt paying for college is at the top of your list. Even if you have a solid plan to pay tuition, fees, and books, it is worth your time to investigate other methods in case your current one falls through. Despite what many think about the costs of college, community college tuition is a real bargain and may be one of the reasons you enrolled. Nonetheless, no matter where you go, it is likely you will have to decide how to pay for the costs you incur.

Scholarships

Winning a scholarship is by far the most rewarding (financially and psychologically) way to pay for college because it is literally free money—you don't have to pay it back. There are thousands of scholarships out there for needy and accomplished students. All you have to do is find them. To find the ones that match your profile, get the word out that you are looking. Talking with friends, family, employers, and college officials is a great way to start the process. They may know of obscure scholarships that will fit your needs perfectly. Another way to get information is to talk to the financial aid officers and counselors at your college. They have access to and knowledge of scholarships that fit the college's student profiles (e.g., single-parent and transfer scholarships). Other effective methods for finding scholarships include investigating sources at the library and searching the Internet. Searching print and Web-based databases will provide you with more than enough information; your only problem will be narrowing your focus.

When planning your college budget, it may be worth your time to investigate part-time work, internships, and other opportunities.

Whatever you find out there in books, in counselors' offices, or on the Internet, do not pay for information about scholarships. There are services that claim, for a fee, to match your qualifications with scholarship qualifications. You can get free help from high-school and college counselors as well as libraries and Internet searches. No reputable scholarship requires that you pay a fee to apply and very few legitimate scholarship services require payment. The website FinAid!, www.finaid.org, provides information about different types of financial aid for college students as well as tips for avoiding scholarship services scams. According to the website, any service that guarantees to match you with a scholarship or that offers you an award that you did not apply for is likely to be a scam. To search for scholarship information, many colleges recommend www.fastweb.com as a great starting point to find scholarships that match your accomplishments.

Grants

By definition, grants are financial assistance that is not paid back. A common federal grant is the Pell Grant, which is awarded for either full-time or part-time enrollment. To determine your eligibility, talk with your financial aid counselor or visit any of the various websites that provide government financial aid information. When you research Pell Grants, you will find that there is a limit to the amount of the award ($4,000 in 2002–2003). Your college will receive the money and then disburse it to you once classes start. Because of recently enacted federal requirements about grants and student loans, colleges may wait several weeks before paying students. The reason for the delay is to ensure that students remain enrolled in classes (rather than taking the grant money and never returning). If you are expecting to receive your grant the first day or week of classes, you should make alternative arrangements to pay bills (including your bookstore bill).

Another type of grant a student can receive is the Federal Supplemental Educational Opportunity Grant, which is available to those who demonstrate an exceptional need. According to the U.S. Department of Education (2002–2003), the difference between a Pell Grant and an FSEOG is that "each participating school will receive enough money to pay the Federal Pell Grants of its eligible students. There's no guarantee every eligible student will be able to receive an FSEOG." The procedure to follow for an FSEOG is similar to the Pell Grant; your eligibility determines the amount you receive, and your college will disburse the money to you after the semester starts.

You must maintain good academic standing at your college to remain eligible to receive grant money. If you apply for grant money, be sure to make note of the minimum GPA you must have in order to ensure your eligibility to receive future grant money.

Student Loans

In the event you are not eligible for grants, investigate students loans. The idea of taking out a loan to attend college makes many students shudder because they don't want the added pressure of paying them back. If you can avoid student loans, then by all means do so. However, receiving a student loan sometimes makes more financial sense in the long run.

Federal student loans are typically low interest and can be paid back over 10 years. For families that would otherwise have to deplete their savings or borrow against retirement or their homes to pay for college, a low-interest student loan is actually better for them financially. Most loan programs allow you to defer payment (but you may accumulate interest) until after you graduate. You can sometimes defer payment further if you remain unemployed after you graduate.

One type of federal loan is the Stafford Loan, which comes in subsidized and unsubsidized versions. A *subsidized loan* is one where the government pays the interest for you while you are in college. Once you graduate and start making payments on your loan, you will pay interest as well. The government does not make interest payments for an unsubsidized loan. You may, instead, pay the interest while you are in college (usually a small amount) or you can wait until after you graduate to make payments, but your interest will be *capitalized,*—the interest is added to the principal amount of the loan.

A federal Perkins Loan is a loan between you and your college. The Perkins Loan allows you to borrow money ($4,000 per year up to $20,000 for 5 years) that you do not have to repay until 9 months after you graduate or drop below part-time status. One benefit of a Perkins Loan is that you may be able to cancel up to 100 percent of the debt if you meet certain criteria. For example, if you choose to teach upon graduation in a "teacher shortage" area or if you serve as a full-time nurse, you may be eligible for cancellation of your loan.

PLUS, which stands for Parent Loan for Undergraduate Students, is another method for receiving money to help pay for college. If you are fortunate enough to have parents willing to take out a loan to help you pay for college, a PLUS is a possible option. In order to qualify, you must be a dependent student, which means your parents support you financially. PLUS loans are provided by the government or by private lenders. Parents who take out a PLUS loan are usually trying to make up the difference between the cost of tuition and the financial aid package their children receive. The parents are ultimately responsible for repaying the loan, which can begin as early as 60 days after they receive it.

Military and Veterans Financial Aid

Being a member of the military can be especially helpful when paying for college. There are numerous benefits for active members and veterans as well as their dependents. To find out about military benefits, talk to a financial aid officer. If you already have military service, contact a local service branch for more information.

Work–Study

Work–study is a program that allows students to earn money while they work on campus. The reason it is called "work–study" is that the jobs may allow you to study when you work. Most work–study positions, however, are similar to office assistants and you will be busy for most of the time you work. In order to work in such a program, you must be eligible for federal work–study money, and you are limited to a certain number of hours you can work each week. Not everyone who is eligible for work–study can find

Consider how understanding your personality style or learning preference can help you through challenging situations.

You are an extroverted student whose learning style preference is read/write. You received a grant to attend college the first semester, but you have to find other means to pay for college if you intend to complete your two-year degree and transfer to a four-year university. You are even considering graduate school, if you can afford it all. You are not sure what your options are at this point. What can you do to secure your college future?

NOTES

*PERSONALITY + LEARNING STYLE = UNDERSTANDING SITUATIONS

a position on campus, however. Each department and area of the college advertises, hires, and manages work–study positions; sometimes, hiring can be competitive. There may be specific requirements (such as computer skills) that a candidate must meet before being hired. Because some positions require working with students' personal information, work–study students must also pledge that they will abide by the college's privacy standards.

The benefits of participating in work–study include earning some money to help pay your expenses and working closely with college employees. By getting to know professors and administrators better—and working for them—you may have access to valuable advice and information. To investigate whether or not work–study is available to you, talk with your financial aid officer. She will review your eligibility and help you apply for on-campus employment.

Tuition Waivers for Employees

Before you exhaust all ways of paying for college, look into what your employer may pay for. Large corporations sometimes offer financial assistance to employees, although there may be stipulations that you work for the company for a certain amount of time after graduation. If your employer doesn't offer scholarships to employees, ask if they are interested in doing so. They will benefit from employees who further their education. Finally, your college may offer tuition waivers for college employees. Some students take jobs at colleges just for the benefit of taking classes for free or at a reduced cost. If you need a part-time or full-time job while in school, check out the openings at your community college.

Creating a Budget

Whether or not you rely on financial aid to pay your tuition bills, creating a budget will help you meet your financial and personal goals. A budget doesn't have to be a dirty word. In fact, it is relatively easy to create a budget. The hard part is following it. First, create a customized budget sheet. Exhibit 13.2 offers a sample you can start with.

Once you identify the categories that fit your lifestyle, gather all of the bills and paystubs you have and add up your expenses and income. It is a good idea to look at three months' worth of bills to get an accurate picture of your expenditures. If you have any bills that are paid less frequently than

EXHIBIT 13.2   *Sample budget form.*

CATEGORY	ESTIMATED AMOUNT PER MONTH	ACTUAL AMOUNT PER MONTH	DIFFERENCE
Income			
Source 1 (wages/salary)			
Source 2 (scholarship, financial aid, etc.)			
Source 3			
Income Total			
Expenses			
Mortgage/rent			
Utilities			
Car payment/transportation			
Insurance			
Groceries			
Household items			
Clothing			
Gas			
Car maintenance			
Cell phone/pager			
Eating out			
Entertainment			
Healthcare (medications, doctor's visits, etc.)			
Credit cards or loans			
Total Income			
(Total Expenses)			
Net Income			

once a month, convert them to a monthly expense. For example, if you pay $240 for car insurance every six months, your monthly expense is $40 ($240 divided by 6 months).

One key to an accurate budget that helps track your spending is to be honest about your expenses. That means you should write down every dollar you spend on snacks or supplies. You may find that you spend $25 a week ($100 a month) on unnecessary items. The more you can track unnecessary items, the better you can control your spending.

After you get an accurate picture of your income and expenses, start setting short- and long-term financial goals. Because you are in college and probably trying to keep expenses to a minimum, you may think that creating financial goals is a difficult undertaking. On the contrary, start setting small short-term goals first. For example, your first short-term goal might be keeping a monthly budget and making adjustments periodically. Another short-term goal could be to gather all of the documents about your financial aid and keep them organized until after you graduate. Meeting these two goals will help you reach larger goals down the road.

In addition to making a list of short-term goals, write down your long-term financial goals. One of your long-term goals could be financial freedom and security. To reach that long-term goal, make a list of short-term goals and start working toward them.

Critical Thinking
EXERCISE 13.4

What is your financial plan for paying for college? If you are receiving financial aid (e.g., grants, loans, tuition waivers), how is it enabling you to pay for the expenses of college?

Companion
Website

Keeping Records

To make it through college with the minimum of problems, it is wise to keep all of your forms, class papers, and receipts. Keep copies of test scores such as ACT, COMPASS, or ASSET; vaccination records; semester grades; transcripts from other colleges; financial aid forms; and scholarship awards. Whenever you talk with someone on campus or over the phone, you should take notes of names, dates, and major ideas. Also, file away any important announcements and documents you receive from a counselor, financial aid officer, or advisor. At a later date, you can throw away any materials that are unnecessary. In the meantime, keep your materials in a safe place.

For class work, keep exams, papers, or homework in a folder even after the class is over. If you have the space, consider keeping records of all your classes, including syllabi and handouts. For financial aid and tuition bills, keep copies of all forms and receipts for all purchases, including books, in a folder. Keep your class work and finance records separate so you can easily find what you need. When you do need the information, take it with you or keep it near the phone when you make a call to the school. After you talk with someone on campus, add details of the conversation to your files; include the names of people you talked to and the dates of the conversations.

What If College Isn't for You?

There is tremendous pressure on those who do not have higher degrees to get them. Every high-school student hears the pitch from parents, counselors, and teachers: Go to college or you won't be anybody. Adults in the workforce know that a college degree can be the difference between doing the same job until retirement and being promoted. Some people even consider going to college a right; if it isn't a right, it is an important part of the American dream.

But not everyone needs to go to college. Yes, college is a great place to continue your education and to make your career dreams a reality. There are also numerous indirect benefits to pursuing higher education—you can improve your health and your financial well-being because you know more about yourself and the world around you. Nonetheless, going to college is not the only key to success. There are many vibrant, intelligent, successful people who did not complete a college degree.

How will you know if college is not right for you? It may be difficult to tell, and you shouldn't quit if you are unsure. The best way to discover how you feel about being in college is to ask yourself a series of questions. Then, talk about your responses with a college counselor, advisor, or trusted friend who can give you good advice.

- Who wants me to go to college?
- Do *I* want to be in college?
- How do I feel when I am in class?
- How do I feel when I am studying?
- How do I feel after I take an exam?
- What do I want to major in? Why?
- What do I want to do with my life? Do I need a college degree to do it?
- What do I value about higher education? What can it do for me?
- What is my passion?

Take your time answering these questions. You may find that your discomfort with college is really a fear about a new beginning and the unknown. Being apprehensive about a new program or a new environment is perfectly normal and does not necessarily indicate you are not right for college.

On the other hand, you may know very clearly that you do not want to be in college at this point in your life. College may not be right for you *right now*, which means you should consider returning when you know for sure it will be your top priority. Many people put off going or returning to college until they can make the decision for themselves. One of the benefits of waiting is that you will be more mature and more responsible—more likely to complete your degree.

Time to Move Forward

Why should you be concerned about what you will be doing after you graduate or transfer from your community college? The answer is simple: Although it seems like forever until graduation, the time will go by quickly. If you have one eye on the future and what you want to do after college, you can make wiser choices while you are there. Therefore, it is a good idea to take some time to envision what life *after* college will be like for you.

Although there are many options open to you once you graduate, this section focuses on three potential "life after college" areas, which may overlap: transferring to a four-year university, joining (or rejoining) the workforce as a graduate, and becoming involved in the community as an ambassador for the benefits of higher education.

Deciding to Transfer

Even if you do not plan to earn a four-year degree any time soon, it is never too early to begin thinking about transferring to a four-year university. The end of each chapter has a section called "From College to University," which focuses on issues involved in transferring to a four-year university. Those sections provide you with specific information to help you cope with the move if you decide to do it. When you do transfer, review those sections. The following information, though, will help you prepare to transfer. Your first step is to talk to counselors and professors at both schools well before you graduate from your community college and enroll in another school. They can advise you about the details of transferring, from getting your transcripts sent over to choosing a major and degree plan.

Before you make any decisions about continuing your education at a four-year university, start searching for one that meets your needs. If you have several in your area, then your best bet is to start looking at their degree programs, their student population, and their tuition—to name a few considerations. Request a catalog from each university and take note of the admission requirements, their basic classes (to compare to one you have already taken), and their financial aid and student services. Once you narrow your search to a few viable options, consider visiting the campuses. Before you visit, call and make appointments with the department chair, admissions counselor, and financial aid officer. If you have time, write a list of questions to ask when talking to these individuals.

When on the campuses, check out the layout of the buildings and take note of the differences you see between your community college and the universities. Getting familiar with the campus you will attend will keep you from getting confused—or from being late—during the first few days. Determine where student parking, the library, the bookstore, and the student union are located. If you have time to wander around campus, look for notices from student organizations that pertain to your interests and possible majors. You may find that the college you are visiting has strong membership in an important career club. Those kinds of extracurricular activities can be as beneficial as a program with a good reputation in the community.

Another consideration when transferring is the acceptance of the courses you have taken. Articulation agreements ensure that students can complete degree requirements at one college and transfer their course credits smoothly to another institution. Your community college may have articulation agreements with universities in the area, which means you can complete an associate's degree and then transfer as a junior to complete your four-year degree. A benefit of an articulation agreement is that you don't have to worry about matching community college courses exactly with their counterparts at the four-year university. Instead, you can concentrate on completing the requirements needed for a two-year degree, and then move straight into upper-level courses at a university. It is always wise to check articulation agreements between the institutions; knowing ahead of time that you have to take a few more classes because they won't all transfer will reduce your stress once you get there.

Making the Leap to a Four-Year University

If you made the decision to transfer and are preparing yourself for the change, here are some tips for transferring—use them as a checklist:

- Request a catalog from the transfer school. Read through it carefully and write down any questions you have about the courses you need to take to complete a degree in your major.

- Apply for financial aid early. Your transfer school may have earlier deadlines to complete financial aid forms.

- Explore the possibility of transfer scholarships. Talk with counselors and financial aid officers at both institutions about possibilities. If you have chosen a major, talk to the department's chair about tuition assistance for majors. Some programs provide financial aid to entice people to major in a certain field.

- Request that your transcript be sent to your transfer school after graduation.

- Request that your transfer school evaluate your transcript when they receive it.

- Ask for recommendation letters, if they are needed, as soon as possible.

- Take note of student organizations, honor societies, and activities that could help you network in your field.

- Get involved as soon as you can.

Making that move from a community college to a four-year university is a big step, but it is no more difficult than the step you took to start school. With some help from your family and friends, you can make that leap.

Critical Thinking

EXERCISE 13.5

What steps for transferring to a four-year university do you think are the most important? Which ones will be the most difficult? For the difficult ones, make a list of resources or ideas to make the transition smoother.

Companion
Website

Asking for a Recommendation Letter

When you make that decision to transfer, you may need a recommendation letter for scholarships, financial aid, an on-campus job, or admission into a special program. If you have cultivated a good relationship with a professor or administrator at your community college, it is easier to ask for and receive a recommendation letter full of specific information about the quality of your work and your character.

When considering someone to ask, choose a person who has had the chance to see you at your best. If you worked closely with a professor or spent many hours talking with a counselor, ask him to write a recommendation letter for you. The better the person knows you, the better the recommendation letter will be. In addition, give this person at least two or three weeks to think about the quality of your work, recall specific examples, and write a polished letter. If you are on a tight deadline, such as a week, be honest with the person and give him a chance to decline the opportunity. If he does agree to write a recommendation letter on such short notice, be sure to provide him with all the necessary materials to complete it properly, including an addressed, stamped envelope and the correct forms. You may want to include a brief resume so that he can speak specifically about your accomplishments.

Once your recommendation letter is written, write a thank-you note to show your appreciation for the favor. A verbal or e-mail message of thanks is acceptable, but a more formal, handwritten note that expresses your gratitude is highly recommended. Finally, when requesting a recommendation, take the necessary steps to ensure you do not read it. If you must hand-deliver the letter, ask that it be sealed in an envelope first. The reason you should not request a copy or attempt to read it is that doing so jeopardizes the honesty of the individual writing it. Committees that evaluate recommendation letters want truthful descriptions of your abilities and strengths; if they know you saw the recommendation letter, they may doubt how accurate the description is.

Practice

EXERCISE 13.6

Write your own recommendation letter for a scholarship. In your letter, describe your accomplishments and long-term goals. Include any obstacles you overcame successfully.

Companion
Website

Going to Work

For those who are not moving from one school to another, graduation from a community college means getting into or back into the workforce. Even if you worked the entire time you took classes, it is still a good idea to review the process for finding and getting the job you want.

Career Counseling

Long before you start thinking about graduating and finding a career, visit your career counselor. Preparing for a career takes longer than a few weeks, and the more planning you do, the smoother the process will be. Each college offers different services in their career centers, but most provide access to interest inventories, which can help you pinpoint those careers you are best suited for. Most career centers also provide "career libraries" that have information about different types of careers, the duties, and the pay potential. In addition, career centers may offer help writing a cover letter and resume and tips for interviewing for a job.

Although your college's career center can offer you many services, there is some assistance they cannot provide. Career counselors will not place you in a job, and they will not choose a career for you. The best they can do for you is give you the information you need—and plenty of it; you have to do the rest to ensure you get a job after graduation.

Resumes

There are actually two parts to an effective resume package: the resume and the cover letter. A resume is a page or two that lists your qualifications and accomplishments. Preparing a cover letter is discussed later. Both should be printed on high-quality paper and a good printer. Also, proofread both your cover letter and resume carefully for errors.

Many books and services are available to help you prepare a good resume, so check a variety of sources. The following are a few of the essential elements that should be included in your resume:

- Your name, address, phone number, and a professional e-mail address.
- State a clear objective. For example, your objective may be "To work in a sales position for a pharmaceutical company" or "To use my knowledge and skills to manage employees effectively."
- Provide information about your educational accomplishments. If you have not completed your degree, note the anticipated graduation date: "Associate of Arts; anticipated graduation: May 2009."
- Provide information about your work history.
- Include any pertinent extracurricular activities, organizations, or awards. If, for instance, you received a scholarship for college, put that information in your resume.
- Provide a list of references or a statement that says references are available upon request.

Exhibit 13.3 is one example of a resume—there are other ways to grab an employer's attention. Choose a format that is easy to read and is professional, and try to keep your resume to one page.

Practice

EXERCISE 13.7

Create your own resume on a separate sheet, using the headings provided.

>   Contact Information:
>
>   Objective:
>
>   Education:
>
>   Work Experience:
>
>   Volunteer Work/Honors and Awards:

>   References:
>
>   1.
>
>   2.
>
>   3.

Companion Website

INTEGRITY MATTERS

Always provide accurate, truthful information in your resume and cover letter. Highlight your accomplishments without exaggerating them.

EXHIBIT 13.3 *Sample resume.*

Charles Kimpler

1234 Broadway Street
Anyplace, US 01234

555-555-1234
ckimpler@anyplace.edu

OBJECTIVE

To use my experience and education to work as an accounting manager.

EDUCATION

Associate of Applied Science in Accounting
Juno Community College

May 2006

EXPERIENCE

Bookkeeper, Mays and Associates

August 2004–present

- Send invoices to clients
- Pay invoices from clients
- Maintain general ledger
- Supervise one staff member

Work-Study, Financial Aid Office
Juno Community College

January 2004–July 2004

- Filed financial aid applications
- Maintained communication with students through newsletter

HONORS AND AWARDS

Accounting Award for Outstanding Student

May 2005

President's Scholarship

August 2002–May 2005

Volunteer of the Year, Humane Society

October 2003

References Available Upon Request

Cover Letters

A cover letter accompanies a resume and explains in detail how your qualifications match what the employer is looking for. As with a resume, keep your cover letter brief and to the point. Why is this important? Many employers simply scan these documents to see if candidates meet the minimum qualifications and then decide, pretty quickly, whether or not to interview them. The more concise your resume and cover letter, the easier it will be for potential employers to determine whether or not you are right for the job.

When writing a cover letter, be sure to address a specific person. Do not start your letter with "Dear Sir or Madam," or worse, "To Whom It May Concern." If you do not know to whom to address the letter, call the company and ask for the correct person's name, along with the correct spelling. If you are sending cover letters to different employers, be sure to proofread your letters and resumes for any references to other people or companies. For example, you do not want to write a letter to Dr. Judy Pile and refer to her company as Chemistry Solutions if she actually owns Ingram Enterprises.

Exhibit 13.4 is an example of an effective cover letter that could accompany the resume in Exhibit 13.3.

Career Fairs

Career fairs are a good way to get information about jobs and employers in your area. If your college sponsors a fair, then be sure to take advantage. However, do not just show up and wander around. Whether you are graduating next month or next year, it pays to approach a career fair with the goal of making contacts and learning more about area businesses.

When you attend a career fair, follow several steps to make the most of your visits with potential employers. This list is just a start; you can get more tips from your college counselors on how to maximize your time at a career fair:

- Dress professionally. Don't show up in a t-shirt and sweats. Carry a professional-looking bag (no backpacks!) and a folder with copies of your resume. Neatness counts.

- Do your homework. Find out what companies will be present at the fair and research the ones that interest you. You can find out more about them through their websites or searching in the library.

- Avoid asking "And what does your company do?" Your research should tell you what the company does.

- Choose a few booths to visit. Instead of blanketing the fair and hitting every representative, be selective and limit yourself to those companies you want to work for.

- Write a standard introduction, practice it, and then use it when you meet someone at the fair. Make the introduction brief (state your name, your interests, and any relevant experience you may have) so you are not clogging the line.

- Be energetic and positive. Recruiters and employers want eager, exciting employees, not people who are dull and boring.

EXHIBIT 13.4 *Sample cover letter.*

Charles Kimpler

1234 Broadway Street
Anyplace, US 01234

555-555-1234
ckimpler@anyplace.edu

October 1, 2006

Dr. Judy Pile
Ingram Enterprises
6789 Levi Lane
Anyplace, US 09876

Dear Dr. Pile,

I am responding to your advertisement in the *Tonitown Times* for an accounting specialist at Ingram Enterprises. As you will see from my resume, I have earned an Associate of Arts degree in accounting from Juno Community College, and I have experience working as a bookkeeper for a local company.

My additional experience as a work-study in the financial aid office at Juno allowed me to improve my people skills as well as understand how an organized and efficient office works.

I hope you will find that both my education and experience fit the position advertised. If you would like to interview me, I can be reached during the day at 555-555-1234. I look forward to hearing from you.

Sincerely,

Charles Kimpler

Charles Kimpler

Internships

An often-overlooked option for community college students is the intern-ship. An internship is a supervised position that allows a student to receive on-the-job training. Usually, internships are unpaid, which makes them less attractive to students who need to work in order to pay bills. However, your college may offer college credit for internships. This may be a good way to get closer to your degree *and* explore careers. Another idea is to volunteer once or twice a week at a place of business. If you can afford a few hours a week or can trade college credit for an internship, then you should investigate the benefits of interning.

Why are internships such a good opportunity for college students? One reason is that internships allow you to work in a field you may be interested in pursuing. In addition, internships can help you explore the different ways a major can be used in the workforce. For example, an English or journalism major may want to participate in an internship at a newspaper or as a proofreader at a company. A networking major may want to intern at a small business to get practical experience with computer networking issues on a small scale. These opportunities give you firsthand experience using your degree.

Internships also allow you to network with others who can help you find a job once you graduate. Even if you decide that you don't want to work in the same area as your internship, you will have contacts who can help you find a job in other fields. An internship can help you refine your career goals.

If your college sponsors a career fair, be sure to attend, with the goal of making contacts and learning more about area businesses.

If you decide to do an internship, treat it as a job. Some employers rely on interns to complete certain projects each year, and they expect you to be serious about the position, even if you do not get paid. Always act and dress professionally. Keeping a good attitude and being self-motivated are excellent ways to shine during your internship. In addition, you should meet regularly with your supervisor to ask questions and get guidance on projects. Most of all, make the best of your unique opportunity.

Interviewing

Another important component to launching a successful career is interviewing for a job. If your winning resume gets you an interview, you are halfway to getting a job. There is, however, still some work to do before you can negotiate a salary.

- Do a little research. Check out the company's website or search for company information that may have appeared in the newspaper. Find out what they do and where they are going.

- Practice interview questions with your friends or family. Try to simulate the interview process by sitting across from the person practicing with you. Ask that person to note any fidgety habits and unclear answers.

- Dress professionally and pay attention to details. Keep your nails clean and short. Check hems and cuffs for tears and stains. Make sure your clothes are clean and pressed and that your shoes are polished. For women, be sure there are no runs in your hose and that your heels are not scuffed.

- Arrive early. Introduce yourself to the receptionist and prepare to wait.

- Listen carefully to the interviewer's questions, pause before answering, and speak slowly and carefully.

- Look interviewers in the eye when speaking.

- Sit up and lean forward slightly. Show by your body language you are interested and relaxed, even if you are nervous.

- Avoid fidgeting with a pencil or paper and tapping your fingers or feet.

- Highlight your strengths. Even if you do not meet all of their qualifications, you can persuade them that you can do the job.

- Avoid asking about the salary. Instead, ask about the job responsibilities and benefits—the interviewer may provide a salary range as part of the process.

- Ask what the time line is for filling the position. Knowing when the company is making the final decision helps you prepare for the next step.

- Thank everyone you meet and follow up with a thank-you note to each interviewer (see Figure 13.5). If you do not know how to spell their names, call the receptionist the next day to get the correct spelling.

EXHIBIT 13.5 *Sample thank-you letter.*

Charles Kimpler

1234 Broadway Street
Anyplace, US 01234

555-555-1234
ckimpler@anyplace.edu

October 12, 2006

Dr. Judy Pile
Ingram Enterprises
6789 Levi Lane
Anyplace, US 09876

Dear Dr. Pile,

Thank you for interviewing me yesterday. I enjoyed meeting you and your colleagues and learning more about how your company works.

After speaking with you, I am more firmly convinced that I am the best person for the job. My education and experience are a great match for what the position demands. I enjoy professional challenges, and I think your company provides the type of opportunities I am looking for.

Please feel free to contact me at 555-555-1234 or ckimpler@anyplace.edu. I look forward to hearing from you.

Sincerely,

Charles Kimpler

Charles Kimpler

Interviewers want to hire people who are energetic, polite, professional, and appreciative. Put your best face forward and try to relax and enjoy the process.

Collaboration

EXERCISE 13.8

Working with a classmate, write several standard interviewing questions and practice interviewing each other. If you have time, practice interviewing each other in front of the class and have your classmates rate the interviewee.

Companion Website

Other Considerations

All college career counselors want students to walk into high-paying jobs the day after graduation, but the reality is much different. Students who major in sought-after fields, such as information technology and health services, sometimes do not find the jobs that they thought were plentiful. Also, the reality of what someone can earn in an entry-level position is often much different than what students imagine. There are many job listings that promise an unbelievable salary for little or no education or experience. Unfortunately, for many college graduates, the pay that they are offered is much less—although there is potential for earning more.

To keep yourself grounded—and to avoid disappointment—make a plan for what you will do if you don't waltz into a dream job immediately. To write your plan, answer the following questions:

- Are you willing to take less money if the opportunity is good?
- Are you willing to relocate for a better job?
- Are you willing to take a job in a different field than what you expected?
- Are you willing to repackage your skills and knowledge to be considered for different types of work?

Reflection

EXERCISE 13.9

What kinds of challenges do people face when looking for a job? What, if anything, do you anticipate as your challenges when you meet your career goals?

Companion Website

Also, start building your network of friends, family, coworkers, classmates, and acquaintances, if you have not already been working on it. Let them know you are about to graduate and will be looking for a job.

Finally, consider the process you must go through if you are to find the right job for you. Getting a job, then, requires that you:

- Consider what fields best suit your skills, personality, and dreams.
- Actively plan and look for work.
- Attend workshops and information sessions that provide assistance with resume writing, interviewing, and networking.
- Prepare a solid resume.

- Network with friends, family, and acquaintances.
- Follow up job inquiries with a phone call or letter.
- Remain positive and flexible.
- Stick to your goals.

Considering the Community

Although your focus during college is on yourself and moving on to another degree or to a new job, you should also look for opportunities to improve your community. One of the purposes of higher education is to improve the lives of individuals so that the community benefits as well. It is essential that educated community members give back and make improvements.

Giving Back

Now may not be the time to encourage you to help your college financially, but you should start considering how you can continue to support your school after graduation. For a college—or any educational institution—to successfully improve the lives of the people in its community, it must depend in part on its graduates to make a good name for themselves and give back using their time, talent, and financial resources. There are a variety of ways you can contribute to the education of those who will surely follow in your footsteps.

A Walking Billboard

First, by being a productive, educated member of society, you are already giving back to your college. Because higher education's mission is to improve a community by increasing the knowledge of its population, we all benefit from students who complete degree and certificate programs and continue to lead productive, happy lives. The skills and knowledge you obtained in college are a good advertisement for the school. College public relations officials want successful alumni to represent the college because they are the best kind of marketing.

Mentoring Others

As you know, community college students are special. They often overcome overwhelming personal and financial obstacles to attend college, and some get lost along the way, thinking that college is too difficult for them. Many of them, perhaps you too, need a mentor to help them stay on track. Once you are confident you can manage college or once you graduate, think about looking for others who need a mentor. Some obvious candidates are people in your family who could benefit from enrolling in a certificate or degree program. Maybe you know friends or coworkers who are too scared to return to school because they don't know if they can compete with the younger generation, or they may believe they cannot afford to go to college. As a mentor, you can share what you know about how to manage going to school with other obligations. You are proof that others can do it—and do it successfully.

Giving Time and Talent

Colleges do not survive on tuition and fees alone. The reality is educating students is expensive—as private college tuition shows us—and thankfully for students, colleges receive money from other sources to cover the total costs of education. Funds raised by companies and individuals as well as federal, state, and local money all help the college function and keep tuition low. The college, then, depends on the generosity of others to make it possible to provide you with a bargain for your education.

You may want to consider giving back to your college after you graduate. It doesn't have to be any time soon and it doesn't have to be a monetary contribution. For example, consider creating an alumni network that encourages employers to donate to the college, or consider sitting on a panel that looks at ways to increase the college's visibility in the community. You can donate your time and your knowledge to help the school raise more money to benefit students such as you.

The End Is the Beginning

It is almost a cliché to say that "commencement" means "a beginning" rather than "an ending." Many graduation speakers address that point each year: When you graduate from college, you are beginning the rest of your life. For community college students, however, the difference between being in college and going off to a career is not that clear. In fact, both a career and college, for most community college students, are very much intertwined. Therefore, it may seem that there is no distinct beginning and ending for you. However, once you do graduate with a certificate or degree, think about your future as a beginning.

What is left for you once you graduate? In addition to transferring, there is always graduate school or professional school. Why not go as far as you can with your degree? You may think now that a master's or a doctoral degree is out of your reach, but with each semester, you are getting closer. Once you meet your goal of graduating with an associate's degree or certificate, you will see that all it takes is goal setting, time management, and a desire to meet your goals.

Another "beginning" to the end of your degree from your community college is lifelong learning. Not only can you use the research and information literacy skills you learned in college, but you can also access materials through alumni borrowing privileges at the library. In addition, you may be more

---

Reflection

EXERCISE 13.10

Have your values changed since you started college? If so, explain.

Companion Website

interested in and informed about guest speakers and community events sponsored by your college. At the very least, you have a network of instructors, counselors, and advisors to call on when you need advice about career changes or information about anything.

Mission, Values, and Goals Revisited

In Chapter 2, you wrote down your values, goals, and mission statement. Do you still have that information in a convenient location? If so, get it out and reflect on how well you met your original short-term goals and how close you came to reaching your long-term goals. Have your values changed any? Or have they been strengthened by your achievements? Have you followed your mission statement? Is there anything you would change about your statement?

To answer these questions, spend time reflecting on your achievements over the past semester. Hopefully, your mission and values did not chang much in the past weeks, but if they did, make a new list of values and rewrite your mission statement. Now is the time to revisit your long-range plans and make necessary adjustments. Keep a record of the short-term goals you achieved and create a new list. Keeping up with what you accomplished serves as a reminder of your success. Here is an example of a new list:

GOALS I MET

1. Completed my courses with above average grades.
2. Created a study group with classmates.
3. Kept up with my commitments on the job.
4. Paid my tuition.

NEW SHORT-TERM GOALS

1. Get registered for next semester.
2. Speak with a counselor about career possibilities.
3. Make at least two As in my classes.
4. Take more time to relax.

Once you revise your short-term goals, you may notice that your time line for reaching your long-term goals needs adjusting as well. Keeping your list in a convenient location and looking at it every day or week will help you stay on track.

You Made It This Far

You not only reached the end of this book, but you are also on your way to completing a semester in college. You did it! You showed a commitment to learning by reading the chapters and completing exercises, and you demonstrated endurance and successful goal setting by staying in your classes and doing the work. No doubt, there were moments you had to work really hard and you may have even doubted yourself a time or two. Be assured, though, that because you have completed one leg of your journey to self-fulfillment, you will be able to make the rest of it. Congratulate yourself for a job well done, and continue on the path to your dreams.

Learning Styles Application

This chart lists the four learning styles and tips based on the chapter's main ideas. Locate your learning style and read the corresponding tips to maximize your success in college.

VISUAL

Visual learners need visual images to help them understand their finances. Seeing how much money you are spending on which items can make sticking to your budget easier. Graphing how much money is spent on different necessities or creating a visual representation of the pitfalls of overspending will assist you.

AURAL

Aural learners often interview well because they are good listeners and can remember and react to verbal communication. You may need help expressing yourself on paper in your resume and cover letters. Talking through the process of writing can help you get your ideas on paper most effectively.

READ/WRITE

Those whose learning style strength is read/write find reading a college catalog and degree information very helpful when planning a degree. Researching careers and the required education and experience will also help you have a better understanding of what it will take to achieve your career goals.

KINESTHETIC

Kinesthetic learners learn best by doing. Participating in internships or work–study positions in your programs of study is extremely helpful because you are able to experience, through activities and interactions with others, what a career in the field might be like. You should seek opportunities to gain experience.

Path of Discovery

What, if anything, might keep you from completing your degree? What would be your plan for getting back into college to meet your education goals?

FROM COLLEGE TO UNIVERSITY

Preparing for higher costs

It is very likely that you will see a change in how much college costs when you transfer to a university. If you chose the local community college because the tuition is cheaper, you may be paying twice as much for tuition at the four-year school. In addition to tuition, you may also see added fees that you didn't have at your community college: Fees for athletic facility use, sporting events, campus organizations, and labs are possible additions to your expenses. Be sure to read the catalog carefully and add the fees to the cost per credit hour to get an accurate picture of what you will be spending per class.

Despite the increase in tuition and fees, you may notice that your bookstore expenses stay the same. Although the price of books can be a significant portion of your overall college expenses, it is unlikely that you will experience an increase in cost. The exception to this statement is if you are taking upper-level science and computer classes that require weighty textbooks and additional software. Those books can be as much as $100 each. An advantage, however, to transferring to a larger school is that there are more people from whom you can buy used books. Take note of special discounts for used books in the bookstore and look for flyers on bulletin boards that announce books for sale.

FROM COLLEGE TO CAREER

The benefits of returning to work before continuing your education

There may be a time when you must interrupt your college career to return to your full-time job. Balancing financial and education goals may be too difficult to handle at the moment, which may mean that your financial needs take priority. If this happens to you, there are many ways to deal with the transition back to the world of work while still keeping your eye on returning to college:

- Realize that going back to work doesn't have to be forever. Just because you are unable to return for more than one semester doesn't mean you never will.

- Talk to your employer about your desire to get a degree. You may be surprised by her support. There may even be financial assistance for employees who take college classes.

- Talk to your family and friends about your need to further your education. Someone may be willing to help you with finances, scheduling, and family duties.

- Set a time line for returning to college. If you need to work a semester to earn more money to pay for tuition, then be sure to keep up with registration periods and college announcements.

- Save your money. Even if expenses are not the reason you returned to work, putting aside money in a "college fund" makes it easier to re-enroll in college. You won't have any excuses for not being able to afford the increased costs.

- Look for scholarships and financial aid for working adults. Some states are creating grant programs for nontraditional students who work full time in order to increase the number of college graduates in their states.

- Keep connected with former classmates and instructors. If you are aware of what is going on at the college, you are more likely to return because you feel as though you never left.

Chapter in Review

1. What are the different methods of paying for college?

2. In what ways have you already mentored others who want to attend college or are just starting their college careers? How have you influenced younger people to value education?

3. What are your new short-term goals? How do they connect with your long-term goals? Have you had to make any adjustments this semester? If so, why? If not, what have been doing to stay on track?

4. What do you want to do with your life after you graduate? How will your goals change? How will your mission change?

Case Scenarios

Read the following case scenarios and determine what each person should do. Refer to the information in this chapter as you write a description and plan of action for each student.

1. Laura paid for her first semester of tuition with her savings, but she is looking for other ways to pay for the rest of college. She doesn't qualify for any grants and is not sure what her options are. Explain to her what choices she has to pay for college without incurring too much debt.

2. Brian's dream is to own a horse farm, but he doesn't think he can afford his dream, so he is in his second semester as a radiology technician because it is a job with a steady income. Also, Brian doesn't want to quit school to follow his dream because he values an education. What advice can you give him about following his dreams?

3. Lawrence is ready to graduate with a degree in networking, and he has been circulating his resume with the hope that he can roll right into a job after graduation. Because Lawrence lacks experience in his field, he decided

to exaggerate some of his responsibilities as a work–study student in the Information Technology Department and as an intern at a local advertising company. What would you tell Lawrence before he sends his resume out to prospective employers?

Research It Further

1. Search for a website devoted to helping you discover the right career for you, such as www.solutionskills.com/index.html. Research a career that interests you and collect information about the education needed, the pay you can expect, and the career potential. Present your findings to your class.

2. As an individual, or in a group, research the qualifications and requirements for the different loans and grants that your college offers. With the information, create a one-page sheet for each type of financial aid that can help students remember the differences between each type.

3. Investigate the entrance requirements of two 4-year universities in the area. Find out what GPA they require for transfer students, what types of scholarships and financial aid are available, and what kinds of degree programs they offer. Make a brief presentation to your class.

4. What, if any, alumni services does your college offer? If they offer very few or none at all, brainstorm a list of ideas that you would like to see implemented and present them to an administrator who can give you feedback on what is possible. Then, report to your class which suggestions can be implemented and which cannot.

Reference

U.S. Department of Education. (2002–2003). "The Student Guide." Retrieved August 27, 2003, from www.ed.gov/prog_info/SFA/StudentGuide/2002-3/fseog.html.

Academic calendar. A list of important dates, including vacation breaks, registration periods, and deadlines for certain forms.

Academic probation. A student whose GPA falls below a designated level is placed on academic probation. If the GPA does not improve, the student may be prohibited from registering for classes for a designated number of semesters.

Adjunct instructor. An adjunct instructor is not a full-time college employee; she usually teaches only one or two courses.

Analytical thinking. Thinking that involves breaking apart the problem and the possible solutions to examine them fully.

Asynchronous communication. Asynchronous communication means that two people do not have to be online at the same time. Tools such as e-mail and discussion boards are asynchronous communication methods.

Articulation agreement. An articulation agreement is a signed document stating that one college will accept the courses from another college.

Audience. In essay writing, the audience is the person(s) you are addressing.

Bloom's Taxonomy. Six levels of learning behavior, developed by Benjamin Bloom, that are considered part of the cognitive domain: knowledge, comprehension, application, analysis, synthesis, and evaluation.

Bursar. A bursar is the person at your college who handles tuition and fee payments.

Catalog. The catalog is a book that provides students with information about the college's academic calendar, tuition and fees, and degree/certificate programs.

CD-ROM. A portable storage device that can store a large amount of files and programs and can be carried and used in different computers; it can be also be used to save files if using a writable CD-ROM.

Central processing unit (CPU). The CPU processes all of the instructions sent when you create a document or save a file.

Chat room. An electronic method of communicating with other people in real time.

Co-requisite. A co-requisite is a course taken at the same time as another course. For example, if Intermediate Algebra is a co-requisite for Physical Science, then both are taken during the same semester.

Cornell system. A system for taking notes in which you draw an upside-down "T" on your paper. The space to the right is for taking notes; the space to the left is for adding questions and highlighting important points; and the space at the bottom is for summarizing the material.

Course objective. A goal the instructor identifies for the student to meet after the course is completed. For example, a course objective could be to use MLA documentation properly.

Cover letter. A cover letter accompanies a resume and outlines how your qualifications match the advertised job requirements.

Creative thinking. The act of creating ideas to solve problems.

Critical thinking. The ability to use specific criteria to evaluate reasoning and make a decision.

Cryptogram. A word puzzle that involves creating a "code" to be deciphered.

Curriculum. Curriculum is the term used to refer to the courses you must take in a particular field, or it can refer to all of the classes the college offers.

Dean. An administrator who is in charge of faculty or a college division.

Developmental classes. Developmental classes, sometimes referred to as remedial classes, focus on basic college-level skills such as reading, writing, and math. Students who earn a certain score on standardized tests such as the ACT and COMPASS exams may be required to take developmental classes before enrolling in college-level courses.

Discussion board. An electronic method of interacting with other people by posting messages and reading posts from other people.

Family Educational Rights and Privacy Act (FERPA). This act, also referred to as FERPA, ensures that your education records, including test grades and transcripts, are not shared with anyone without your consent.

Floppy disk. A portable storage device that cannot hold a large amount, but can be carried and used in different computers; allows you to alter files after you save them.

Full-time student. To be considered a full-time student, you must take at least 12 hours a semester.

Full-time worker. To be considered a full-time worker, you must work at least 40 hours a week.

Grade point average (GPA). GPA is the number used to determine a student's progress in college. It refers to the number of quality points divided by the number of hours a student has taken.

Hard drive. A disk that stores and reads stored data; storing a file on a hard drive is the same as storing it in the computer.

Information literacy. Information literacy requires individuals to recognize when information is needed and locate, evaluate, and effectively and ethically use the information.

Knowledge. Knowledge comes from taking information in, thinking about it critically, and synthesizing your own ideas about what you read or saw.

Long-term goal. A goal that takes longer to complete (a year or more) is considered a long-term goal.

Major. The area you are focusing on for your degree. If you want to teach third grade, your major might be elementary education. (See also Minor.)

Matching questions. Test questions with one column of descriptors and another column of words or phrases are called matching. The student matches the word or phrase with the appropriate descriptor.

Meta-search engines. Meta-search engines search other search engines based on the terms typed in.

Memory stick. A memory stick (or thumb drive, pin drive) is a small portable storage device that holds a large amount of files and programs and can be carried and used in different computers; it also allows you to alter files after you save them; connect to a USB port to access files.

Minor. A second area of emphasis in your degree. A minor usually requires fewer classes and is not as intensive as a major. For example, if your major is marketing, but you want to learn more about running your own business, you may minor in business or accounting.

Mission statement. A mission statement declares what a person or institution believes in and what that person or institution hopes to accomplish.

Multiple-choice question. A multiple-choice question provides a statement or question and the correct answer must be determined from a list of possibilities.

Numberplay. A puzzle that uses a combination of letters and numbers to create a common saying or phrase.

OK5R. The OK5R reading strategy, developed by Dr. Walter Pauk, stands for Overview, Key Ideas, Read, Record, Recite, Review, and Reflect.

Objective question. A question that presents a limited number of possible answers.

Part-time. Part-time status describes students taking less than 12 credit hours a semester.

Prerequisite. A required course or score that must be completed or achieved before enrolling in a course.

Priority. Something important at that moment.

Provost. A high-ranking college administrator.

Quality points. The number assigned each grade. For example, an A is worth four quality points, while a B is worth three.

Registrar. The official record keeper of the college.

Remedial classes. See Developmental classes.

Resume. A document that states a person's education and work experience. It also contains a career objective and contact information.

Search engine. A search engine searches web pages based on the terms typed in.

Short-term goal. A goal that can be accomplished in a short period of time (a week or a few months) is considered a short-term goal.

Stress. Stress is a physical and psychological response to outside stimuli.

Student handbook. A college publication that outlines what the college expects of the student.

Subjective questions. Test questions that require a student provide a personal answer are considered subjective. Usually, there are no "wrong" answers to subjective questions.

Syllabus. A document that contains an overview of the course, including objectives, assignments, and required materials as well as the instructor's policies for attendance, exams, and grading. It may also contain the college's policies on disability accommodations and academic dishonesty.

Synchronous communication. Synchronous communication requires that two people be online at the same time. Internet-based synchronous communication includes chat rooms.

T system. See Cornell system.

Time management. Refers to the strategies someone uses to use time effectively.

Topic. The subject of a piece of writing.

Transcript. A record of the courses you took and the grades you earned. Transcripts also note your GPA.

Transfer. Transfer refers to moving from one school to another. Students who transfer must apply for admission to the second school and must request their transcript(s) be sent to the new school.

Values. Values, a part of your belief system, provide the foundation for what you do and what you become. For example, if you value financial stability, look for opportunities to earn money and provide a secure future for yourself.

Wordplay. A word puzzle that uses a combination of letters, symbols, and numbers to create a visual play on words.

Work–study. A federal program that allows students to work at their college while taking classes. Students must qualify for work–study money and meet college department requirements for work.